THOSE ARE
REAL
BULLETS

Also by Peter Pringle and Philip Jacobson

Insight on the Middle East War
(with the *Sunday Times* Insight team)

Year of the Captains: An Account of the Portuguese Revolution
(with the *Sunday Times* Insight team)

Also by Peter Pringle

The Nuclear Barons
(with Jim Spigelman)

SIOP: The Secret US Plan for Nuclear War
(with William Arkin)

Chernobyl: The End of a Nuclear Dream
(with the *Observer*, London)

THOSE ARE REAL BULLETS

BLOODY SUNDAY, DERRY, 1972

Peter Pringle & Philip Jacobson

GROVE PRESS
New York

For Eleanor and Annie

First published in Great Britain in 2000 by Fourth Estate Limited, London

Printed in the United States of America

FIRST AMERICAN EDITION

Library of Congress Cataloging-in-Publication Data

Pringle, Peter.
    [Those are real bullets, aren't they?]
    Those are real bullets : Bloody Sunday, Derry, 1972 / Peter Pringle & Philip Jacobson.
        p.   cm.
    Includes bibliographical references.
    ISBN 0-8021-1680-9
    1. Londonderry (Northern Ireland)—History. 2. Demonstrations—Northern Ireland—Londonderry—History—20th century. 3. Political violence—Northern Ireland—Londonderry—History—20th century. 4. Massacres—Northern Ireland—Londonderry—History—20th century. 5. Northern Ireland—History—1969-1994. I. Jacobson, Philip. II. Title.

DA995.L75 P75 2001
941.6'21—dc21   00-063621

Grove Press
841 Broadway
New York, NY 10003

01 02 03 04   10 9 8 7 6 5 4 3 2 1

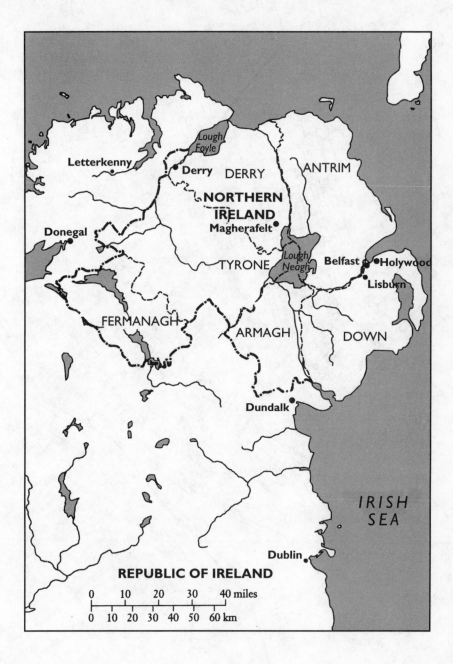

Street map of Derry in 1972 showing the direction of the Bloody Sunday march.

Contents

Prologue

This book follows the events of a single day in the Troubles of Northern Ireland – Bloody Sunday, 30 January 1972. In the Bogside of Londonderry, British paratroopers shot twenty-seven unarmed Catholics, five of them in the back. Thirteen died.

The killing ground is now hard to imagine. The flats on Rossville Street where five young men were gunned down around a rubble barricade have been demolished. William Street, where the first shots wounded a man and a boy near the Nook bar, has been rebuilt with neat maisonettes where the burnt-out buildings once stood. The scruffy Victorian terrace at Free Derry Corner, where the rule of British law ended and IRA vigilantes took over and where the twenty-four-year-old Bernadette Devlin urged the civil rights marchers to stand their ground against the advancing paratroopers, is now a wide avenue with a grassy intersection; a fancy ramp leads up to the ancient city walls. It is as if some town planner had only one purpose in mind – to destroy the landmarks and wipe out the memories.

Yet no clearance of the killing ground, no new houses, new roads or fresh paint can blur the ghastly images: the picture of Barney McGuigan's body by the phone box outside the flats, lying in a big pool of his blood and brains, his head blown open by the high-velocity bullet of a British soldier.

McGuigan was not an IRA gunman, or even a young stone-throwing rioter. He was aged forty-one, the father of six, and he was killed because he went to the aid of Paddy Doherty, a thirty-year-old plumber's mate who had been shot from behind while crawling on the pavement to avoid the gunfire. For several minutes Doherty lay bleeding to death and crying out for help; 'I don't want to die by myself,' he was saying. McGuigan had taken cover by the flats and wanted to go to Doherty, but was restrained by others sheltering with him. 'I can't stand this any longer,' McGuigan said. 'If I take a white handkerchief and go out they'll not shoot me.' He came out with his hands up, waving the hanky. He had taken only two steps before the paratrooper fired.

If the soldiers who killed McGuigan and Doherty fired aimed shots, as all the soldiers insisted they did, then they must have known what they had done.

But a British government inquiry by the Lord Chief Justice, Lord Widgery, never positively identified the killer of either man. Perhaps it was the anonymous paratrooper known to the Widgery inquiry only as Soldier F, who had been firing in the direction of the phone box. Or perhaps it was Soldier H, who had been pulling so recklessly on the trigger of his 7.62mm assault rifle that he couldn't account for nineteen of the twenty-two rounds he fired that afternoon. Lord Widgery wrote of the shot that killed McGuigan: 'I cannot form any worthwhile conclusion on this point.'

Bloody Sunday marked a crucial turning point in the Troubles that flared anew in 1968. The fury among Catholics produced a queue of volunteers to swell the depleted ranks of the IRA. A terrorist war was launched, bringing assassinations; bombs to Belfast, Birmingham, Westminster and Whitehall; arms shipments were smuggled from Libya and millions of dollars were raised to buy arms from the Irish community in America. More than 3000 people died in the conflict over the next quarter-century.

In the grim array of atrocities committed in the name of Irish Republicanism and Ulster loyalism, the death toll on Bloody Sunday is not the highest for a single incident, but the killings stand apart. They were not random casualties from a terrorist bomb in a pub, the assassination of a member of parliament, or a sniper's shot at a policeman on patrol. The thirteen unarmed men, seven of them teenagers, were killed as part of a deliberate plan, conceived at the highest level of military command and sanctioned by the British government, to put innocent civilians at risk by authorizing the use of lethal force during an illegal civil rights march.

Only two other incidents in Britain present an historical comparison with Bloody Sunday – one dating from an earlier phase in the harsh chronicles of Anglo-Irish relations: the shooting of twelve spectators at Croke Park football ground in Dublin by British troops in November 1920. On English soil the only parallel is the so-called 'Peterloo Massacre', when demonstrators seeking parliamentary reform were charged down by cavalry in Manchester, in August 1819. In the annals of atrocities committed by the state against its own people, Bloody Sunday takes its place alongside India's Amritsar, South Africa's Sharpeville, Mexico's Tlatelolco and America's Kent State. 'Something in all of us died that day,' said Ms Devlin.

The British government was at war with the IRA and the Widgery inquiry was a propaganda exercise that ignored civilian evidence; failed to examine the circumstances of the fourteen who were wounded; was unwilling to allow examination of key army documents and never looked at crucial photographs, or examined shots fired by soldiers other than paratroopers. Widgery's lamentable conclusions were even contradicted by the evidence he did accept.

A generation later, Tony Blair's Labour government took the unprecedented step of reopening the inquiry, this time under Lord Saville, to establish the 'truth' of what happened on that day. Widgery was urged by the Prime Minister of the day, Ted Heath, to bear in mind the need to win the public relations battle over Bloody Sunday and he obliged. Lord Saville is working under no such constraints; he has time and funds – thirteen million has already been spent – to conduct an exhaustive inquiry.

It is a daunting task, not least because memories have dimmed and several of the key players are now dead, but also because it requires the rank-and-file soldiers and senior officers who apparently lied on oath to Widgery to re-examine their stories. For these reasons, some would argue, the enterprise is bound to fail: the 'truth' that Lord Saville seeks is simply unattainable.

It did not help Lord Saville's quest when the British courts ruled that the paratroopers will remain anonymous. They will be known, as they were in Widgery, as Soldier A, Soldier B and so on. In a sense, though, this is unimportant. If Soldier A admits to firing the shot that killed McGuigan, the inquiry's aim is satisfied, even if he remains unidentified. But will this soldier also admit that he was mistaken in suggesting McGuigan had a gun or a bomb? And will he confess that he shot a man waving a flag of truce?

Will the marksman who shot Paddy Doherty from behind admit, now, that he fired at an unarmed man crawling away from the shooting?

And what about the wounding of Peggy Deery, mother of fourteen children, the only woman hit on that day? Will the paratrooper who blew off the back of her left leg now admit he shot her by mistake? He could not, surely, have fired at her on purpose because she had nothing in her hands and was wearing a skirt, a black, shiny, wet-look fur-trimmed coat and boots to match. None of the soldiers' testimony mentions seeing such a target, yet Mrs Deery was only about twenty-five yards away from them.

Then there is the mystery of the four nail bombs found on the dead body of seventeen-year-old Gerald Donaghy. Each roughly the size of half a brick, the crude devices made of gelignite wrapped round a bag of nails were 'discovered' by the RUC in Donaghy's blue jeans. Yet two doctors and several civilians had examined him previously and found nothing in his pockets. The search for the 'truth' of this strange incident would appear to involve the police recanting previous sworn testimony. Is this likely?

The forensic evidence is being re-examined by the new inquiry using more sophisticated techniques than existed in 1972. At least four of the dead were shot from the rear and one – perhaps two – were shot twice. Will reopening the forensic files show that seventeen-year-old Hugh Gilmore's death was caused by one bullet or two? If so, will the soldier who fired those two shots come forward? Can new forensic evidence, or eyewitness accounts, prove that John Young, Michael McDaid and Willie Nash were killed by paratroopers firing from Rossville Street, or by soldiers of another regiment in snipers' nests on the city walls? Their wounds suggest that either is possible.

What will be heard from army officers who drew up the master plan to arrest rioters and seek a confrontation with the IRA? The evidence demonstrates that the operation was ill conceived in preparation and went disastrously out of control. Are they now likely to admit this?

Finally, will volunteers of the IRA, or other freelance gunmen, now give evidence of what they did on that day? Will it demonstrate that they fired only in self-defence, as they have always claimed, and did not provoke the paratroopers into the extreme reaction that caused the killings?

As the inquiry gets under way, the millions of pages of revised testimony, government and military documents now made available or declassified under regular archival reviews, do not offer conclusive answers to these questions, or even, forgive the pun, produce a smoking gun.

Before it is all over – at least a year from now – tens of millions of pounds will have been spent interviewing witnesses and sifting through files, collecting photographs and making a virtual reality model of the killing ground, but most of the money will have gone on lawyers' fees. Politicians will complain about lawyers becoming unreasonably, and unfairly, rich and certainly rewards for the outside solicitors have been relatively easily gained. Most of the legal work has been interviewing civilian eyewitnesses or soldiers first interviewed twenty-eight years ago.

The value of these interviews is questionable, as we have found. The memory plays tricks; events can be erased, or embellished. The civilian eyewitnesses now remember things – sometimes quite startling things – they had not put into their original statements, and they cannot recall other events they initially described. A reasonable person might reluctantly conclude, on the basis of the evidence so far, that the relatives of the dead and wounded may never establish beyond a reasonable doubt the legal truth of what happened.

The public will wonder whether the money has been wisely spent. They will ask whether a judicial review of the inadequacies of Widgery would have been a more prudent course, achieving the same ends. For most of the relatives, the goal now is justice not revenge. An anonymous soldier cannot be convicted of a crime, and no evidence of criminal activity offered by a witness can be used in a subsequent prosecution.

Lord Saville has been at pains to say that he will not be passing judgement on Lord Widgery – he starts with a clean sheet of paper. But that assertion is frankly unrealistic. The Saville inquiry, if it succeeds, will by its very nature constitute a condemnation of Widgery.

Even so, reopening the investigation is a political and judicial landmark – the first time an official inquiry set up under the 1921 Tribunals Act has been revisited. In the context of the civil rights struggle of Catholics in Northern Ireland, the new inquiry represents a remarkable turnabout; their voices will now be heard.

Whatever the result, the new inquiry is bound to focus public attention on the intimate and tragic human story. It requires a minutely detailed reconstruction of twenty-four hours in the life of a city in revolt; a community which incorporated in one small place named the Bogside all the underlying social and political reasons for the three decades of armed conflict.

The British army's operation in Derry on that Sunday

foreshadowed the ultimate failure of its military response. It also brutally portrayed the folly of using the shock troops of the Parachute Regiment in a civilian role and exposed the terrifying destructive power of the high-velocity bullets in their assault rifles—bullets which two weeks before Bloody Sunday the army high command had recommended should not be used in crowd control because of the risk of collateral damage.

One of the primary sources of evidence of what happened on Bloody Sunday lay untouched for twenty-seven years in the archives of one of Britain's oldest newspapers, the *Sunday Times*. Under its then editor, Harold Evans, the Insight team, of which we were members, carried out a lengthy investigation of the events of that day. Five days after Widgery's report, the paper published a 12,000-word Insight report which challenged Widgery by concluding that, although the IRA did fire, the paratroopers' response was 'out of all proportion to what they were facing', and 'reckless in the extreme'.

On 12 April 1998 the *Sunday Times*, under new management, handed over to the Saville Inquiry Insight's entire collection of notebooks, memos, statements of civilians, confidential interviews with government officials, the British army and the IRA, plus more than 500 photographs

Lord Saville asked us to assist the inquiry in authenticating the archive, which we have done as far as we were able. Seeing this material after such a long time was strange indeed: names, dates and places long forgotten but crucial to a complete history of Bloody Sunday. The material also presented us with a problem: the interviews in which Lord Saville expressed most interest were those with members of the IRA, or concerned with matters related to the IRA. All these interviews were conducted in confidence; they were given on the understanding that we would not divulge the names of the interviewees and we asked Lord Saville to respect that journalistic undertaking. He declined to do so, but we stand by our pledges unless and until they are rescinded by the interviewee.

We have agreed to appear as witnesses to the Saville inquiry, but only on this condition. What follows is the first full narrative of Bloody Sunday, updated with additional material produced by the Saville inquiry, declassified secret official documents and new interviews in Derry.

Peter Pringle and Philip Jacobson,
London, 30 January 2000

I

The Alarm

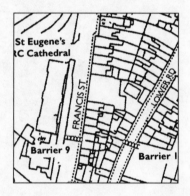

The atmosphere was so relaxed and cheerful that
I decided to leave my medical bag in the car

Dr Raymond McClean, Derry GP,

on the day of the march

FATHER O'NEILL RAISED the alarm during midday mass at St Eugene's Cathedral. From his room in the parochial house, he could see soldiers moving into positions in Lower Road, just outside, and parishioners had called to say that convoys of troops were crossing the River Foyle over the Craigavon Bridge. He ran across to the cathedral, went straight up to the altar, where Father Daly was bringing mass to a close, and whispered his urgent message into Daly's ear. British soldiers were putting up barbed-wire barriers on William Street and Little James Street. Armoured cars packed with paratroopers in their red berets were lined up in Clarence Avenue. The cathedral was surrounded. Snipers with telescopic sights fixed to their rifles were moving into sandbagged positions on the walls of the old city, and a water cannon had been spotted filling up from a fire hydrant in Strand Road. An army helicopter was circling overhead. It seemed like the Bogside was being invaded.

Father Daly tried to keep calm. Everyone had heard that massive reinforcements would be arriving from Belfast for the Sunday afternoon march and there were rumours that the paratroopers were coming to 'crack heads'. At the end of the mass, Daly told the congregation about the soldiers outside and urged people not to panic; just to walk home as though it were an ordinary Sunday. If they were going on the march, as he hoped they would be, he pleaded with them to make it a peaceful protest. He would be there to help, as usual, if things went wrong.

11

Across the Bogside, at the Long Tower Catholic church, Father Bradley offered a special prayer during mass for the safety of the marchers. He had seen army snipers taking over upstairs rooms at the Derry City Social Club on Bishop Street, and moving into a derelict house on Nailor's Row, just below the city walls. The snipers overlooked the flats in Rossville Street, the new maisonettes in Glenfada Park and Abbey Place, the Bogside Inn and Stanley's Walk, where the Derry Provisional IRA had its headquarters. These army sharpshooters had a clear line of sight to 'aggro corner', the scarred intersection of Rossville and William Street where there was always trouble from the youths who threw stones. The show of force was massive and menacing; there had been nothing like it since the British soldiers arrived in Londonderry two and a half years earlier.

On nearby Barrack Street, troops were building a barrier of wooden knife rests and barbed wire, and one young boy had been arrested for kicking a soldier. In other streets around the Bogside troops had arrived in armoured personnel carriers known as Pigs, and groups of youths were already pelting them with stones.

After mass, Father Bradley went to a house where the family was huddled around a radio listening to the army's messages – a strictly illegal act considered by the authorities to be eaves-dropping on official secrets, but everyone tuned in on marching days. The upper-class English accents of army officers, so different and foreign-sounding, reported the confrontations as though they were sporting events, which in a way they were: 'About fifteen chicos stoning OPs [observation posts] 2, 3 and 4. Baton rounds have been fired and a few hits scored.'

In undecipherable army codes, the same voice announced the arrival of each military unit:

Hello, Zero, this is 54 Alpha, positions 18, 19, 20, 21, 22 and 23 are now complete. 24 will be completed in about five minutes, over.

I UDR sitrep. A coy, B coy, C coy. S1 moving in now. S2 in position. Y3 moving in now. Y4 in position.

How many positions the army was occupying and where they were you couldn't tell. It seemed like a lot of troops for such a small place. And the list of the regiments sounded like an honour roll of some distant battle on foreign soil – Coldstream Guards, Royal Regiment of Fusiliers, Royal Green Jackets, Royal Anglians, 22nd Light Air Defence Regiment, Royal Artillery and, in reserve in case of trouble, the élite soldiers of the 1st Battalion, The Parachute Regiment (the Paras).

The Paras' convoy of trucks and armoured cars, which had left Belfast before dawn, was due to reach its base location at Drumahoe, three miles outside Derry, at 10 a.m. One of the paratroopers, who was a radio operator in the machine-gun platoon, recalled what happened the night before the Paras came to Derry. In their barracks at Holywood, a pretty little town on Belfast Lough, the lieutenant in charge of the platoon told them they were to carry out internal security duty in Derry the next day. According to the radio operator, the lieutenant painted a lurid picture of the mayhem the IRA had caused there: 'Several hundred soldiers had been hospitalized and not one arrest had been made.'

He looked around at his colleagues in the barrack room and saw delight on their faces.

After all the abuse and nights without sleep, frustrations and tension, this is what they had been waiting for.

We were all in high spirits and when our Lieutenant said, 'Let's teach these buggers a lesson – we want some kills tomorrow ...' this was tantamount to an order (i.e. an exoneration of all responsibility).

We set off in a convoy across Northern Ireland. It was a beautiful sunny day, patches of snow were still to be seen.

When we arrived at Derry we parked our vehicles in the back of the town and debussed. We knew that the Creggan 'was an IRA fortress, conning towers, machine-guns and barbed wire as well as land mines guarding its approaches. The people of Creggan had not paid rent and hijacked all their food for several years.' A technical hitch was discovered on the way. The Paras lost their radio link with army headquarters in Derry; the set was faulty.

After the Paras had come, the road blocks went up along the seventy-mile route from Belfast. At 9.35 a.m. the Royal Green Jackets reported: 'Op SPONDON in op.'

Operation Spondon was a standing plan to seal off the area along the border with the Irish Republic.

Father Bradley's parishioners told him they refused to be intimidated by the presence of so many soldiers; if the British army came out in force that afternoon, then so would they.

Supporters of the march, as well as troops, were coming in from all over Northern Ireland, according to the army's radio. At 10.45 a.m. British army headquarters in Lisburn reported: 'Three buses left 1000 hrs, full of women and children. Taking South route down the Falls Road [Belfast's Catholic ghetto].'

Leaders of the civil rights movement were also on their way, including Derry's young firebrand socialist, Eamonn McCann, and Bernadette Devlin who, at twenty-one, had become the youngest woman ever elected to the British Parliament, as MP for Mid-Ulster. She could draw a crowd in Derry. When she was sent to jail for six months for taking part in the Battle of the Bogside, even moderates and conservative Catholics protested; by that legal reckoning they were all criminals.

Other civil rights leaders were flying into Belfast from London. Lord (Fenner) Brockway, the former socialist MP, lifelong anti-imperialist and human rights campaigner, arrived in the same plane as Tony Smythe, general secretary of the National Council for Civil Liberties. To avoid army checkpoints Brockway drove a circuitous route, mostly through the Republic. Even so, his car was stopped and searched three times before they reached Derry. Smythe took the more direct route through Maghera and Dungiven, staying on Ulster roads, and was stopped so many times at road blocks that he missed the march altogether.

At 10.31 a.m. the army radio reported: 'One, maybe two, buses bound from Belfast to Portadown and Cookstown to Derry. Expected to pick up B. [Bernadette] Devlin and Austin [Currie, the Nationalist MP for Tyrone] at Cookstown.'

In fact, Devlin was driving to Derry with McCann, as the army would shortly find out. Each time the couple drove through military checkpoints, the army radio reported their progress: '12.45 p.m.: Bernadette has passed through road block in Cookstown.'

Devlin and McCann had heard there would be a good turnout for the march and were also sure there would be violence, and possibly even some shooting; as they approached Derry they were even guessing at how many might be shot.

In Derry, most people expected trouble at 'aggro corner', the Bogside gateway to Derry's commercial district. Shoppers approached this important intersection from the south along Rossville Street, from the west down William Street and from the north through Little James Street. Four years of riots at the corner itself had taken their toll; no shops or bars remained intact; they had been gutted and firebombed, their fronts now crudely boarded up with corrugated iron, their walls covered with graffiti. The pavements had been torn up to make chunks of concrete to hurl at the troops.

The 'hooligans', 'yobbos' or 'chicos', as the army variously called them, would gather each day at this intersection among the burnt-out or derelict buildings, where there was a plentiful supply of missiles – stones, bricks, slabs of pavement, iron bars, bottles, tin cans and lead pipes – to hurl at the troops. If the youths were IRA volunteers they had access to home-made bombs, nails wrapped in gelignite, which were lethal weapons in the army rule book and soldiers were permitted to shoot to kill if they saw anyone throwing them.

But most afternoons the youths chucked stones, and the soldiers fired rubber bullets and canisters of CS gas. In a city which, prior to 1968, was famous for its low crime rate, rioting became a daily ritual, creating local heroes out of those who took on the army. The spectacle made good television and the youths would sometimes take a break to see themselves on TV in a local bar. Then they would come back and start again.

When a stone found its mark they cheered and when a rubber bullet hit home the soldiers cheered. Sometimes, if the stoning was too rough, the troops rushed the youths and, if they could catch them – which generally they could not – in the warren of narrow streets and alleys, they arrested them for riotous behaviour. The rioting would usually end without bloodshed – stones would miss their targets or bounce off the soldiers' plastic shields; the rubber bullets, which were capable of inflicting fatal wounds or putting out an eye and smashing teeth, mostly caused nasty bruises, or bounced harmlessly down the street. The riot would end when the youths tired and went home for tea, or when it rained, whichever came first. Only twice in two and a half years had unarmed youths been shot by real bullets.

Word of the arrival in Derry of the paratroopers spread quickly and was especially unnerving for those who had seen them in action the weekend before at Magilligan, an old army camp on a sandy head-land near Lough Foyle, where internees were being held. The marchers went there in a fleet of hired buses singing 'We Shall Overcome', not knowing the Paras had been sent to meet them. They scrambled across the dunes and along the strand to the barbed-wire fence around the camp, where the army told them they could go no further because it was Ministry of Defence property.

The presence of the Paras was not immediately apparent to the crowd and the atmosphere was at first good-humoured. The Green Jackets' commander offered tea and buns if marchers agreed to follow a route up to a barrier at the camp's entrance (where an enormous airport-style foam dispenser was stationed in case of trouble).

But when a group of protesters headed towards the barbed wire, the Paras were waiting for them. The *Guardian* newspaper's correspondent, Simon Winchester, provided a graphic description of what happened next.

'A dozen paratroopers opened fire with their gas guns. Volley after volley of rubber bullets flashed and flittered across the sand: a score of demonstrators hit by the bullets crumpled up into the sand . . . for half an hour there was bitter hand-to-hand fighting.' The crowd snatched up sticks and rocks from the beach, the troops responded with more rubber bullets at point-blank range.

Under the eyes of the television cameras and press photographers, a few of the Paras appeared to lose control completely. One was pictured swinging his rifle like a club, others had to be held back physically by fellow soldiers from attacking demonstrators. Some marchers claimed that a Para officer struck one of his own men, while a press photographer heard a Green Jackets soldier exclaim: 'Christ, we're here to stop the protesters, not kill them.'

When dusk fell, the marchers gave up and went back to the buses, several of them nursing bad cuts and bruises. This was the first time Derry people had clashed with the Paras and it seemed to them to be a deliberate 'get tough' strategy on the army's part. Everyone saw the confrontation that evening on TV and many wondered apprehensively if the same hyper-aggressive element would be deployed in Derry the following weekend.

The word at the British Legion Club during the week was that the Loyalists had organized a counter march, also to end at the Guildhall, and if people wanted to avoid trouble they should stay away. By Saturday the warnings had hardened: the Paras were coming and there were going to be killings. Army officers who were friendly with some of the nurses at Altnagelvin Hospital, the big medical centre in the Protestant Waterside, had warned Catholics not to go on the march because there would be blood spilled.

Paddy Doherty had been caught up in the mêlée at Magilligan. He lived with his wife, Eileen, and their six children in Hamilton Street on the southern edge of the Bogside, and when he heard that the Paras had arrived in Derry on Sunday morning he told Eileen she shouldn't go on the march; there was bound to be trouble. 'The paratroopers are a bad bunch of bastards,' he warned her.

The Dohertys were veterans of civil rights marches and at the centre of the 1969 riots. When that battle was over, Paddy had come home, filthy dirty and tired out, but he and the other volunteers had held the line: the vicious police attack had been beaten back and the army had been called in to restore peace. It was a triumphal ending for the Bogsiders, however brief, because the Royal Ulster Constabulary (RUC) had lost its authority. 'It's the best holiday I've ever had,' Paddy told Eileen. In those days, he used to talk a lot about the IRA and Eileen had the feeling he had been asked to join up, but he never did. He respected the volunteers' right to take up arms, he said, but would never do so himself.

Unlike so many Bogside men, Paddy Doherty had something to lose. After leaving school at fourteen he had held odd jobs in construction, one of them in England on a big tunnelling scheme in Penrith. He returned home with a pay packet and the hope that he would be able to find work in his home town. In contrast to England's booming economy with strong trade unions, jobs in Derry were few and the unions weak; even if work was available, the wages were generally low. Some employers recruited women and youths under eighteen in order to pay them less. One electronics firm continued its under-eighteen policy until late 1996 when it sacked 1500 employees at one hour's notice and then closed down.

New industries were not coming to Derry. Between 1945 and 1966 only two in a total of 224 new industries set up in Ulster went to Derry, Ulster's second-largest city. Even Ulster's second university, for which Derry had an obvious claim, was given to Coleraine, a smaller, more prosperous and overwhelmingly Protestant city thirty miles to the east of Derry. In this atmosphere of despair, some men chose unemployment and state benefits in preference to low-wage jobs.

Paddy Doherty was hard-working, and lucky. For the last six years he had been employed at the American-owned DuPont synthetic rubber factory, starting as a labourer and rising to be a plumber's mate. He was popular and conscientious and he had a nickname, 'Skelper'; it didn't mean anything – except to distinguish him from all the other Dohertys. Now aged thirty-one, he had been married for eleven years; Eileen had been the girl next door when they were growing up. Doherty was the figure of authority in the family; he only had to call the children once and they came. Eileen respected him and almost always took his advice, but on this day she insisted on going on the march. She felt as strongly as he did about internment; that this inhuman law of locking up people without trial had to be thrown out. Paddy had agreed to be a steward on the march, so he had to go. If the stewards could not control the young stone throwers, then trouble was inevitable.

After lunch, Paddy and Eileen left their house and strolled up the hill to the Creggan, a post-World War Two council house estate. Rows of white stuccoed, two-storey houses, indistinguishable from one another, spread out from the new St Mary's Catholic church, a row of shops, a modern school and dilapidated playing fields. It was bleak and uninviting. Apart from Central Drive, the names of the streets, which were wider and longer than any to be found in the warren of Victorian terraces of the Bogside, were all named something drive or something gardens, a concept which was in the name only. Evidently, the will, or the money, to pretty up the estate with trees and shrubs was not there; not even for the cemetery. The best the residents could do was to put up wicker fences, or a hedge, round their front doors. On days when the army's armoured cars dared to penetrate the barricades, young boys pelted them with stones, just like they did in the Bogside. But the army had not been in the Creggan for some months.

Paddy and Eileen took an unusual route, cutting through the cemetery to the open ground known as the Bishop's Field, a patch of grass where the marchers were now assembling. Doherty took out his white handkerchief and tied it round his arm to show he was a steward, said 'Cheerio' to Eileen and went off to join the other stewards. Eileen said, 'Cheerio, see you later' and watched him go, cheerful and excited about the day. Remembering what he had said about the paratroopers, she joined her sisters at the back of the march. It was the last time she saw Paddy alive.

As people gathered at the Bishop's Field, there were as many women as men, which was a new development for Derry. Sunday was traditionally a day when Catholic mothers, exhausted by the burden of tending to their large families, stole two hours after lunch for a stroll and a natter, often in the Creggan cemetery.

A visit there, on the hill overlooking Derry and the River Foyle, was a genuine pleasure for these women. The view is splendid and the cemetery is a huge open space filled with memories of the large, interrelated families of the Catholic ghetto; it provided a fund of stories for good 'craic'. Dreams of a better life, in this world or the next, were spun on such afternoons. If the children had to come because there was no one at home to look after them, hide and seek among the gravestones kept them happy.

Four years of the uprising had presented these women with a

new Sunday afternoon pursuit: marching with the men. On occasion, they even marched by themselves. In May 1971 Roisin Keenan, daughter of Derry's IRA veteran Sean Keenan, started the Women's Action Committee whose first public protest against British army brutality saw 300 women march through the Bogside to an army post in the centre of the city.

Some husbands still would not let their wives go on demonstrations, but no such restriction had ever applied to Peggy Deery, a thirty-eight-year-old widow with fourteen children, one of the ghetto's better-known victims of life's injustices. She had turned out for the first protest against housing conditions in 1968 and had been on every march since then.

Peggy Deery was born in 1933 in Limewood Street in the heart of the Bogside, the last of five children. Her parents had been born in the Bogside and when they first married they lived in Miller's Close, which was separated from Bridge Street by a pub called Buckets of Blood. Her father and her two older brothers had fought in World War Two, which helped boost the family income. Her mother sold home-made toffee apples and, out of season, squares of toffee in wax paper. Peggy and her sister Nellie worked in Derry's shirt factories. Nellie had five children, and seventeen miscarriages and still-births, and Peggy had sixteen children, including three sets of twins (two children died at birth). After they married, Peggy went to Portsmouth with her husband Patsy, who painted ships for the navy while Peggy worked in a bleach factory. But they missed the extended family life of Derry; there were no grannies and aunts and uncles, no family support when you needed it in a land where the Irish labouring class was mocked and vilified.

Peggy and Patsy returned to live in tenement rooms in Magazine Street, just inside the city walls. As the family grew, so did the strains on the marriage and then Patsy was diagnosed with cancer of the spine. He died in October 1971 after a long illness that caused him and the family to suffer greatly. By then Peggy had at long last been given a council house, an aluminium-sided bungalow – with its own bathroom and a patch of grass in Swilly Gardens on the top of Creggan Hill.

Desperately poor and permanently in debt, Peggy Deery was among the leaders of the rent strike against internment. Her oldest boy, Paddy aged sixteen, had recently joined the youth wing of the IRA. On a fine day like this Sunday there was no way Peggy Deery would miss the march.

After making her family Sunday lunch, Peggy put her eldest daughter, Margie aged fourteen, in charge of the children and dressed up as though she was going on an outing. She put on a black, mock-leather, wet-look coat, which had fun-fur trimming around the hem, and shiny black boots to match. Then she walked the few hundred yards to the Bishop's Field and joined her nieces, Rita and Sandra. Owen Deery, Peggy's eleven-year-old son, accompanied his mother, even though she had told him not to come; she was embarrassed that he had a large hole in one of his shoes and told him to go home. She even gave him some money to leave the march and buy something in the shop. But to Owen it was like a day out and he tagged along. It was to be Peggy's last public protest.

Among those who thought of staying at home to watch football on television was Barney McGuigan. A forty-one-year-old unemployed painter who lived with his wife and six children in Iniscairn Crescent on the edge of the cemetery in the Creggan, McGuigan was a big, caring man who used to do maintenance work for Monarch Electric, but had lost his job when the company closed because of the Troubles. Now, he had turned his varied skills to helping the community and he had a reputation for being able to fix anything from a broken window to a motor car – his own automobile was a distinctive, lurid shade of blue, painted by himself. He was an amateur stone mason and, if you couldn't afford the prices being charged by the professionals for a gravestone, McGuigan would carve you one for free in his back garden.

There was no community centre and nothing for kids to do in the area of the Creggan where the McGuigans lived. His oldest boy, Charlie, who was nearly seventeen, had just passed five O Levels and was expecting the results of another. A younger son was at St Columb's College, the Catholic grammar school. The youngest, in primary school, had just won a handwriting contest. The McGuigans were doing well.

The flats opposite Barney's house were in a bad state, with street lights smashed, and he had started the Bligh's Lane Tenants' Association. Bligh's Lane led down into the Bogside and was the one street in the entire Free Derry area that had a police station – manned by two RUC officers with 200 British soldiers there to guard them.

After ten-o'clock mass with the family at St Mary's in the Creggan, McGuigan attended two funerals of friends, conducted by Father Daly from the cathedral, and then settled in front of the telly. Shortly after the football began, however, his sister arrived and said she was going to join the march, so he decided to go with her. McGuigan told his wife that he would be back before she cooked the tea. When he left home, she gave him a rag soaked in vinegar as protection against CS gas. She always did that when he was going into the Bogside and there was a likelihood of trouble. Before leaving Barney told his son, Charlie, that in no circumstances was he to go on the march, there was too much chance of it turning violent. A friend of Charlie's suggested they could still go down to the town to see what was happening without being on the march and so they set off anyway.

II

City Under Siege

The Bogside is now a community in revolt

> *Father Anthony Mulvey, Report of Tribunal of*
> *Inquiry into Violence and Civil Disturbance in*
> *Northern Ireland, 1969*

Bogside was once a street, now it is a condition

> *Seamus Deane*

SUNDAY, 30 JANUARY 1972, broke over the north coast of Ireland crisp and clear with a fresh southerly breeze, a day when the soft greens of the Inishowen mountains come magically alive in the winter sun, hinting of spring. On such days, if you stand on the sand dunes at the mouth of Lough Foyle you can see Scotland, so they say. To the south, inland down the lough, lies the ancient city of Londonderry, one of the most beautiful natural harbours in all of Ireland. Over the centuries Gaelic chieftains, medieval earls, English kings, Catholics and Protestants have fought viciously for control of the settlement and it's easy to see why. It is a 'holy city', of sorts.

Perched on a hill rising 120 feet above the River Foyle, it commands views west to Donegal, and east and south to the heart of Ulster. The hill was once protected from the mainland by a bog so waterlogged that English invaders in 1600 described the settlement as an island. It was covered with oaks and known as 'the Derry', from the old Irish daire, modern Irish, doire, meaning 'oakwood', or 'oakgrove'. Protestant planters from the city of London developed the fertile Foyle valley and the name was changed in their honour by royal seal to 'London'derry – a prefix Irish Catholics never accepted and most people who live there, Catholic or Protestant, call it plain Derry.

In the seventeenth century the English planters built massive walls around the settlement – a six-foot-thick outer layer of local schist, quarried from the hill, with a twelve-foot earthen rampart.

These fortifications became a symbol of Protestant domination. In 1689, when England's Catholic King James II was battling William of Orange for the British throne, James laid siege to the city, but a Protestant citizens' army kept the king's men at bay and the walls were never breached.

As the city grew, streets of tiny terraced houses sprang up outside the walls – Nailor's Row and Tanner's Row and Fish Lane. The Irish Catholics built two churches, the Long Tower on the legendary site of the monastery of St Columcille, Derry's religious founder, and later the much grander St Eugene's Cathedral whose sheer size and grand spire marked the advent of established Catholicism. But the Catholics were left in no doubt as to who was in charge. The names of the colonists were nailed to the streets: English kings and queens – William, Mary, James, Victoria – or English generals – Marlborough – or great British victories – Waterloo, or the Protestant governor of the city during the siege, the Rev. George Walker. The British garrison was housed in Ebrington Barracks, a nineteenth-century fortified site across the River Foyle.

The bog between the hill and the mainland became the Catholic ghetto, known as the Bogside.

The 1921 partition of Ireland placed the city of Derry four miles inside the new statelet of Northern Ireland, whose population was sixty-seven per cent Protestant, or Unionist, and thirty-three per cent Catholic and Nationalist. In Derry, before partition, anti-Unionists had traditionally returned a majority to the local council, but the constituency boundaries were redrawn in a dazzling gerrymander that put the Unionists in control, and kept them there. Despite a growing Catholic majority (it is now fifty: fifty) the Protestants always won local elections by twelve seats to eight.

In the Bogside a severe housing shortage and searing unemployment went uncorrected – somewhere between twenty and thirty per cent being out of work. The forlorn images of physical and moral decay were everywhere; unemployed men hanging around on street corners, spending money they didn't have in betting shops and pubs, taking to their beds for weeks on end; mothers who had no money to put a decent meal on the table, or the will to clean their houses; youths taking to hooliganism and vandalism. In the local poet Seamus Deane's words: 'Bogside was once a street. Now it is a condition.'

In 1968, the Catholic working class rose up against this human misery, taking inspiration from the poor blacks of the US ghettos and the segregated townships of apartheid. The young socialist theoreticians saw themselves as 'Ulster's white negroes'.

At first the protests were about jobs and housing: 'One Man – One Job' and 'One Family – One Home'. Demonstrations, pickets, sit-ins, teach-ins, rent strikes – all the bugle and bluster of a Sixties citizens' revolt pumped new life into worn-out bodies. They marched, sang songs, held meetings, formed organizations which split and splintered, printed leaflets and painted anti-British slogans on the walls of their slums. It seemed to those who lived in this ghetto that overthrow of the institutions of power was now a real possibility: this was not a revolt of neo-Marxists posing as 'red brigades', or élitist radicals on the Left Bank, or disciples of Danny The Red, this was a genuine citizens' uprising. The masses were on the move, as they were in the American South.

The government soon clamped down; marches were banned; march organizers were arrested, refused to pay fines and were imprisoned, just like their fathers, uncles, grandfathers and great-uncles before them. But the defiance of British rule by this new wave of protesters was no longer the stuff of folklore, of ballads and yarns, sung and narrated in front parlours and pubs – although there was always some of that, of course.

In the exuberant congregation gathering at the Bishop's Field on this Sunday, one famous Bogsider was conspicuously absent. He was John Hume, civil rights leader, self-styled voice of moderation, non-violent follower of Martin Luther King, 'spoiled priest', teacher, one-time smoked salmon entrepreneur and Stormont MP for the new centrist political group, the Social and Democratic Labour Party. The SDLP civil rights platform included the reunification of Ireland but through the consent of the majority, not the gun. Since the first march in 1968, Hume had deliberately set himself apart from the more militant protesters – and especially from the IRA. On this day, Hume was expecting violence and had deliberately stayed at home.

The eldest of seven children, Hume knew as much as any Bogsider about poverty and discrimination. His mother could only write her name and his father was unemployed for twenty years after World War Two.

Yet, in a way, Hume was privileged. He had the good fortune to reach school age at a time when Britain's post-war education acts gave the working class a chance to attend fee-paying secondary schools – in Hume's case St Columb's College.

It was founded by the Catholic clergy of Derry in 1879, primarily to prepare students for the priesthood. Early graduates formed the professionals of the emerging Catholic middle class (the alumni now include the Nobel Prize-winning poet Seamus Heaney and Seamus Deane).

Two graduates of St Columb's were to make a political differ-ence in the Sixties Catholic uprising, not only in Derry but across the province. They were John Hume and Eamonn McCann. In place of the military campaigns of the old-style IRA, they led protests that offered solutions through mass civilian demon-strations and self-help reforms; their ambitious goal was to use the issues of jobs and housing to transcend the sectarian divide and provide a bridge to unite the Catholic and Protestant working classes. Unification of Ireland, should it come, would be evolu-tionary – through the will of the Northern majority.

Hume was invariably photographed at the front of the crowd, priest-like, persuading everyone to sit down in a peaceful protest and leading the singing of 'We Shall Overcome'. In measured tones, calculated not to inflame passions, he negotiated with police or army officers demanding the crowd disperse or be arrested. Once they arrested Hume himself.

As the Derry action groups proliferated, Hume sided with the business and professional class, among them Michael Canavan and Ivan Cooper. Each would become a member of the SDLP. Canavan was a founder member with Hume of the Derry Credit Union and also owned a chain of bookmakers' shops, a pub and a salmon-processing factory. Cooper, a Protestant, was a member of the young Unionist Party in the early Sixties, but left to join the Derry Labour Party. Hume, Canavan and Cooper appealed to an important sector of conservative Derry Catholics because they were seen as reasonable, mature, well-connected and intent on non-violent demonstrations.

To succeed (where the old-style militarism of the IRA had failed), the new protest movement had to attract, and keep, this important middle ground of Catholic opinion, which included the Church. In these early days the clergy viewed attacks on the army as too dis- ruptive of the social fabric, leading to vandalism and criminal activity. They urged a restoration of control by forces of the crown – the RUC and the army – and they blamed the 'communist' ten- dencies of the young socialist left for leading the youth astray.

McCann was the symbol of such leftward leanings. Like Hume, he was for peaceful protests, but he had fire in his belly, uncom- promising rhetoric and a starkly different image. A self-styled revolutionary socialist, he saw Hume and his group as 'middle- aged, middle-class and middle-of-the-road'.

McCann plunged into the radical politics of the day. He, too, had grown up in the Bogside, but after St Columb's College he had studied history at the University of Belfast, where he was a member of a militant group of socialists, who eventually coalesced under the banner of Peoples' Democracy. Their aim was an all- inclusive revolution.

In Derry, this approach had greater appeal than elsewhere in Northern Ireland, especially Belfast; the intimacy of Derry seemed to blunt the knife-edge of sectarian hatred in a way that always appeared impossible in the meaner religious enclaves of Belfast. Derry was a softer city and the Catholics had a better sense of their own identity; they were a more self-supporting and common-sense community.

McCann's generation of schoolchildren were not taught to hate Protestants; they resented them, of course, because they barred unification with the South, and they engineered and controlled the instruments of discrimination against Catholics. And every 12 August, they marched in memory of William of Orange and threw pennies from the city walls at the less fortunate Bogsiders. The pennies were missiles of contempt.

While Hume worked instinctively from the top, seeking an alliance of Catholic and Unionist moderates, McCann's vision reflected the youthful radicalism of the times: flamboyant direct action – sit-ins, pickets and squats. Hume's approach was too soft, too slow for McCann. He left Derry for a while to edit the socialist *Irish Militant* in London, returning in 1967, as a member of the left wing of the Labour Party to set up a direct-action housing group. The Derry Housing Action Committee started with twenty members who were so headstrong they split twice within the first few months; one group complained it was 'too political', the other that it was not political enough.

Derry's desperate housing problem gave McCann's group great opportunities for publicity. Young Republicans, loosely organized by the Bogside-born Finbar O'Doherty, an indefatigable pamphleteer, marcher and protester, helped fend off bullying bailiffs used by landlords for evictions. The most famous case was that of Ellen (Nelly) McDonnell. Aged forty-eight, she lived at 17 Harvey Street, just below the city walls, with her son and daughter. Her husband had died prematurely after being wounded while serving with the British Army in the North African Desert during World War Two. The young Republicans took up her case, moved into the house ahead of the bailiffs and barricaded the door, but an RUC Special Branch officer, posing as an inspector from the electricity department, tricked his way inside and Nelly McDonnell defended her home by hurling crockery at the police. She lost the fight, but was found another place to live and her spirited defence spurred others to greater opposition.

O'Doherty would write, 'We viewed ourselves as Ulster's white negroes – a repressed and forgotten dispossessed tribe captured within a bigoted, partitionist statelet that no Irish elector had cast a vote to create . . .' Older, traditional Republicans complained of the youth group's extremism and its 'communistic ideas'. The Bishop of Derry, Neil Farren, warned young people not to let themselves be led by the mob.

The mass demonstrations began. The first march in Derry was on 5 October 1968. McCann and fellow-activist Eamon Melaugh chose a deliberately provocative route starting in the mostly Protestant Waterside, over the Craigavon Bridge across the Foyle and into the Diamond, the main intersection in the town's shopping centre. They borrowed the duplicator at the Derry Canine Club, to turn out stirring leaflets calling on the working class to 'Unite and Fight', 'Class War, not Creed War' and 'Orange and Green Tories Out', 'Police State Here'. The march was banned by Stormont, which only served to give it more publicity.

They were hoping for thousands but only 400 turned up at the Waterside railway station. It didn't matter, the police were so brutal that the march made history anyway. Constables blocked the marchers in front and behind, and without warning started swinging their batons. Gerry Fitt, the Nationalist MP, was one of the first to have his head bloodied, followed by fellow MPs Austin Currie and Eddie McAteer. Many were felled in the mêlée, poles and placards went flying. About one hundred ended up in hospital. For the first time, the police used a water cannon, which had such force that it washed the demonstrators clean across the

Craigavon Bridge over the River Foyle. Rioting at the Diamond continued into the night. McCann, Melaugh and Finbar O'Doherty were arrested the next afternoon, charged with contravention of the government's ban.

Images of the baton-wielding police clubbing unarmed demonstrators and MPs were shown around the world, stirring up the Catholic population as never before. The police acted 'without justification or excuse', the Cameron Commission would later conclude. The Northern Ireland Civil Rights Association, or NICRA, had achieved its first real victory. Predictably, Stormont's Home Affairs Minister, William Craig, charged that the march was 'a Republican front' for the IRA and communists. There was some truth in the charge.

The next big confrontation with the police – the three-day Battle of the Bogside – in the summer of 1969 was so violent that in response to a request from Stormont the British Labour government sent troops to 'aid the civil power' in restoring law and order. After the battle, Father Anthony Mulvey, a Catholic priest and pioneer of housing reform, now declared the Bogside was a 'community in revolt'. On a gable end of St Columb's Street appeared the defiant words: 'You Are Now Entering Free Derry.'

This icon of the revolution was beamed worldwide and locally Bogsiders tuned into their own propaganda; Radio Free Derry, the 'Voice of Liberation', began broadcasting calls to 'join your vigilante patrols' while not forgetting 'to love one another and keep cool'.

This tiny area of the United Kingdom became a symbol of the 1960s struggles for civil rights; the name Bogside took its place with Paris, Prague, Birmingham and Selma. It was a place where a new volunteer army of Irish Nationalists set aside the gun and took to the streets in mass civil disobedience.

In four years this uprising achieved more social progress than in the past four decades after partition, but by the beginning of the Seventies the instruments of repression and discrimination, the armed police of the Royal Ulster Constabulary and the Northern Ireland parliament at Stormont with its unassailable Unionist majority, were as entrenched as ever.

In the ultimate act of civil disobedience, the citizens of the Bogside and the Creggan, 33,000 in all, declared themselves independent from the civil authority and sealed off their ghetto from the rest of the city with barricades of rubble, slabs of concrete, old bedsteads, iron girders, planks of wood with rusty nails, burnt-out trucks and cars. Inside this Catholic enclave the rule of law did not exist. Young IRA volunteers, in black balaclavas and combat fatigues, manned the barricades with an arsenal of weapons from bygone campaigns, rusty and unreliable, some unable to fire a bullet when bullets were available, which was not often. Even so, the police and army entered the Bogside at their peril; there was always one gun that worked.

Such an affront to the Northern Ireland parliament at Stormont, the constabulary and the forces of the British crown became too much to bear; new repressive measures were introduced.

In August 1971 Stormont implemented the second tool (after the gerrymander) of Protestant domination: internment of 340 rebels without trial. In the Bogside and the Creggan, sixteen men were picked up in dawn raids, including the veteran Republican, Sean Keenan. The numbers were few, but in the intimate community of the Bogside everyone knew someone who had been 'lifted'. Internment united the ghetto and over the coming weeks, as reports came from the prison camps of ill-treatment and torture – cruel and unusual punishment, the European Court of Human Rights would call it after an inquiry – the focus of demonstrations turned from housing and jobs to the Special Powers Act and institution of power, the Unionist-controlled Stormont parliament.

The law allowing internment without trial was passed after partition as the Civil Authorities (Special Powers) Act (Northern

Ireland) 1922. It was renewed annually until 1933, when the Stormont parliament made it permanent. Known as the Special Powers Act, it allows the suspension of any and all of the basic liberties, from habeas corpus to freedom of the press; permits arrest on suspicion, searches without warrant; allows curfews, a ban on meetings, marches, assemblies (including fairs and markets); permits punishment by flogging, denies trial by jury and dispenses with the holding of inquests on 'any dead bodies found in Northern Ireland'. The application of these powers was subject to fewer safeguards than the Emergency Powers Act which the British Parliament passed at the start of war with Germany in 1939 – and there was little risk of judicial pusillanimity in enforcing the Act because by the 1970s the Protestants held a permanent majority in the High Court.

After August 1971, council house tenants refused to pay their rent in protest against internment. The strikes were enthusiastically embraced by the poorest Bogsiders who used the money saved to put meat on the dinner table. The government retaliated with a new law, the Payment for Debt (Emergency Provisions) Act, Northern Ireland, 1971, which punished rent strikers by deducting monies from their social security and pension benefits on which so many Bogsiders relied. A shooting war broke out between the IRA and the army. The confrontation escalated. By year's end, another wave of demonstrations was launched.

In the bowl of the Bogside, overlooked by the city walls and a new council house estate in the Creggan, the deafening boom of the bombs, the thump of rubber bullet guns and the sharp crack of modern high-velocity rifles were heard every day, sometimes several times a day. If you lived in the middle of this bowl, in the high flats rising nine storeys above Rossville Street, or the new maisonettes in Glenfada Park, or Columbcille Court, or Abbey Place, it was like being in an echo chamber where the sound of bombs and gunfire was all around and you had no idea where it was coming from.

The civil rights marches had eclipsed the IRA; its daring exploits before partition, and in the failed 1950s campaign, were frozen in time. Neither the IRA, nor the Nationalist Party for that matter, had put forward any new ideas to draw in the new wave of civil rights protesters. As John Hume put it, '. . . they reiterated the principles of the heroes and if you voted against them, you voted against the patriot dead.' In McCann's view, 'They were living out too urgently the ideals to which, tacitly, we were all committed.'

To the Nationalist Party, political life was either Orange or Green and activism confined to waving flags and chanting slogans. Created after partition, the party's avowed aim four decades later was still to remove the border. Party officials complained loudly about the way Catholics were treated, yet offered no constructive, let alone bipartisan, solutions. Trade union groups argued that the urgent social need was jobs, not reunification, but the Nationalists shouted them down: 'We don't want their jobs and houses, we want our freedom.' Union leaders were branded by the Irish patriots as communists – and, although they were essentially Labourites, the label stuck.

Local Republican veterans such as Paddy Shiels, Neil Gillespie and Sean Keenan were regarded by the new breed of reformers and radicals 'with guilty pride', as McCann put it. Their exploits had been of an especially stage-Irish nature – 'courageous, amateur, comic, intermittently savage'. A local story illustrates the theme.

On the east shore of Lough Foyle – the Ulster side – the IRA decided to plant a bomb at the British military camp at Ballykelly, originally an airfield. The target was chosen more for its accessibility than its strategic importance. The plan was to row two boats ten miles across the lough from the Donegal shore, plant a massive delayed-fuse bomb of gelignite against the wall of one of the army buildings and escape before it went off by rowing back across the water.

The six recruits were country boys from Cork and Limerick who under orders joined the Limerick Rowing Club, a posh Anglo-Irish establishment, and sculled furiously up and down the Shannon river to tone up for the task. When judged fit enough for action, they journeyed north and set out, in a blinding snowstorm, in two boats across Lough Foyle. As they approached the eastern shore, floodlights of the army encampment suddenly switched on and, fearing they had been detected, they quickly changed course and rowed downstream for a while

In the end they dumped their bags of gelignite with charges set against a building that, in the darkness, loomed so large they thought it must be important. They made their retreat back across the lough crammed into one boat, because the guard they had left on the shore had been restraining the second boat with the butt of his rifle and when he lifted it to challenge the returning warriors the craft drifted away. Halfway across the lough an oar broke, but the massive explosion heartened them. Back in the Republic they were picked up by the Irish police scavenging food from a farm and interned. It was only then that they learned the building they had blown up was one of Ulster's ancient monuments, a Napoleonic Martello tower.

By 1967 the IRA, in the words of its chief of staff, Cathal Goulding, was virtually finished. 'In August of that year we called a meeting of local leadership throughout the country to assess the strength and we discovered we had no movement.' Circulation of the IRA's newspaper, the *United Irishman*, once close to 100,000, had dropped to 14,000. The IRA certainly held no appeal for the likes of John Hume, but nor did it attract the self-proclaimed socialist revolutionaries like McCann. Goulding knew that to survive the IRA had to attach itself, in some way, to the new civil rights movement. 'The first job is to organize the people in civil agitation [over] housing and civil rights; issues like that. Our job then is to defend these people.' In other words reforms first; violence second, if the reforms were not implemented. The IRA would eventually split over the issue of which came first into the Provisionals, who wanted to keep going with the campaign of violence, and the Officials, who primarily sought social change.

Goulding attended the first secret meeting of NICRA in 1966 but there was never any question of the IRA taking control: NICRA's leadership was composed of middle-class Catholics, a handful of communists and a number of well-known Republicans who were not IRA volunteers and would never have accepted orders from Goulding. The Unionist government in Stormont, the British government in Whitehall and the British army would always claim that NICRA was an IRA front, but this was too simplistic. The Cameron Commission came closest to the truth, perhaps, observing that 'while there is evidence that members of the IRA are active in the organization, there is no sign that they are in any sense dominant or in a position of control or direct policy . . .'

In Derry, left-wing Republicans revived the IRA by involving volunteers in housing evictions and other social activism – precisely the direction Goulding wanted them to go. But the more violent the police action became, the more attractive were the rallying cries of older Derry republicans like Sean Keenan. 'We have only two cheeks and we have turned the other for the last time,' he said after demonstrators on the Belfast–Derry march on New Year's Day 1969 ran into the RUC ambush at Burntollet Bridge, and the hated B-Specials (police reservists) had run amok that night in the Bogside.

As the mass protests dissolved into violence in the summer of that year, the issues of British rule, the new presence of British troops and the goal of a united Ireland returned to centre stage. To most Republicans in Derry this now seemed to be a decisive moment in history, the best opportunity ever to topple the state. It became harder and harder for moderates like Hume to advocate non-violence.

On 19 July 1969, they buried Samuel Devenney, a middle-aged man who had been viciously beaten by police three months earlier in his own home in William Street. The funeral was attended by 15,000 people, according to the Protestant newspaper *Londonderry Sentinel* – more than attended most civil rights protests. Next month the Battle of the Bogside confirmed what many already believed: Free Derry could no longer be defended by stones and barricades; the vigilante groups had to be armed. The civil rights movement and advocates of non-violence took a back seat while a new IRA campaign of bombings and shootings was cranked up.

It took a long time – almost a year – before the first shot was fired at a British soldier in the Bogside. It was not a matter of fetching the tommy-guns down from the attic, or digging up buried caches of ammunition. In the IRA's Derry armoury only a small number of weapons worked – a few revolvers, some Thompson sub-machine guns smuggled into Ireland with the Cork football team in 1921, a number of pre-World War One rifles and a Martini Henri .303. No more than a handful of men knew how to shoot.

Towards the end of 1969, Sean Keenan opened up his contacts with the Dublin government and took the first of several trips to the United States looking for guns and money, and the Irish government arranged for some Derry men to have weapons training at an Irish army base across the border in Donegal. But these efforts were short-lived, ending in the 'arms trial' of Irish government ministers and exposure by the press of the training sessions, which halted abruptly. In early January 1970, the Irish police raided a house in Donegal and found seven Derry men and a machine-gun left lying on a sofa.

The same month the IRA formally split into Provisionals and Officials, the Derry 'Provos' led by Sean Keenan openly criticizing the 'ultra-left' politics of the Officials, and the young radicals in the Officials accusing the Provos of weakening the Republican movement by splitting off. If anything, the Provos had the upper hand in the community, which distrusted the leftist tilt of the Officials.

The Derry Officials announced they would 'take action against collaborators with the British occupation forces in the Bogside' and gradually moved away from the leftist alliance that included young socialists still seeking reforms like Eamonn McCann. He was accused of not being revolutionary enough, to which he replied, '. . . the transformation necessary to implement these reforms is a revolution.' The success of the Republican revival in Derry depended, to a large extent, on Derry's youth (boys *and* girls) who increasingly were being picked up by British troops for 'riotous behaviour', often on flimsy evidence, and jailed for up to six months. They were ready to join up; the ranks of both IRA factions swelled with volunteers, many of whom were not even old enough to vote.

The steady flow of recruits coincided with the moderate Catholic community's rising rejection of the army's authority; many of the middle-class who had welcomed the troops as a buffer against the RUC now saw them as an army of occupation, harshly, sometimes brutally, enforcing laws that still discriminated against Catholics. This was the key change that allowed the new militarism to flourish. By not condemning the uprising, the clergy began to play a greater, though still strictly non-violent, supportive role.

By the summer of 1970, the Provisionals were ready to start their bombing campaign. The Belfast Provos struck first but it took the Derry volunteers a few weeks to catch up because of an early setback. Three middle-aged Derry Provos blew themselves up (and killed two girls aged nine and three) while putting together a bomb in a house in the Creggan.

The first IRA shots in Derry were fired at British troops in Bishop Street after riots in August 1970; all six bullets missed their target. For the next eleven months only a handful of isolated shots were recorded and nobody was hit: weapons and ammunition were still in short supply. It was hard to say who was responsible for the shooting because neither wing, Provos nor Officials, would own up to the attacks.

The first bomb in Derry was exploded at an electricity sub-station in William Street in September 1970. A month later two gelignite bombs were thrown over the perimeter wall of an army base in the Strand Road. In 1971, bombings of buildings in the city centre and car hijackings became a regular addition to the daily stone-throwing. In Belfast, the systematic shooting of British soldiers started in early 1971.

In August, after internment, the level of violence escalated across Northern Ireland. By year's end the Provisionals were losing a war of attrition in Belfast and seeking an excuse to return to mass protests on the streets. They proposed a series of marches against internment and in defiance of the permanent ban on demon-strations. NICRA and the Official IRA, looking at a wider picture and keen to keep the initiative, proposed ending internment as the first step to a lasting peace. Their proposals were ignored by the Tory government of Edward Heath, so they also planned a series of marches. One of them was to be in Derry – the crucible of the revolt.

The question, literally, was how far to go? Should the march be kept inside Free Derry and avoid confrontation with the troops, as the John Hume faction advocated, or should it try to break out of the Bogside and hold a protest meeting at the Guildhall, the old symbol of repressive Protestant rule? This was the preference of the Creggan faction, led by Bridget Bond, one of the driving forces behind the rent strikes.

NICRA organizers from Belfast found open warfare between the two factions – typical of Derry's political fragmentation and split leadership. A week before, the two sides agreed on the route: it should start in the Creggan, go down to Free Derry Corner, up again to St Eugene's Cathedral and then down William Street. The idea was to pick up supporters en route.

At aggro corner, the moderates favoured making a right turn into Rossville Street; the Bond faction wanted to keep going down

William Street to rattle the barricade in the hope of ending up at a meeting at the Guildhall. The word was spreading fast that the IRA would leave its guns behind.

The Provisionals and the Officials told the NICRA organizers they would not engage the troops for fear of starting a firefight in which civilians would be harmed. They believed the army might use the march as a pretext to invade Free Derry – launching an attack in the Creggan estate after the marchers had left their homes and descended into the Bogside. The Creggan, with its wider avenues and streets, was more vulnerable to a military assault than the Bogside's narrow lanes and derelict houses that provided cover for IRA snipers. Both wings of the IRA planned to keep their weapons in cars patrolling the Creggan for the afternoon. Strict orders were given to volunteers to fire in self-defence, and then only if it did not endanger marchers.

On the eve of the march Dr Raymond McClean, a Derry doctor who was part of the John Hume faction, went with his brothers-in-law, Danny and Micky McGuiness, to the Rocking Chair bar in Waterloo Street, then a reliable source of information about current activity of the IRA.

McClean had a conventional middle-class upbringing as a bright, hard-working Catholic schoolboy. He went to St Columb's, was a brilliant student, footballer and star boxer at Dublin University, graduated from Dublin's Royal College of Surgeons. He also served as a medical officer in the Royal Air Force, part of the time in the Middle East. On returning to Derry in 1958, he worked as a GP in the Bogside among the chronically sick and the poverty-stricken families of slums like Nailor's Row and Walker's Place. McClean saw first-hand the grass-roots effects of the gerrymander and he became a dedicated community activist.

McClean left the pub that night assured there would be no violence, at least from the IRA, but he still wondered about the paratroopers; he had seen them in action at Magilligan. He arrived home later that evening, worrying about the next day. He would say later,

> I admitted to myself that I was secretly relieved that I would have no responsibility for crowd control during the march, as the march was being organized and stewarded by NICRA, of which I was not an active member. I could not put my finger on the basic source of my discomfort, other than the fact that apparently the paratroopers were coming to Derry for the day. I couldn't clearly understand the reason behind that decision.

On the Sunday afternoon, after an early lunch, Dr McClean put his bag of emergency equipment in his car and drove to the Creggan with Micky and Danny McGuiness to join the others assembling at the Bishop's Field.

People were in a good mood; the blue and white civil rights banner was unfurled and looked splendid, even though it was rather difficult to control in the freshening southerly breeze. All kinds of people turned up: labourers, shopkeepers, barmen, doctors, accountants, lawyers, plus an equal number, it seemed, of women, teenagers and schoolchildren. The atmosphere was so relaxed and cheerful that McClean decided to leave his medical bag in the car.

A contingent of Catholic paramedics from the Knights of Malta, the Dublin-based Red Cross, was on hand. Some were dressed in their traditional grey military-style uniforms and peaked hats with white canvas first-aid bags. They looked like an army medical corps from the First World War. Others wore white coats. These volunteers always turned out wherever there were crowds – football matches or civil rights marches – and were known, affectionately, as 'the blood-suckers'.

Teenagers joined the Knights of Malta because it was something to do and there was a good social life; they took an eight-week course and then had weekly meetings. Their commanding officer in Derry, a teacher named Leo Day, was expecting trouble after Magilligan and had asked for thirty volunteers, ranging in age from seventeen to seventy. Some of them wanted to wear their steel helmets but, apprehensive as he was, Commander Day vetoed that: 'We are not going to war.'

If war was not exactly on the minds of the hard-core hooligans in Derry, some were certainly looking forward to a good afternoon riot. Among them were sixteen-year-old Sean O'Neill, John Duffy and their comrades, who were regulars at aggro corner and considered rioting to be good 'craic'. They used to plan disturbances in advance; a notice went up one day on Abbey Street, 'Rioting Begins at 2 p.m. Sharp' and never came down.

Sean and John were known as 'frontliners'. They both had nicknames: Sean was 'The General', sometimes 'Firebomb'. The knowledge they knew they were costing the British exchequer a small fortune by keeping troops on the streets made the gassing and the occasional bruises from rubber bullets worth putting up with. On this day they were out to avenge the beating the marchers had taken on the strand at Magilligan a week earlier.

Right on schedule, the flat-topped coal lorry belonging to McGlinchey's, almost brand-new and glinting in the sunlight, arrived to lead the procession and to carry the civil rights dignitaries and the loud-speaker system. All that was needed now was someone to say it was time to go.

At 2.45 p.m. Kevin McCorry, a NICRA organizer from Belfast, climbed on to the lorry and told the driver to set off down the hill; the stewards tried to keep the marchers in line, but Derry's youth raced to the front, relishing a clash with the troops. The youths took no notice of a group of stern women from Belfast, led by Madge Davidson, who were trying to shepherd people into tidy rows. 'Let's show that Belfast can march,' cried Ms Davidson. 'Come on there, five abreast, get in line.' Bernadette Devlin and Eamonn McCann chuckled at the women – and at the amplifiers on the back of the lorry which were not working. McCorry was issuing orders, trying to keep control. 'Anyone in front of the lorry is not part of the march,' he announced, but his voice was lost to all but those beside him. And even if the others had heard, they would not have taken any notice. People were in such good humour, the turnout was terrific, the sun was shining. It was more like a Sunday outing to the beaches of Donegal than a political demonstration.

As the marchers wound down from the Creggan, people were coming out of their houses and joining in. When they passed checkpoints and army barriers, the soldiers radioed back crowd estimates to headquarters: their figures started at several hundred, but it was difficult to gauge true numbers because the crowd was so spread out. The police were calling in varying numbers: 1000 entering Southway, then 2000 and 'in excess of 3000' by the time the march had reached William Street. At Free Derry Corner, as the coal lorry turned back up the hill, a group of a hundred or so youths broke away from the march as it turned up Westland Street and moved across in front of the Rossville flats towards aggro corner.

Among them were 'the General' and his comrades. In their pockets they had two army-issue CS gas canisters which troops had fired at them a couple of days earlier but which had failed to explode. Today they were going to send them back to the army.

III

Operation Forecast

I am coming to the conclusion that the minimum force necessary to achieve a restoration of law and order is to shoot ringleaders among the Derry Young Hooligans

General Robert Ford, Derry, 7 January 1972

The outcome of this weekend could have very long-term effects on the campaign

Lt. Col James Ferguson, CO, 22nd Light Air Defence Regiment, Derry, 28 January 1972

SHORTLY BEFORE 2 P.M., Chief Superintendent Frank Lagan of the RUC drove through the security checks at Ebrington Barracks, the Victorian headquarters in the Waterside of 8 Infantry Brigade. As head of the force's 'N' division, Lagan was responsible for policing Derry and had been invited by the local army commander, Brigadier Pat MacLellan, to follow the progress of the march from the army's operations room. He was carrying last-minute intelligence from his sources in the Bogside.

With less than an hour to go before the march left the Bishop's Field, Lagan, one of the most senior Catholics in the RUC, had been tipped off that the NICRA organizers would not attempt to break through the army barrier at the bottom of William Street and march to the Guildhall. Instead, the procession would be halted by stewards at aggro corner and be made to turn right along Rossville Street. The rally with the speakers would be held at Free Derry Corner.

Lagan was immensely relieved. He knew that any attempt by the marchers to force the William Street barrier and possibly enter the city centre would result in prolonged rioting, and the longer the riot the greater the temptation for freelance gunmen, ignoring IRA orders to fire only in self-defence, to take pot-shots at the massive concentration of troops surrounding the Bogside. The presence of the paratroopers had heightened the risk. Lagan assumed that Brigadier MacLellan would also be delighted by NICRA's change of plans.

Once inside the Ebrington compound, Lagan was escorted direct to MacLellan's headquarters, which comprised two connecting offices adjoining the Operations room. As Lagan arrived, radio messages were coming in over the brigade's radio net from troops manning barriers around the city.

Lagan found MacLellan deep in conversation with his immediate superior, Major-General Robert Ford, Commander of Land Forces (CLF) for Northern Ireland. Ford controlled day-to-day operations of three brigades from the army's headquarters at Lisburn, near Belfast; his presence in Derry was a measure of the significance the army attached to the day's operation.

The two officers had just finished a working lunch when Lagan approached them with his urgent information, but instead of welcoming the news Ford immediately turned his back on him and MacLellan followed suit. Without saying a word, they strode into the adjoining room, where other headquarters staff were gathering.

Lagan recalled that he was left standing by himself in MacLellan's outer office. Through the open door he could see his own superior from Belfast, Assistant Chief Constable David Corbett. Without consulting Lagan again, they all left through a door on the far side of the room.

As a Catholic and a local police officer, Lagan was outside the political–military establishment in Belfast; it was hard for him fully to comprehend the underlying frustrations of senior army officers who were desperate to find a military solution to Derry's no-go area. Had the Bogside been a rebellious enclave in a distant British colony, it would have been brought to heel long ago. Instead, the Northern Ireland army command was watching the progressive destruction of Derry's commercial district by a rebellious band of teenagers. It was profoundly humiliating for commanders in charge of troops equipped with highly sophisticated weapons, who had extensive experience of internal security operations.

In a report to his superior, General Harry Tuzo, Ford had

identified the so-called Derry Young Hooligans (DYH) as the underlying problem and flagged the NICRA march this Sunday as a potential flashpoint. Any large-scale confrontation with the DYH would present an opportunity for the army to assess the likely reaction to military invasion of the Bogside. The code name of Ford's plan seemed prophetic: Operation Forecast. The army had prepared for confrontation, but Lagan's latest information suggested that serious trouble could still be avoided.

For several weeks the army's high command in Northern Ireland had been secretly discussing how to deal with the increasingly embarrassing and unacceptable problem of the no-go area of the Bogside and the Creggan – and especially of the roving bands of stone-throwing youths who rioted every afternoon, disrupting business and keeping shoppers out of the commercial centre. MacLellan's orders, since he arrived in Derry at the end of October 1971, had been 'progressively to restore the rule of law', but instead the Catholics had built more barricades (there were at least thirty, of varying effectiveness, in the Bogside and the Creggan). The afternoon mayhem at aggro corner had also become more frequent and more intense, with nail bombs and petrol bombs, and a dramatic increase in the number of shots fired at troops by each wing of the IRA. The RUC maintained only a token presence at the sole military post in the area on Bligh's Lane, halfway up the hill to the Creggan. Far from being reduced, the boundaries of the no-go area were actually expanding beyond the northern 'front line' on William Street. Once a busy street packed with small shops and bars, it now looked like a street in the blitz with the jagged remains of fire-bombed houses, a wrecked cinema, a derelict bakery and a disused shirt factory boarded up with corrugated-iron sheets which the rioters used as shields. Only two shops were still open for business.

General Ford was under tremendous pressure, from local business owners, mostly Protestants, from Stormont politicians and also from the Chief of the Defence Staff in London, General Sir Michael Carver. All looked to Ford for a plan to deal with Derry's defiance of authority, yet there was no obvious military solution.

Carver himself accepted that suppressing the Catholic enclaves would require a major military operation incurring many casualties, most of whom would inevitably be civilians. In the end, such action would merely inflame the unrest in the whole of Northern Ireland and infuriate the Irish Republic without producing a lasting solution in Derry.

In mid-December 1971, in a memo to British defence chiefs, Ford had wrestled with three options: containment of the Bogside and Creggan linked to a much tougher line on unrest outside the no-go area; large-scale military operations inside the Catholic enclave; or the establishment of a permanent military presence in Free Derry – in other words, an invasion.

Ford had become convinced that the local IRA in Derry was emerging as a serious threat. Adventurous exploits reminiscent of the Fifties campaign were being undertaken. During the week of 12–18 January, for example, the army and the IRA fought a running gun battle in the city cemetery up in the Creggan. An open, mostly treeless area, the only cover worth having was behind the more impressive gravestones. Even so, an army helicopter on a routine reconnaissance mission came under fire from there. A military patrol was deployed and in the clash that followed the gunmen – there must have been more than one – fired about a hundred rounds while soldiers returned forty-nine shots. The army thought that four IRA men were hit, and a fifth 'kill' was claimed later from the Bligh's Lane post.

Two days after Ford's visit, in an operation that seemed to herald a sudden new influx of IRA recruits, 157 sets of combat clothing, which had been sent by the army to Peerless Dry Cleaners in the city centre, were stolen. A press report suggested the uniforms were spirited over the border, where IRA volunteers were being trained for an operation dressed as British soldiers.

Ford had no doubt that his third option – invasion of the no-go zones – made military sense, even if it would require at least three extra infantry battalions. An energetic, hands-on soldier, he set great store by maintaining the 'offensive spirit'. First commissioned into the 4/7th Dragoon Guards – a smart cavalry regiment whose chargers had long since given way to tanks – Ford fought with distinction during the Second World War, earning a Mention in Despatches. Now forty-eight, imposingly tall and forceful by nature, he was considered a high flyer.

Ford already had a tour in Northern Ireland under his belt, although that was between 1966 and 1967, when soldiering there was altogether less eventful. At the time, Lisburn was known as 'Happy Valley' for its splendid hunting, shooting and fishing opportunities. Ford was appointed Commander of Land Forces just seventy-two hours before the introduction of internment on 9 August 1971 had plunged the province into a terrorist war.

Ford concluded in his memo that the potential political fallout of an invasion precluded its implementation. Like Carver, he thought many civilians would be killed – 'and much will be made of the slaughter of the innocents' – while military incursions with lots of soldiers into the Catholic enclave would produce only marginal returns and drive the community further into the ranks of the IRA. Aggressive patrolling increased the risk that troops would have to shoot into crowds. He chose to continue the policy of containing the no-go area – even though it meant tacit acceptance of the open revolt.

But in the first week in January Ford returned to Derry for a second opinion. In a 'personal and confidential' report to General Tuzo, the General Officer Commanding (GOC) and the overall commander in Northern Ireland, Ford took a markedly tougher line. He was shocked, he wrote, to find Brigadier MacLellan and Chief Superintent Lagan admitting that 'The Front', the northern boundary of the no-go area along William Street, would soon be moving north, not just by one block but two – into the residential areas of Great James Street and Clarendon Street. This meant that Derry's main shopping centre would, in MacLellan's and Lagan's view, 'become extinct during the next few months'.

Most of the bomb damage, Ford learnt, was being done by teenagers carrying five- to ten-pound bombs of high explosive in handbags. Typically, they would arrive undetected in Derry's main commercial street, Strand Road, by dodging in and out of derelict buildings leading out of the Bogside, thus avoiding any checkpoints on the main thoroughfares. They would then slip into the shopping crowds so that the regular three-man infantry patrols – fourteen were on the streets at any one time – could not spot them. Once in the crowd, the bombers were often given protection by the shoppers, Ford complained. 'The vast majority of the people . . . not only give no help to our patrols but, if they saw a youth with a very small bag which might contain a bomb, they would be likely to shield the youth's movements from the view of our patrols.'

At a meeting with shopkeepers and businessmen from the Strand Road, Ford had listened to 'the usual pessimistic message' about the bombers and stressed the need to have security guards checking bags at the entrances to their premises. He had also agreed to block off one of the alleys leading into Strand Road and look at the possibility of placing more observation posts on the tops of high buildings. Ford ended the meeting by giving what he called, 'the usual encouraging talk about the Province as a whole'. But the traders were not impressed. They had told him their businesses were on the point of collapse and they gave him a wish-list, including military occupation of the Bogside and Creggan with shoot-on-sight curfews and the permanent evacuation of the Rossville flats, a complex, Ford noted wryly, that contained '5000 inhabitants and a soldier has never entered them in the history of Londonderry'.

Such action was out of the question in the short term; an

invasion of the Catholic strongholds would take several months to plan and an evacuation of the flats in co-ordination with the local authority would probably take a year to implement. Even so, the situation had been communicated to the top brass; the commercial future of Derry depended on drastic action now.

Significantly, Ford identified 8 Brigade's immediate problem, not as IRA gunmen and bombers, but the hard-core Derry hooligans running wild in William Street and its environs. He noted that attempts by the army to disperse the rioters with rubber bullets and CS gas were increasingly futile 'because [they] operate mainly in open areas where they can avoid the gas (and some have respirators, many others makeshift wet rag masks) and in open order beyond the range of baton rounds'. Efforts to arrest the youths inevitably drew troops into the snipers' 'killing zones'. If mounted patrols went into the Bogside in armoured cars, the 'Pigs' were often mobbed by 'yobbos', which meant troops had to follow on foot, exposing themselves to sniper fire.

Ford described the DYH as

gangs of tough, teenage youths, permanently unemployed who have developed sophisticated tactics of brick and stone throwing, destruction and arson. Under cover of snipers in nearby buildings, they operate just beyond the hard-core areas and extend the radius of anarchy by degrees into additional streets and areas. Against the DYH [. . .] the Army in Londonderry is for the moment virtually incapable [sic]. This incapacity undermines our ability to deal with the gunmen and bombers and threatens what is left of law and order on the West bank of the River Foyle.

Ford's identification of the young hooligans as the decoys for the IRA's gunmen and bombers led him to suggest a new tactic. As he saw it, the army could no longer pacify them with the existing 'minimum force' methods of using batons, rubber bullets and CS gas.

In a brutally frank assessment he said that he was coming to the conclusion that the level of force now required for the restoration of law and order was 'to shoot selected ringleaders among the DYH, after clear warnings have been issued'.

Such action would represent a drastic change in the rules of engagement in Northern Ireland. Never before had a senior officer suggested that unarmed civilians could, in certain circumstances, be shot.

Existing regulations, set out in the so-called 'Yellow Card', permitted soldiers to shoot to kill only when they could identify a target that immediately threatened their lives – gunmen, nail bombers or petrol bombers. The instructions on the 'Yellow Card', which was carried by all soldiers on duty, were drawn up by the Ministry of Defence, the Treasury Solicitor and the Army Legal Service, and emphasized that firing should always be a last resort – the doctrine of 'minimum force'.

The first version of the Yellow Card issued in September 1969 had recognized that soldiers had a common-law duty, no different from the ordinary citizen, to aid the civil power in restoring law and order, by force if necessary. There was a similar duty to help prevent crime and effect lawful arrests, using 'reasonable force'. The question of giving a warning before opening fire was hardly addressed, so a revised card was issued in January 1971. It authorized soldiers to shoot at anyone carrying a firearm who was thought to be about to use it and refused to halt, or at a person throwing a petrol bomb. Whenever possible, a warning had to be given, but troops could open fire without warning if that was the only way to save themselves or other people from harm. Only aimed shots were allowed. The card was revised again in November 1971, permitting automatic fire against identified targets 'when considered by the commander on the spot to be the minimum force necessary'.

Since the majority of the youths who rioted at aggro corner were mostly stone throwers, they would not be legitimate targets, according to the Yellow Card. In addition, they were often accompanied by onlookers, happy to find some good 'craic' on the way home from school, shopping or work, so picking off ring-leaders of the DYH would be difficult without putting innocent civilians at risk. And if soldiers were using the British army's standard infantry weapon, the self-loading rifle, or SLR, there was a potential problem with what the military calls 'collateral' casualties. Although Ford believed that the army would be justified in using the SLR, he was concerned about 'the devastating effects of this weapon and the danger of rounds killing more than the person aimed at'.

Specifically designed for use on the modern battlefield, the SLR fired standard Nato 7.62mm ball ammunition, either on automatic or single shot. Maximum accurate range was around 450 yards, but bullets had been known to carry up to three miles. Travelling at 2750 feet per second, they could punch straight through an iron railway line at close range. Opening fire at a target in a crowd posed a clear risk of killing others. As one paratrooper on duty in Derry put it, 'A gunman is not going to stop the bullet.'

Ford suggested to Tuzo that it was time to consider adapting SLRs to fire a smaller .22 high-velocity bullet, which would still be lethal to its primary target but posed less of a threat of collateral damage. He wanted these weapons to be issued to units on riot duty to 'engage' ringleaders, and revealed that thirty such rifles had already been delivered to 8 Brigade for 'zeroing' – ensuring their accuracy with practice shots – and 'familiarization training'.

If such tactics were adopted the army would, in effect, be reverting to the uninhibited internal security methods used against insurgents in far-away corners of the British empire – the 'shoot one round at the big black bugger in the red turban' approach, as one officer put it. But in Derry, British troops would be firing on their fellow citizens in front of an increasingly watchful media and a proliferation of human rights groups.

Although Ford was the first to articulate a need for much sterner measures in Northern Ireland, he was not alone among the defence establishment in believing the soldiers could not cope under the present rules.

At the Ministry of Defence, officials assessing the extra troops required to enforce the ban on marches had concluded that current force levels could not cope with 'more than two or three large-scale demonstrations at any one time'. As there was no immediate hope of securing reinforcements merely to impose the ban on marches, their answer was 'additional measures for the physical control of crowds'. Inevitably, such measures involved the use of firearms: 'Disperse or we fire.'

One realistic policy paper concluded, 'It would not be the gunmen who would be killed but "innocent members" of the crowd. This would be a harsh and final step, tantamount to saying "all else has failed" and for this reason must be rejected in extremis. It cannot however be ruled out.'

Any commander in Northern Ireland had to be part soldier, part public relations man and Ford, aware that his proposed new measures were controversial, emphasized that proper authorization would be needed to use the .22in modified rifles. Ford also alerted Tuzo, in the same memo, to the upcoming illegal protest march from the Creggan to the Guildhall originally planned for Sunday, 16 January but which was later postponed to 30 January.

Although Ford did not say so, the march was expected to degenerate into violence, with the young hooligans to the fore, and there was a possibility that the situation would justify employing marksmen to pick off ringleaders. Operation Forecast would involve sealing off the Bogside with the heaviest troop concentration ever seen in Derry. Army snipers with telescopic sights would ring the Catholic enclave; paratroopers armed with SLRs were poised to carry out an arrest operation and engage IRA gunmen or bombers, if they came under attack.

As the military preparations for containing the march got under

58

way, the mood in the army's Lisburn headquarters was hardening perceptibly; the assault troops of the Parachute Regiment would be on hand to execute the new, sterner measures that Ford was suggesting.

The army's plan was drawn up on the likelihood of confrontation and violence from the DYH. If there was no confrontation, as Superintendent Lagan believed would be the case following the change in the route of the march, the paratroopers would not be justified in penetrating the Bogside, making arrests or 'engaging' the ringleaders.

So, was the Derry police Chief's news unwelcome because it could cause the army to rethink its plans?

The no-go zone in Derry, and the bands of stone-throwing youths who patrolled its perimeter, had been a headache for the army since trucks carrying eighty men of the Prince of Wales's Own Regiment rolled into Waterloo Place on the late afternoon of 14 August 1969 in response to a request from the Northern Ireland government to come to the 'aid of the civil power'. In the House of Commons later that day the Labour Home Secretary, James Callaghan, assured MPs that soldiers sent to Northern Ireland would act impartially between Catholics and Protestants. He also intimated that they would be withdrawn immediately the 'limited operation' was over. However, few believed they really would be back soon – and certainly not by Christmas.

The first British troops to set foot in Derry put on a good show of being nice to the Catholics. Sean Keenan was among influential local Catholics who readily established close contacts with the military.

But while the army's hearts-and-minds campaign began promisingly, it encountered growing opposition from hard-line Republicans. The increasing use of snatch squads to make arrests within the Bogside was a particular cause of friction. Sean Keenan's twenty-year-old son was arrested (and subsequently jailed) for telling soldiers trying to move him on, 'No bastardin' British troops will move me,' he told them.

When the singer Dana, a Derry girl who was representing the Irish Republic, won the 1970 Eurovision Song Contest, the army laid on a party to welcome her back. According to one senior officer, 'Yobbos ruined it and turned it into a riot.' Other accounts suggested that soldiers had taunted Catholic youths that Dana sang for Britain because Derry was British and always would be.

And for all the genuine goodwill, the seeds of future conflict were being planted. Step by step the army was becoming a permanent feature in everyday life in Derry, effectively policing – and increasingly controlling – the overwhelmingly Catholic population. An army that cut its teeth on counter-insurgency campaigns in the jungles of Borneo and Malaya, Aden and the deserts of Oman was now required to enforce the law on fellow Britons, most of them reluctant to obey orders.

The riot drills that the troops practised assiduously at a disused airfield outside Belfast were a peculiarly colonial inheritance. Tactics rarely went beyond adopting a box formation to minimize casualties under a hail of missiles, then advancing to lay a strip of white tape across the road and unfurl a banner reading 'HALT OR WE WILL OPEN FIRE'. The first time one officers' unit rehearsed that drill, the banner they checked out from the quartermaster's store turned out to be in Arabic.

The risks of deploying soldiers as ad hoc policemen became glaringly apparent in September 1969, when scuffles between Catholic and Protestant students at a technical college near Derry city centre mushroomed into a more serious confrontation. Troops quickly separated the sides, but through ignorance of the sectarian geography of Derry, shepherded some Protestants into an area where angry Catholics had gathered.

In the ensuing brawl a middle-aged Protestant, William King, dropped dead of a heart attack. More than 2000 people turned out for his funeral and Derry's Loyalists acquired a martyr as potent as

Samuel Devenney had become for local Republicans earlier in the year. As communal tensions mounted, the army took a decision that was to have profound consequences.

Without consulting any of the Catholic civic organizations, a 'peace ring' was erected around the main approaches to the commercial zone from the Creggan and Bogside. In sharp contrast to Belfast's new peace line – thrown up to keep warring communities from each other's throats – the barriers and checkpoints seemed to many Catholics to be intended to seal them off from the rest of the city. The impact on the community, above all its multitude of bored and unemployed young people, was far-reaching.

In the first week of the peace ring six youths were arrested for disorderly conduct and subsequently convicted. Some had objected strenuously to having their cars searched, others resisted when soldiers prevented them from visiting stores, cinemas and clubs in the city centre.

As the army's role in policing Derry expanded, Catholics began to wonder if they had not been reclassified as restless natives, to be put down by British might like many an imperial outpost. Unease grew with the appointment in September 1970 of Brigadier Frank Kitson as commanding officer of 39 Brigade. Kitson, the acknowledged guru of counter-insurgency and a target of the Left, made his impact felt quickly, pursuing a 'punchy' line on the streets of Belfast that endorsed the muscular interventions of the more aggressive units, especially the paratroopers. He was himself awarded the Military Cross 'for valour' during his service in Northern Ireland (the full official citation is still classified secret). But Kitson, now Sir Frank, a retired general, had no discernible influence in the Derry of 1970.

The army's first major clash with Catholics in Derry – at the end of October 1969 – finished with a baton charge against a crowd protesting outside a police station. Among those arrested was nineteen-year-old Martin McGuinness, passionate Republican, future commander of Derry's Provisional IRA and today Education Minister in Northern Ireland's power-sharing executive. (McGuinness was bound over by magistrates.) By the end of 1970, violent encounters between troops and Catholic youths chafing at the restraints of the peace ring were increasingly common. A Republican paper suggested facetiously that 'Don't Fence Me In' had replaced 'We Shall Overcome' as the Bogside's communal anthem. More ominously, there were claims that tainted evidence from soldiers was being used to secure rioting convictions (a mandatory six-month sentence for rioting was introduced).

In the Waterside, Derry's edgy Protestant community was following events closely. The destruction in the commercial centre was hitting Loyalist pockets hard. When they were not complaining about the army for being too soft on Catholics, they worried about sectarian clashes erupting in vulnerable pockets like the predominantly Protestant working-class Fountain district tucked under the city walls, on the edge of the Bogside. But much to the relief of the overstretched battalions of 8 Brigade, local Loyalists seemed to have no desire to emulate their turbulent brethren in Belfast.

Yet despite the growing alienation of mainstream Catholic opinion, the military appeared to believe that things were going rather well in Derry. In early 1971 General Ford sounded positively upbeat. Overt army activity was at a low level while the hooligan element had been isolated from responsible Catholics and the IRA, undermanned, poorly equipped and lacking funds, could do little more than lie low.

From the start of the Northern Ireland crisis Harold Wilson, the British Prime Minister, and his cabinet had been uneasy about the consequences of committing troops. Every Ministry of Defence intelligence assessment forecast that there would be an unstoppable escalation in the number of soldiers required. The government also worried about being manoeuvred into rubber-stamping the policies of Protestant hard-liners.

The cumbersome division of responsibility for security in Northern Ireland did not help matters. Stormont, the Ministry of Defence and the Home Office all had overlapping responsibilities. Day-to-day security matters were overseen by the army's Director of Operations Committee.

The top brass at Lisburn quickly discovered that the Stormont government had its own agenda. Each Monday, the Joint Security Committee (JSC) of the Northern Ireland government, which had to approve military operations, met at Stormont Castle, an overblown neo-classical building set in its own grounds in east Belfast. And each Monday the cabinet ministers and senior police officers who sat on the committee would urge the military commanders present to clobber the Catholics.

At the time the troops arrived in the province the GOC was Lieutenant-General Sir Ian Freeland, an upright, athletic man not renowned for agility of mind and known to his subordinates as 'Smiling Death' because of his custom of issuing punitive orders with a smile. Freeland was soon under heavy pressure at the JSC to do something about the Catholic no-go zones. The politicians wanted the barricades cleared and the Irish Republic's tricolour that fluttered above them torn down.

At one meeting in Stormont's cabinet office, where an oversize oil painting of Arcadian country scenes hung above the fireplace, Freeland finally lost patience with the civilians telling him how to do his job. It would be a simple enough military exercise to occupy the Bogside, he agreed. 'Three hours to take over, and about three years to get out again. Is that what you want?' For a long moment there was stunned silence.

Freeland's successor in the spring of 1971 was Major-General Harry Tuzo, an Oxford-educated gunner with a fine war record. Then in his mid-fifties, beginning to contemplate retirement, he was told, 'Buckle your safety belt, you're going to Northern Ireland.'

Tuzo's appointment owed much to the lobbying of Sir Michael Carver, then waiting to take over as Chief of the General Staff

(CGS), the top job in Britain's military hierarchy. In Tuzo, Carver saw the qualities of 'toughness, resilience, breadth of outlook and rapidity of mind' that the GOC's job now demanded. He also considered his protégé's genial and outgoing temperament – Tuzo was a keen sportsman who was equally at home with music, literature and the theatre – an important asset in a post that increasingly involved rubbing shoulders with politicians and the media. Carver and Tuzo shared the view that since soldiers were trained to shoot to kill, they should not be asked to fire either over the heads of a civilian crowd or to shoot to wound. If the army was used on riot control duty in situations that did not justify the use of firearms, troops should be restricted to tear gas or rubber bullets.

At Tuzo's first JSC meeting he made it abundantly clear that while the army was in Northern Ireland to support the Stormont government, he would not permit his troops to be used for purely sectarian ends. A senior civil servant was amused by how twitchy Tuzo made the politicians; it was their first encounter with an intellectual soldier and they sensed that he would run rings around them.

At a subsequent meeting one Stormont minister, Captain William Long, complained indignantly that soldiers were too slow to catch rioters. 'Why can't you put them in gym shoes so they run faster?' he asked Tuzo. The GOC gazed for a moment out of the large bay windows overlooking Stormont's well-kept lawns, then murmured in a dismissive way that he would give the matter some thought. (Some units did subsequently experiment with gym shoes, but not to much effect.)

On Carver's first day as CGS, early in April 1971, he and Tuzo were summoned to 10 Downing Street for a meeting of the Cabinet Committee on Northern Ireland, known as Gen47. By then, Edward Heath's Conservative government had been in power for almost a year and, as the situation in the province deteriorated, he had come under increasing pressure from

Stormont's newly elected Unionist Prime Minister, Brian Faulkner, to take a harder line with the Catholics.

Gen47 was composed of senior British cabinet ministers and was effectively responsible for making all key political decisions affecting the province. At one meeting at Downing Street, Carver was shocked by some of Faulkner's wilder suggestions for dealing with the IRA. By one account he wanted undercover army squads to kidnap known IRA men from their boltholes across the border. Carver thought the measures Faulkner proposed were guaranteed to create serious problems with the government of the Irish Republic.

Carver made it clear that he could not, and would not, order soldiers to do anything that brought them into conflict with the law. He was equally unbending when Lord Hailsham, the Lord Chancellor, pressed for the army to adopt what amounted to 'shoot-to-kill' policy in Northern Ireland.

Citing an antique legal statute, Hailsham argued – as the government's senior law officer – that anyone obstructing the armed forces in the course of their duty was *ipso facto* an enemy of the crown. It seemed to Carver that Hailsham thought this would justify troops shooting such people dead, whether or not they were under attack themselves. Although Carver did not take him seriously, he suspected that other senior ministers present were ready to go down that road. Predictably, Faulkner seized on Hailsham's suggestion.

Meanwhile, the shooting war was heating up in Belfast. On 6 February 1971 Gunner Robert Curtis of the 94th Location Regiment, Royal Artillery, was killed by machine-gun fire, the first British soldier to die in Northern Ireland.

In Derry, despite severe unrest, there were as yet no gun battles and neither the army nor the IRA had killed anyone. At the beginning of July, however, shots were fired at soldiers after a riot, then more shots followed at army posts. Before the week was out, troops had killed two civilians in circumstances so contested by eyewitnesses that John Hume and his fellow SDLP MPs withdrew from Stormont after the British government refused to set a public inquiry into the deaths. The city began the slide into a full-scale guerrilla war.

The Anglians patrolling the Bogside on the night of 7 July 1971 were understandably jumpy. A few days earlier two rounds had been fired at troops confronting rioters in the William Street area. Then two observation posts were attacked by gunmen who loosed off about a dozen rounds. It was the first time in several months that the army had come under fire, and it seemed to signal a new and more violent phase in the IRA's Derry campaign.

The army log recorded that the Anglians spotted a man with a rifle in William Street, where troops were being bombarded with stones and petrol bombs. He was challenged and ordered to halt, the log recorded, but moved to a new position and took aim at the patrol. A soldier then shot him from close range.

The man who fell was Seamus Cusack, an unemployed welder aged twenty-eight; the crowd immediately rushed him away, leaving a huge pool of blood but no trace of a weapon. Civilian eyewitnesses said Cusack was unarmed when the bullet severed his femoral artery. He was still alive when a private car delivered him to Letterkenny hospital, twenty miles away across the border in the Irish Republic, but died shortly afterwards.

Cusack might have survived had he been rushed instead to Derry's well-equipped Altnagelvin Hospital, only a few minutes away on the east bank of the Foyle. But by now, many Catholics routinely avoided going there, or to other local hospitals, for treatment of injuries sustained in riots. They feared that doing so could result in them being reported to the security forces and taken to court.

Those who knew Cusack were adamant that he had no connection with the IRA and his death sparked off even more intense rioting. The following afternoon, as rioting broke out again and two or three gelignite bombs were thrown at troops without causing serious injury, an Anglian marksman killed Desmond Beattie, a jobless nineteen-year-old, with a single shot in the chest. The army claimed that Beattie had fired on soldiers first; eye-witnesses who saw him fall with blood pouring from him emphatically denied that. No weapon was recovered by troops and subsequent forensic tests found no evidence that Beattie had fired a gun or handled explosives.

The killings of Cusack and Beattie effectively ended any possibility of co-existence between the security forces and the majority of Derry's Catholics. In a little under two years, soldiers who had originally been hailed as liberators had become hated occupiers. And worse was to come.

The introduction of internment marked the point of no return for the army, alienating the last remaining pockets of moderate Catholic opinion. At SDLP meetings in Derry, the local doctor Raymond McClean listened with amazement to the fiery oratory of people who had previously shunned any form of activism. Overnight, they turned into agitators, backing rent strikes and rattling collection cans for 'the men behind the wire'.

Yet internment was neither the army's decision, nor its choice. As Tuzo made clear in an interview a few days earlier, he regarded it as a distasteful weapon of last resort and dubious value – 'the Unionists' panacea'. But when the proposal was put before Heath, Tuzo could not come up with a military alternative for checking the violence. Heath traded internment for a six-month ban on all marches, including the imminent Protestant Apprentice Boys procession on 12 August.

Sixteen men from Derry were 'lifted' before dawn on 9 August 1971, tripping the Catholic enclaves' early warning system into a frenzy of blaring car horns, whistles and clanging dustbin lids. Among them were at least five senior Provisionals, including Sean Keenan and three senior Officials, one the commanding officer.

Even so, army misgivings about the list of suspects provided by the RUC Special Branch being out of date were roundly substantiated – among the 342 people picked up around the province was Liam Mulholland, aged seventy-seven, who had been imprisoned in 1929. Another on the RUC's list was blind and another had died. After two days 104 detainees were released.

But while the old guard leadership in Derry was hard hit, a fresh generation of young recruits, largely unknown to the security forces, were standing by to take over. Prominent among these new 'players' was Martin McGuinness. That evening, as some thirty new barricades sprang up in the Bogside and Creggan, well-armed IRA men were patrolling openly and shooting attacks on troops intensified.

Two days later, on 11 August, the first British soldier to be killed in Derry was picked off by a sniper as he repaired a perimeter fence at the vulnerable Bligh's Lane post. The army's response was to throw some 1300 troops, backed by armoured cars and helicopters, into the Catholic enclaves with orders to dismantle every barricade they found.

In Belfast the Provisionals were also on the offensive. During August there were 131 bomb attacks, 196 in September and 117 in October. Towards the end of August, with Belfast still burning, General Tuzo (by now Sir Harry) flew by helicopter to Derry to meet a group of prominent Catholics who had withdrawn co-operation with the security forces in protest against internment. At a hotel outside the city, Tuzo and Howard Smith, a former diplomat who was the UK Representative in Northern Ireland, listened to a litany of complaints from political moderates and con-servatives about the military's conduct in Catholic areas.

Then, out of the blue, Tuzo made a startling offer, promising to halt all military operations in Derry for a month if they could deliver peace in that time. He saw it as a tactical experiment that could easily fail but was worth trying. The politicians on the JSC were understandably less than enthusiastic, but Tuzo guaranteed that if his gambit came to nothing the army would take whatever action was necessary to pacify the Catholic enclaves.

An informal truce took hold in Derry almost immediately, ending some two months of unremitting conflict. The *Londonderry Sentinel* reported that an eerie calm had descended, with the security forces off the streets, the provocative Catholic barricades ignored. The IRA kept up bombing attacks, but its snipers were much less active.

It was more than two weeks before the familiar cycle of unrest in Derry resumed, sparked off by the death of fourteen-year-old Annette McGavigan. Forensic evidence produced at the inquest established that she had been hit in the head by an army bullet. More than 10,000 angry mourners – close on a third of Derry's Catholic population – turned out for her funeral and the rioting that followed it lasted several days. By the late summer of 1971, Ford acknowledged bleakly, the security forces were facing 'an entirely hostile Catholic community'.

The genesis of Operation Forecast lay in the headlong descent of Derry into what General Ford succinctly described as 'violence on a large scale'. Until then, getting to grips with Belfast was the main priority for Unionist politicians and the military, followed by security along the troublesome border with the Irish Republic. Some insiders had the impression that a 'let Derry burn' lobby was active behind the scenes at both Stormont and Lisburn.

Brigadier MacLellan may have felt the same way after learning that the three extra battalions – comprising some 2000 soldiers – he expected to accompany him to his new command had been diverted to Belfast. Without them it was utterly unrealistic to expect 8 Brigade to achieve much more than keeping the lid on Derry.

The Brigade Commander's diary, a detailed log containing daily 'situation reports' from each of its units, made alarming reading. Between early July and mid-December – a period encompassing the sharp increase in IRA activity that followed internment – troops and police in Derry came under fire on average fifty times a week and suffered twenty-two casualties, including seven dead.

Since the start of MacLellan's tour of duty at the end of October 1971, IRA snipers had become far more active, with the use of automatic weapons increasingly common. The number of attacks on the security forces with nail and gelignite bombs had also risen sharply, to the point where foot patrols were being targeted virtually around the clock.

Meanwhile, the city's commercial centre was under siege. Pubs, betting shops and post offices were raided frequently, often for meagre rewards – one stick-up netted just £3.50. Entire office blocks were destroyed by bombs, cars hijacked at gunpoint. Between the IRA and regular criminals from the Catholic enclaves, wailed one prominent Protestant, 'They're making a burnt-out barbecue of our town.' Derry's fragile economy was slowly being strangled.

By 11 October 1971, two full companies of Anglians – some 200 men – were required to make just six arrests in the Rossville Street area. Another big operation two weeks later was no more successful. Between August 1971 and January 1972, arrests for riotous behaviour rarely exceeded a dozen a week – and less than half of those charged were eventually convicted in court.

Over the same period, arrests on the lesser charge of disorderly conduct – traditionally used to deal with drunks and minor breaches of the peace – totalled twenty-two, with fourteen convictions. To the army's intense irritation, Derry's magistrates rarely fined anyone convicted on those counts more than £10, sometimes as little as £1. And even then the money was hard to collect, since police required an army escort to pursue scoff-laws in the Creggan and Bogside.

On 26 October 1971, the day before MacLellan was due to take command in Derry, new operational orders for 8 Brigade were drawn up. With characteristic brevity, Ford instructed it

70

'progressively to restore the rule of law in the Creggan and Bogside'. Specifically, he wanted to take the fight to the hooligans by mounting more vigorous arrest operations in the Catholic strongholds. His determination could be judged from his insistence that the army was entitled to open fire 'whenever events demand it and the law permits'.

On the basis of the limited intelligence available, Ford estimated that there were at least forty active gunmen among the IRA's hundred or so volunteers, with some 250–300 hard-core hooligans. Almost thirty barricades existed in the Bogside and Creggan, most of them too formidable for the one-tonne Pigs to smash through. They were manned around the clock by vigilantes whose searchlights and ear-splitting alarms made a sneak attack all but impossible.

In November, 8 Brigade launched a series of battalion-strength operations; one began at dawn and lasted for almost three hours, under continuous attack by rioters. A few weapons were seized and troops claimed to have shot three gunmen and a petrol bomber. But this aggressive new strategy did not impress one company commander. 'We sort of steamed through those areas in a broad phalanx, letting off hundreds of tear gas cartridges and grenades ... doing nothing, really, but irritate people,' he observed.

Under standing orders, commanders were required to be selective in the use of IS (Internal Security) weaponry. The previous July, MacLellan's predecessor had reminded commanders that it was 8 Brigade policy not to use CS gas inside the city unless there was no alternative.

Now complaints about the army's conduct were pouring in. Father Mulvey from the Creggan telegraphed Edward Heath at Downing Street, describing his parish as 'a vast gas chamber' (370 CS cannisters were collected after one army incursion). Local doctors reported that heavy exposure to gas had caused a mini-epidemic of respiratory diseases, especially among children. A racing pigeon enthusiast accused the military of poisoning his prize birds.

At JSC meetings, both government and military grumbled about media bias, often singling out the BBC's Northern Ireland services. The army had never before been involved in a conflict where an incident that took place in mid-afternoon could be on the early-evening television newscasts. One officer likened it to being in a goldfish bowl. The military mind also found it hard to accept that journalists would hobnob with the enemy

The army's own efforts to win the information battle were singularly ineffectual and the RUC's even worse. Things got so bad that soldiers on the confrontation lines began agitating for an improvement in relations with the media. A new section responsible for information policy was eventually installed at Lisburn to develop a more sophisticated approach, but found it uphill work.

In mid-December, with Stormont piling on the pressure, Ford composed his lengthy assessment of the military options in Derry's no-go zones. Carver had visited Northern Ireland a week earlier, returning convinced – despite the rising level of violence – that a window of opportunity might appear for the British government to seize the initiative. He thought mid-February 1972 would be about right.

What he had in mind was reducing military activity to a level which would maintain morale among the troops and the Protestants without provoking the Catholics to an extent which 'causes us severe casualties, further antagonizes them and brings no dividends'.

Derry's 'city battalion' at the time, responsible for the Bogside area, was 22nd Light Air Defence Regiment Royal Artillery (22 LAD). Its commanding officer, Lieutenant-Colonel James Ferguson, provided an insider's account of what this involved.

Taking a day at random from the unit log, 28 December had begun with a dawn chorus of shots fired at the gunners positioned in OP Charlie on the city walls. 'More activity, shots, and bombs thrown during the morning,' the log recorded. At midday, men of 11 Battery came under heavy stoning in William Street and retaliated with CS gas. Shortly before 1 p.m., OP Charlie was attacked with automatic gunfire: trouble continued into the afternoon, with more hooligan activity, more bombs, more CS gas and rubber bullets fired at crowds up to a hundred strong.

The log for the day ultimately recorded thirty-one separate shooting incidents and fifteen nail bomb attacks on 22 LAD troops alone. Next morning Gunner Ham became the regiment's first fatality, killed by a single shot as a patrol worked its way along a track in the Brandywell area near the city cemetery.

IV

The Decision To Put Civilians At Risk

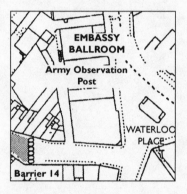

The Containment Line and the area within it are
to be dominated by physical military presence

Brigadier MacLellan's orders, 27 January 1972

Of course my lads are tough; they're known
around the world for that

Lieutenant Colonel Wilford

THE COUNTDOWN TO the army's biggest operation since arriving in Derry began on 24 January. That afternoon, Brigadier MacLellan and the local police chief, Frank Lagan, met at Ebrington Barracks to discuss ways of stopping the NICRA march. MacLellan had been ordered by General Ford during his visit to Derry earlier in the month to produce an outline plan for blocking the demonstration. MacLellan would be the senior commander on the spot, and it was up to him to choose the best place to turn back the marchers, and to make provisions for what would happen afterwards.

A forty-six-year-old officer of the Coldstream Guards, MacLellan had been in Derry for only three months, arriving from a posting on the army staff command in Cyprus. He could not draw up the plan without consulting the veteran RUC officer whose forces would also be manning barriers and who had a wealth of experience of previous demonstrations.

MacLellan hoped that he and Lagan could present a joint front to their respective superiors on the best way to handle the demonstration. Both officers were conscious that the outcome of the weekend could have long-term effects on the campaign against the IRA in Derry and beyond, and that their own reputations were on the line.

General Ford had made it quite clear to MacLellan during his earlier visit that he was dissatisfied with the security situation. It was hardly MacLellan's fault; he was doing the best he could with his limited resources to contain a situation that was rapidly getting out of control. But Ford was not the kind of commander to make allowances for failure. In a painfully blunt memo to Tuzo, he wrote that he was 'disturbed by the attitude of both the Brigade Commander [MacLellan], and also, of course, by Chief Super-intendant Lagan'. He told Tuzo that he had issued MacLellan with 'very firm directions . . . that he is to take all possible steps within his capability to inhibit and deter the operations of the bombers'.

For his part, Lagan was well aware that his Catholic upbringing could sometimes work to his disadvantage in the overwhelmingly Protestant RUC, and in the army high command. He was an unusual figure in the force who had worked his way up through the ranks since joining more than thirty years earlier. Born in County Derry, he was educated at St Columb's and, despite fierce hostility towards the RUC among most Bogsiders, he enjoyed respect among moderate leaders, such as John Hume, and had a wide network of contacts, extending indirectly to the IRA.

Although Lagan knew that some in the military suspected he was 'soft' on the Nationalists, there had never been serious friction between police and army in Derry. He regarded his working relationship with MacLellan as warm and mutually beneficial. They spoke on the telephone most days and met frequently to discuss security issues, dropping into each other's offices without making an appointment.

The march presented problems on several levels. First, it was illegal under Faulkner's ban on public processions, now extended for another twelve months. The army also expected that it would attract far larger numbers – perhaps up to 12,000 – than any of the previous protests staged since Christmas.

MacLellan and Lagan, as the two senior officers on the spot, had to decide how to handle the march without a full-scale military incursion. The essential question – especially in Lagan's mind – was whether it should be stopped at the bottom of William Street, or be allowed to proceed to the Guildhall as planned.

Lagan expected the DYH to attach themselves to the march and anticipated that IRA volunteers would take part, although he did not think there would be 'organized IRA activity'. In other words, no shooting.

The army took a much harder line. An early assessment from 8 Brigade was unequivocal. 'The hooligan element will be present from the start; if not in the van of the march they will certainly be on the flanks and in the rear. Some gunmen are certain to be sheltering behind the hooligan ranks.' Lisburn was convinced that the IRA would use the crowds as cover to open fire on soldiers, either at the barricades, or at the observation posts. Lagan did not put particular weight on this intelligence.

At their meeting on 24 January, MacLellan and Lagan took turns in laying out the possible consequences of different courses of action. Lagan's sources were telling him demonstrators intended to disperse when they reached the fringe of the Bogside and would either attempt to force a number of different barriers at the same time, or slip through the back alleys leading to the city centre.

He warned MacLellan that any attempt to turn back a large number of people at this stage would almost certainly lead to serious confrontations. He told MacLellan that several days of intense violence could well follow. In Lagan's view the best course would be to allow marchers to pass through the Bogside, and be channelled under police and army supervision along the extra hundred yards into the Guildhall square for the rally. The security forces could photograph the organizers of the march and other prominent figures with a view to subsequent arrests for breaching the ban.

With his experience of rioting, Lagan preferred to have strong cases against a relatively small number of people rather than make lots of arrests that might not stand up in court. He said that he would recommend this course of action in writing to his superiors in Belfast. Lagan left the meeting convinced that MacLellan had agreed with him and would do the same with Ford. Their memos, he believed, would be presented as 'joint advice'.

But whatever impression Lagan was left with at the time, MacLellan's recollection of the meeting would differ significantly. He insisted later that he had made it very clear to Lagan that he wanted to contain the illegal march entirely within the Bogside and the Creggan. The army's main objective, he emphasized, was to keep the anticipated rioting as far away as possible away from the commercial area.

As soon as the meeting ended, MacLellan sent a signal to Ford at Lisburn, accurately reporting Lagan's concerns about the risk of bloodshed should the march be prevented from reaching the Guildhall. He also put on record his own view that stopping the march could have very serious repercussions. Without reinforcements, he would have nowhere near enough troops to cope with the situation that Lagan envisaged.

The response from army headquarters was swift. Next day, Ford telephoned MacLellan to inform the Brigade Commander that he should 'assume for planning purposes' that he would be ordered to stop the march; MacLellan's outline plan was required on Ford's desk by 8.30 the following morning. MacLellan made handwritten notes of the conversation:

Cordon Bogside/Creggan approaches
 Blockade covered by snipers with blocks of fed gunners to
 fire volleys [of rubber bullets]
 Must prevent damage to shopping & Protestant areas by
 saturating with troops
 Plan with marked map to be with CLF [Ford] by 0830 Wed
 26 Jan

To man the barriers, observation posts, sniper nests and provide sufficient back-up, MacLellan told Ford that he would need at least two more battalions, possibly three, in addition to Derry's regular garrison of four battalions. Ford had already alerted the King's Own Border Regiment, which had become operational on

13 January as the Province reserve battalion, plus 1st Battalion, The Parachute Regiment.

This was the first MacLellan had heard of the Paras' involvement. His notes recorded: 'CLF [Ford] sees 1 Para in reserve in City to "counter attack" i.e. go round the back to arrest 300–400 rioters.'

Whatever MacLellan and Lagan recommended, Ford had already decided to stop the march and send in the paratroopers' snatch squads.

Lagan was in his headquarters at the Victoria police station when someone from the Chief Constable's office in Belfast left a message with his secretary to say his advice had been rejected. He was never told why.

The decision to make the Paras the spearhead of Operation Forecast was made personally by General Ford. He would always maintain that the reason why he selected the roughest, toughest troops in his command was because they were the only unit available with enough experience in Northern Ireland.

The battalion had been commanded since July 1971 by Lieutenant Colonel Derek Wilford. Intelligent and articulate, Wilford was widely regarded as a rising star. A lean, fit man of thirty-eight, he had spent two years attached to the Special Air Service and trained with American paratroopers at Fort Bragg. His preference for books – he appreciated the classics and could read Latin – over the bar of the officers' mess had earned him a reputation as something of a loner.

In the sour judgement of one officer who served with him in the SAS, Wilford had played the army system masterfully to get ahead. 'If I had been told ten years ago that he would hold the position [commanding 1 Para], I just wouldn't have believed it.'

But Wilford was fully signed up to the macho ethos of the Paras. Soon after he took over, his battalion was heavily involved in putting down the intense rioting that followed internment. He readily acknowledged that his soldiers had a fearsome reputation in Belfast's Catholic ghettos. 'Of course my lads are tough,' Wilford enthused to one journalist. 'They are known around the world for that.'

The Paras were chosen as the strike force in the face of fierce Catholic outrage over their conduct at Magilligan, the previous Saturday. MacLellan can hardly have been unaware – if only through mess room gossip – of the intense hostility towards the paratroopers among Belfast Catholics who had been on the receiving end of their strong-arm tactics. As the mobile reserve unit for 39 Infantry Brigade, Wilford's men were rushed to trouble spots anywhere in the city. They sorted out Protestant crowds with equal vigour.

'Going in hard and ready' was how Captain Mike Jackson, then the battalion's adjutant, liked to describe the Paras' approach to crowd control. The idea was always to inflict casualties, never to receive them and by early 1972, the battalion had not lost a single man. According to Jackson – more widely known today as the rugged British general who commanded NATO ground forces during the Kosovo conflict – no other regiment in Belfast matched the paratroopers when it came to getting results.

That was emphatically not the view of some officers in other 39 Brigade units, who considered the Paras a menace and a liability, too rough and undiscriminating to handle stand-offs with civilians. 'Little better than thugs in uniform,' was one biting judgement. 'I've seen them arrive on the scene, thump up a few people who might be doing nothing more than shouting and jeering, then roar off again.'

During the summer of 1971 at least two commanding officers of Belfast-based regiments took the exceptional step of asking informally if 39 Brigade headquarters would keep Wilford's men off their patches. That had nothing to do with petty regimental jealousies, insisted an infantry captain – even if the Paras habitually derided other units as 'crap hats' and sneered at them for using CS gas instead of getting stuck in during riots.

As the captain acknowledged, the Paras' ferocious training and innate aggression made them superb shock troops. Their reputation for bravery was burnished in Northern Ireland by Sergeant Michael Willets, awarded a posthumous George Cross for saving civilians by throwing himself on a smoking bomb outside a police station. 'But wading into people as if this was jungle warfare simply isn't on in Belfast.'

To an old Belfast hand like Corporal Bert Henshaw of the Green Jackets, using the Paras in Northern Ireland was asking for trouble. On routine patrols, he observed witheringly, they would bang off live rounds just to get across the street. 'They'd call it hard targeting, but I'd call it bad soldiering [because] if you fire a shot at night you don't know where it's going.'

The Paras also had a habit of straying on to other units' patches without proper authority or any advance warning. On one night stake-out, Henshaw's squad was about to open fire on four armed men when he realized they were paratroopers. 'We would have been justified in shooting them dead.'

The civil rights publicity machine had reacted swiftly to the clash at Magilligan, perceived by many Catholics as a calculated attempt to intimidate the protest movement. A defiant press statement from the Derry Civil Rights Association declared that 'this latest act of violence by the authorities strengthens the will of the people of Derry to march in peaceful protest on Sunday next'.

Although army headquarters promised an inquiry, the matter does not seem to have been pursued vigorously, and only one paratrooper ever appeared before Wilford – who was not present at Magilligan – on disciplinary charges. He had been seen on television repeatedly kicking a fallen demonstrator, but Wilford decided that in the circumstances this had been justified. The soldier concerned would be among those on duty in Derry on 30 January.

But what led Ford to select such notoriously belligerent troops to carry out a tricky arrest operation in the Catholic heartland of a city where they had never been in action before? It was not as if he had no other alternative to the Paras. MacLellan's own brigade contained two infantry regiments with a wealth of hard-earned experience of Derry's flashpoints.

Soldiers of the Royal Anglian Regiment had been serving there for a full nineteen months, those of the 2nd Battalion, Royal Green Jackets for more than six months. Both were wearily familiar with the intricate topography of the Bogside and Creggan. And if by early 1972 most Catholics in Derry regarded all British troops as oppressors, they were at least a familiar presence. Yet the main involvement of both the Anglians and Green Jackets on the day of the march was largely limited to manning static army barriers.

Ford's explanation was that the Paras were the only uncommitted troops then available with extensive 'street' experience in Northern Ireland. The battalion's Support Company, which would be pivotally involved on Bloody Sunday, had been in action almost fifty times since the end of November 1971.

The fateful decision to put innocent civilians at risk by inviting a confrontation was approved in a flurry of meetings in Lisburn, Stormont and Whitehall over the next two days.

MacLellan sent his outline plan for stopping the march to Lisburn in the early hours of the night of 25–6 January, to arrive, as Ford required, by 8.30 a.m. Ford had decided against issuing specific orders for opening fire because soldiers were bound in all circumstances to abide by the Yellow Card rules. If no IRA gunmen appeared during the march, army snipers would have no reason to fire. Because of the hooligan threat, Ford told MacLellan to ensure that at least eight riot guns for discharging rubber bullets were available at every army barrier. They were to be fired in salvos of no less than four at a time, because experience in Derry showed that small groups of soldiers could be overwhelmed by determined rioters.

The next day, 27 January, the plan was submitted to the regular weekly meeting of the Joint Security Committee at Stormont. There was particular concern about a 'new rash of attacks on RUC personnel'. (Within hours, an RUC patrol car was ambushed in Derry near the Rosemount police station. Several gunmen drove by in a gold-coloured Hillman Avenger and raked it with shots from an M1 carbine and Thomson sub-machine gun. A police sergeant and a constable were killed and another constable was injured.)

The meeting then turned to upcoming anti-internment marches: one from Dungannon to Coalisland was scheduled for Saturday 29 January, with the big march in Derry on the Sunday. It was agreed that both should be stopped 'at points selected on tactical grounds'. In Derry, the basic plan was to block all routes into William Street and halt the march there. Discussion was brief, according to the notetaker who wrote the conclusions of the meeting. The possible outcome was contained in a single line: 'The operation might well develop into rioting and even a shooting war.'

Ford would be asked later if the danger to civilians had been properly assessed. He confirmed that it was discussed at the highest level; the decision had been that the risk was small enough to be acceptable. But he acknowledged, 'Every operation of this type, of course, has an element of risk.' That was why Operation Forecast had required cabinet-level clearance in London through the Gen47 committee. That same day in London, General Carver, Chief of the Defence Staff, briefed the Cabinet, including the Prime Minister.

There was a brief discussion about what might happen if there was serious violence. In the secret Cabinet minutes Heath himself summed up, saying that the meeting 'appreciated the difficulties facing the army when dealing with peaceful marches. This was essentially a job for the police, but the RUC did not possess the necessary numbers . . .' The reference to possible trouble in Derry was perfunctory: '. . . incidents of confrontation between the army and the civil population were inevitable.' The Cabinet wanted 'maximum publicity' for the arrests and the court proceedings following the march.

That same evening, Brian Faulkner was at Number 10, bouncily optimistic about progress towards defeating the IRA. He was less cheerful about the 30 January march, insisting that while Orange Order marches were banned it would be political suicide to let a civil rights parade go ahead. Faulkner considered it essential that Unionists should see NICRA supporters being turned back by the army on television.

All that now remained was for MacLellan, in consultation with Lagan, to draw up the operational orders. Drafted in the sparse jargon of the military, the eighteen-page Brigade Order 2/72 of 27 January reflected the conviction of the Northern Ireland command that what happened in Derry would provide a strategic blueprint for future security policy.

The mission was simply defined – 'to prevent any illegal march taking place from the Creggan and to contain it, with any accompanying rioting, within the Bogside and Creggan areas of the city'. In no circumstances would demonstrators be allowed to pass through a score of blocking points established around the containment zone.

The intention, MacLellan emphasized, was to deal with the march 'in as low a key as possible and for as long as possible'. Provided the crowd remained entirely within the defined containment area, troops would not intervene. MacLellan had no doubt that bands of the DYH would infiltrate the march and defy attempts by responsible march organizers to control them. He anticipated this would produce intense violence. It was almost certain, MacLellan thought, that nail and petrol bombers and IRA gunmen would move in behind the rioters, probably during the closing stages of the march.

The core of 8 Brigade's plan was to subjugate the Bogside. 'The Containment Line and the area within it are to be dominated by physical military presence . . . the maximum number of soldiers are to be "in the shop window" . . . they are to be covered by deployment of OPs [observation posts] and by a massive deployment of snipers in the anti-sniper role . . . at every vantage point.'

The most critical phase of the operation – the 'scoop-up' by the Paras – would only be launched on orders from MacLellan and he anticipated that the troops would go in on foot.

The final military briefings for Operation Forecast were set in motion on the afternoon of 28 January, when MacLellan held a co-ordinating conference at Ebrington Barracks to deal with matters arising from his orders. It was attended by the commanding officers of all the units that would be involved: Lagan was also present.

MacLellan went through Order 2/72 paragraph by paragraph, stressing the army's intention to hold to the doctrine of minimum force wherever possible. Although he accepted that IRA snipers might open fire on troops during the planned 'scoop-up', he was determined not to endanger peaceful elements in the crowd.

The importance of isolating hooligans was obvious: with the media out in force, the army had no wish to be seen sweeping peaceful demonstrators off the streets. MacLellan doubted that any gunmen would be lurking among the main body of marchers when it reached the barriers. He was prepared to allow plenty of time for rioters to become separated from the bulk of demonstrators, even if that meant fewer arrests might be made.

Paragraph nine of MacLellan's order set out the area in which the Paras' snatch squads would operate. He intended to launch them on two axes, one directed towards hooligans in the area of William Street–Little Diamond, the other towards the William Street–Little James Street area. Wilford's men were to advance rapidly from behind the rioters.

Since a frontal assault would allow people to escape along Rossville Street towards Free Derry Corner – beyond the limits defined for the arrest operation – the hooligans would have to be hit in the flank. Wilford appeared to find MacLellan's orders clear enough; before the meeting, he had borrowed a civilian car to scout out various routes for getting his men into action quickly and he also took a helicopter ride over the Bogside.

While others at the conference asked questions, the Paras' CO had so little to say that one officer present thought he must already have had some kind of private briefing. But Wilford's air of confidence was misleading; he was actually very concerned that his orders did not spell out what would happen 'if the shit hit the fan' and the Paras came under fire.

Wilford would insist later that he had asked for guidance on this and was told – by whom he did not make clear – something to the effect of 'oh well, we'll deal with that when it comes'. It was his greatest regret, he said, that he had not pushed harder for an answer.

Many of Wilford's men were trained in a technique known as 'snap shooting' – getting off aimed shots very fast with intent to kill. Once the scoop-up began they knew there would be precious little time for second thoughts. As one insider put it, 'The blokes would be hyped-up [expecting] a gunman to come . . . suddenly four blokes dash out. Bang-bang-bang! You're talking about split seconds.'

At 10.30 a.m. on the day before the march, Wilford gathered his commanders together at Palace Barracks to hear their operational orders. He told them that the battalion's mission was to arrest the maximum number of rioters and stressed that everything would depend on speedy deployment when the moment arrived.

Wilford said the hard-core Derry hooligans, whom the Paras would be encountering for the first time, were used to rubber bullets and gas but not to the use of rapid snatch squads on their own ground. The paratroopers involved would be covered by others armed with SLRs and rubber bullet guns. Movement would be in 'tactical bounds of no more than twenty metres', with close attention to the flanks and front.

Wilford emphasized that there was every chance of coming under fire from the Rossville flats, 'where there has been so much sniping during previous rioting'. Yet other officers more familiar with Derry considered the risk was greatly exaggerated. Brigade logs showed that just nine of the 1900 rounds fired at troops during the previous three months came from there. Neither MacLellan nor Ford regarded the flats as a particular threat when planning the arrest operation, while Lieutenant Colonel Ferguson of 22 LAD – the city battalion – did not believe they were a hotbed of IRA activity.

With army marksmen permanently stationed in observation posts on the city walls right above the flats, a gunman who opened up would be targeted immediately. OP 'Echo', the observation post on top of the Embassy Ballroom building in the Strand Road, also had a clear line of fire into the flats. The city walls rose some seventy feet above the Bogside, the ramparts being above the highest (ninth) floor of the Rossville flats. A grassy knoll separated the walls from Fahan Street which ran down into the Bogside from Butcher's Gate and from the army's observation posts there was an uninterrupted panoramic view of the Bogside and the Creggan. The Embassy Ballroom building was fifty yards down the Strand Road from the William Street barrier.

Wilford had less to say about his own plans for conducting the scoop-up. He intended to be well forward himself to get an early feel for the mood of the crowd before bringing the snatch squads up to jump-off points. Assuming trouble began around William Street, Wilford wanted to put them in over the back wall of the Presbyterian church, which fronted on to Great James Street.

The riot-hardened troops of Support Company, under the command of Major 236, were to lead the assault. But Wilford did not give him precise details of the role the Paras were to play. In the absence of guidance from his CO, Major 236 concluded that he would be left to decide for himself exactly where Support Company would operate.

Wilford's final exhortation to his men emphasized that the 'scoop-up' relied on speed. 'Move, Move, Move.'

By 2 p.m., a Sioux military helicopter carrying Lieutenant Colonel Peter Welsh, commanding officer of the Green Jackets, was circling at about 4000 feet above the Creggan. Code-named 'Hawkeye', Welsh's job was to provide a running commentary on the progress of the march for 8 Brigade's operations centre. Crucially, he would have to judge when peaceful marchers had separated sufficiently from the hooligan element for arrests to begin.

A second Sioux was also in the air, containing a military cinecamera crew shooting in colour. MacLellan had specifically requested heavy photographic coverage of the march and any incidents that accompanied it. About a dozen army still photographers were in position around the containment line. Their film would be collected for processing in a mobile darkroom while the march was still in progress.

On MacLellan's orders, a major public relations exercise was also under way. Every unit was to ensure that all possible assistance was given to the media in areas where troops were deployed. Belatedly, the army had concluded that it was better to help journalists do their job in the hope that it would produce more favourable reporting.

Around 2 p.m., a Military Police escort team armed with sub-machine guns arrived at Ebrington Barracks to collect General Ford, his 'Information Policy' officer, Colonel Maurice Tugwell, and his aide-de-camp. They set off in his personal Land Rover for a tour of army positions, beginning with an hour-long inspection of the most strategic of the army barriers.

Ford had assured MacLellan that he was present purely as an

observer and did not intend to interfere with the conduct of the operation, but would be following events through the army radio link in his vehicle. MacLellan can hardly have appreciated having a hard-driving superior peering over his shoulder. An old military adage held that 'one over one is never the right chain of command on active operations'.

As Ford discovered at the barriers, the army's preparations left nothing to chance. Extra supplies of rubber bullets (22 LAD drew 3000 rounds) and plastic handcuffs had been issued, together with a powerful battery-powered loudhailer. The Royal Engineers had delivered canisters of foam for dousing petrol bombs and every Pig carried a stretcher.

Each barrier in the area around the city centre had been allotted a code name, seemingly chosen by a bird lover. The Green Jackets were manning 'House Martin' (William Street, number 14) and 'Wood Pigeon' (Waterloo Street, number 15). 22 LAD were allotted 'Garden Bird' (number 12) on Little James Street and 'Little Tern' (number 13) on Sackville Street.

At approximately 3 p.m., Ford made his way to the walls for a view of the Bogside and Creggan, where marchers could be seen assembling. Around him, army 'counter-snipers' were taking up positions at vantage points. A sergeant from 22 LAD armed with a .303 Lee Enfield Mark IV rifle with telescopic sights – considered by marksmen to be more accurate than the SLR – was concealed in the attic of an abandoned house.

Two more soldiers from the regiment, armed with SLRs, were at OP 'Kilo', a platform on the walls near the statue of Governor Walker, and another three manned OP 'Charlie' nearby. To the west of the flats, a marksman with SLR rifle, sniperscope and binoculars, was on the top floor of the Peter England shirt factory with a clear field of fire across William Street.

With the sun out and little cloud cover, visibility was excellent. Two senior police officers from the Renfrew & Bute Constabulary – in Derry on a pre-arranged study visit – could easily read the numbers of cars parked near the Rossville flats through the periscope in one OP.

The last stage of Ford's tour took him to the Anglians' tactical headquarters on the lower level of Craigavon Bridge. Besides checking vehicles, they were to back up the RUC in blocking any attempt by Protestant marchers to cross from the east bank of the river. The Military Police had set up a collection point for prisoners at the bridge: a centre for processing those arrested had been established at Fort George, a former naval dockyard on the Strand Road.

While Ford was with the Anglians, Lieutenant Colonel Welsh in the Sioux – call sign Yankee 61 – radioed that the procession was now under way. Ford went straight to OP 'Echo', above the Embassy Ballroom, squeezing in beside an RUC observer and an army photographer.

As the march set off from the Bishop's Field, a transmission over the army radio from headquarters in Lisburn reported the death of Major Robin Alers-Hankey of the Green Jackets in a hospital in the UK.

That must have struck a sombre note with troops braced for what they had been told was certain to be a confrontation with the young Derry hooligans and the IRA gunmen behind them. Alers-Hankey had been hit by a bullet in the chest during a routine bout of 'aggro' in the Bogside almost three months earlier. A fellow Green Jacket who was now on barrier duty remembered how the crowd had suddenly scattered to allow the sniper a clear shot.

V

Barrier 14

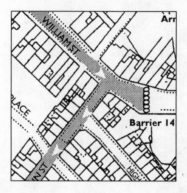

This assembly may lead to a breach of the peace,
you are to disperse immediately

RUC officer to crowd at Barrier 14

Neptune has been used to considerable effect

*Report on army radio net after water cannon drenches
marchers at Barrier 14*

WITH MCGLINCHEY'S COAL lorry leading the way, the demonstration wound down William Street, passed the municipal swimming pool, Harrison's Garage, the burnt-out shell of Stevenson's bakery and on to the junction of Rossville Street and Little James Street where the solid row of Victorian terraces gave way to scorched gaps and the rubble-strewn waste ground at aggro corner.

It was here, for the first time, that the marchers saw the paratroopers with their rifles pointing at the crowd and it was an unfamiliar and foreboding sight. In their camouflaged jump smocks and helmets, they looked very different from the infantry units that normally patrolled the Bogside; some were wearing the regiment's distinctive red beret. Two were lying prone in a sniper's position on the flat roof of the GPO Sorting Office. Others could be seen on top of a wall by the Presbyterian church and half a dozen more occupied a derelict building beside it, where Richardson's shirt factory used to be. The barrels of their SLR assault rifles were sticking out from behind sheets of corrugated iron over the windows.

A group of youths at the front of the march began to jeer and shout obscenities, and give the soldiers two fingers. 'We can see you,' they yelled to those partly concealed in the derelict building. Half a dozen youngsters picked up stones from the waste ground and hurled them at the soldiers, as if by habit. This was their daily battleground and no one took much notice; as usual, the stoning was largely ineffective.

The Coldstream Guards, manning a barricade at the top of William Street, reported over the army radio that the marchers were waving and chanting 'but causing no particular aggro'.

And yet there was something undeniably sinister about the presence of the paratroopers. Dr Raymond McClean was in the middle of the march as it reached the Sorting Office, and his mind went back to the Paras at Magilligan and the clashes on the beach. He noticed now that none of them was in riot gear – the helmets with plastic visors and shields that other regiments used for protection against stone throwers. And he wondered why they had taken up aggressive sniping positions. After all, the enemy – the IRA – had all but publicly announced that it was taking the day off. If that information was freely available in the Rocking Chair Bar on Saturday night, surely British intelligence must have picked it up. So why were so many snipers needed? The way the paratroopers were showing themselves so openly was hardly prudent fieldcraft; in fact, it was downright provocative to any freelance gunman who happened to be on the march with a weapon.

Perhaps they meant to intimidate the marchers. Some students had already encountered rough abuse from Colonel Wilford's men. As they were passing a group of paratroopers in an armoured car, a soldier called out to them through one of the slits in the side of the vehicle, 'We'll get you bastards later.' And when one of the students asked a soldier what it was going to be like down in the town later, he replied, 'If you go down there, you'll get your fucking heads blown off.'

Of immediate concern to the organizers of the march, however, was whether their stewards would be able to make the marchers turn into Rossville Street and prevent a confrontation further down William Street at the army's barrier. Brigadier MacLellan was concerned about that too. At 8 Brigade headquarters in Ebrington Barracks, he seemed to be as apprehensive about what would happen at aggro corner as the marchers themselves.

He radioed Lieutenant Colonel Welsh in the army helicopter: '[It] is important for you to observe whether they now turn down Rossville Street or whether they form in aggro corner with a view to pushing on to their original published meeting place.'

Kevin McCorry, the NICRA organizer, feared that there were not enough stewards at the head of the march to stop those who wanted to cause trouble from continuing to the barrier at the bottom of William Street. To make matters worse, the driver of the coal lorry had made too swift a turn into Rossville Street for the front of the march to keep up. There was now a gap between the lorry and the youths, and they took advantage of it. Without a moment's hesitation they ran on down William Street, yelling, and booing, 'What about the Guildhall? We're going on to the Guildhall.'

In MacLellan's office, the voice of Lieutenant Colonel Welsh confirmed that the stewards had failed to turn the crowd down Rossville Street and towards Free Derry Corner. 'There seems to be quite a few of the crowd breaking away, running down [to the barrier].'

David Capper, a BBC radio reporter, was there and spoke into his tape recorder. 'A crowd of youths has suddenly broken away from the march and they're tearing down William Street leading straight into the heart of the business section of the town . . . '

At aggro corner McCorry jumped down from the lorry and tried to steer the marchers down Rossville Street, but it was too late. 'All hell was breaking loose. Everybody was going purple with high blood pressure,' McCorry recalled later. He yelled to the crowd to follow the lorry, but the loudspeaker system still wasn't working. The stewards tried to hold the line, but the youths surged down William Street, passed Jim Porter's radio and TV shop, the Central Café and McCool's newsagents to the army barrier. They were jeering, making clenched-fist salutes, and chanting anti-army slogans: 'British Bastards', 'Dad's Army', 'What About Monty?'

and 'IRA, IRA'. The television cameras followed. It was 3.30 p.m., according to the RUC.

Hundreds, if not thousands, of marchers now pushed the stewards out of the way and descended into the narrow funnel at the end of William Street where the army had erected Barrier 14. Once there, the only escape was into the narrower Chamberlain Street or an even more confined alley on to the waste ground in front of the high flats on Rossville Street. The first marchers to reach the barrier were trapped. If they tried to bypass the barrier and reach the Guildhall, they would be stopped at Barrier 15 on Waterloo Street.

Each of the two barriers, 14 and 15, was manned by a platoon of twenty men from 'A' Company 2nd Battalion, Royal Green Jackets. The company commander, a major, had placed a lieutenant at each barrier. Unlike the paratroopers they were dressed in riot gear – steel helmets with visors and shields – and held their snub-nosed rubber bullet guns at the ready. In accordance with MacLellan's order army snipers were deployed in houses on William Street, one either side of Barrier 14, and another sniper was covering Barrier 15. But the marchers couldn't see them. Also out of sight in the Strand Road, was a water cannon.

The first marchers to arrive at Barrier 14 pushed right up to the wooden knife rests, which were anchored with concrete blocks and topped with barbed wire; the front marchers were close enough to the soldiers on the other side to shower them with spit. One man started to climb over the barrier and another tried to tear it apart, but the stewards pushed them back. They did their best to discourage the crowd from coming close to the barrier, but the marchers kept advancing. Behind the Green Jackets were the paratroopers with their jump helmets and their red berets, just round the corner.

'English bastards, come out and behave like men,' the crowd taunted the soldiers. 'Come out and fight.'

People were packed in so tight that if you were more than ten yards from the barrier you couldn't see the troops.

Peggy Deery was in the crowd with her nieces, Rita and Sandra. To escape the crush and get a better view, Rita climbed a lamp-post, grabbed hold of the bulb and hung on. Peggy and Sandra decided to leave her there and pushed back through the oncoming marchers to the relative safety of aggro corner. At Barrier 15 in Waterloo Street, a photographer taking pictures got into an argument with one of the soldiers. Barney McGuigan was standing nearby, grabbed him and led him away warning, 'You're going to get yourself into trouble.'

Still the marchers kept coming down William Street. At aggro corner, stewards had given up trying to turn them into Rossville Street and the crowd surged into the bottleneck, building pressure on those at Barricade 14. William Street was jammed. 'It was like coming out of a football match,' recalled Coleman Doyle, an *Irish Press* photographer who was worried that he might get pinned against the barbed wire on the barricade. TV cameras bobbed up and down above the crowd, press photographers held their cameras above their heads trying to take pictures of the confrontation at the barrier; everyone was being pushed and shoved and squashed.

It seemed to those caught in the crush that a riot could break out at any second – ignited by the smallest thing. Bernadette Devlin and Eamon McCann were about twenty feet from the barrier when a small terrier dog, trapped underfoot, started yelping and a group of women panicked, afraid they were going to be bitten.

Any moment, everyone knew, the troops would retaliate with rubber bullets. One of the stewards spoke to the Green Jackets major in charge, pleading with him to wait for them to regain control, but the officer refused. The steward left, throwing up his hands in despair as if to say, 'I can't do anything.'

Before the army could open fire with the rubber bullets, standing orders required the crowd to be warned. If the police were present, as they were, an officer – not below the rank of inspector – had to issue the warning as a representative of the civil power. Inspector Junkin of the RUC now shouted through a loudhailer. 'This assembly may lead to a breach of the peace. You are to disperse immediately.'

The inspector might as well have blown his police whistle and called for the rioting to start. The crowd roared and jeered, and let loose a hail of missiles. Chunks of paving stone, planks of wood, bricks, bottles, a chair with nails sticking out, an iron bar and a fire grate came hurtling over the barrier at the soldiers. A stone knocked the peaked hat off Inspector Junkin's head and the Green Jackets major was cut on the chin by a chunk of concrete. On the army's side of the barricade, TV crews and reporters were also caught in the barrage. An ITN cameraman, Peter Wilkinson, was caught by a brick on the collarbone and his crew were hit in the legs.

The army officers took cover behind the Saracen armoured cars and the police sheltered in the doorway of the old City cinema. Missiles bounced off helmets, visors and riot shields of the soldiers who stood their ground at the barrier, rubber bullet guns and CS gas grenades at the ready.

A handful of stewards kept trying to stop the youths from throwing stones, grabbing the chunks of paving stone from their hands. Even so, the level of the rioting was no greater than usual – and no petrol bombs or nail bombs were being thrown. The army officers didn't seem overly concerned. General Ford had come over from Ebrington Barracks in a Land Rover to act as a military observer on the army side of Barrier 14. He was watching the confrontation and chatting with reporters. He then spotted the MP Austin Currie, introduced himself and the two men had a brief discussion about the hooligans, and the task of the army in maintaining law and order in support of the civil power.

Ford warned those around him to be careful: an IRA sniper had been spotted in an upstairs window of a house in William Street, overlooking the barrier. 'Watch out, when the stoning stops – that's when the snipers will open up,' Ford predicted.

After a few minutes, even the stoical Green Jackets had had enough. The lieutenant ordered up the water cannon, which nosed round the corner like a clumsy green monster with jets of purple-dyed water spewing out of two hoses. All those within a hundred feet were drenched.

David Capper of the BBC spoke into his tape recorder, 'They've brought up the water cannon . . . which is spraying a purple dye over all the marchers .. . the crowd's being scattered by the machine and, er, women and children [are] running in panic, some of them trying to hold their ground . . . looks too like gas has been flung there but the gas unfortunately for the army is blowing in the wrong direction . . . it's blowing back in their faces.'

The crowd retreated in panic and confusion, dripping wet and purple. 'They'll be back,' said General Ford.

Sitting down on William Street, in front of Barrier 14, his arms folded over his knees in peaceful protest, was twenty-two-year-old Jim Wray, a lanky young man in a brown corduroy jacket, black woollen hat with a blue handkerchief tied over his nose and mouth to help against the gas. He was just sitting there, soaked in purple dye and staring at the soldiers behind the barrier. Behind him, youths were still jeering, waving their hands in the air, giving V-signs and hurling any object they could find.

The first CS gas of the afternoon was thrown, apparently by two hard-core rioters. At the corner of High Street and Chamberlain Street, out of sight of the soldiers, they lit the canisters and tossed them over the roofs of the houses in the general direction of the army barriers. They hit their mark.

The Green Jackets radio operator at Barrier 14 received a message from his colleague at Barrier 15 at Waterloo Street saying an army issue CS gas grenade had been thrown by the crowd.

The army also reported a gas grenade thrown from the crowd at Barrier 14 underneath the water cannon. The driver, who was taken by surprise and was not wearing his gas mask, had to retreat, as did the soldiers manning Barrier 14. They quickly donned their gas masks. The Green Jackets lieutenant would later describe the scene: 'We were all completely asphyxiated by the gas and I could see nothing until the gas cleared and I recovered about two minutes later.'

Whether this was caused by one of the canisters hurled by O'Neill and Duffy is not clear. Max Hastings, then a reporter for BBC TV's *24 Hours*, saw two CS gas canisters thrown over the barricade from the crowd. One rolled under the water cannon, forcing the driver to reverse it round the corner and back into the Strand Road.

The gas had now formed a thick cloud, enveloping the 'frontliners'. Capper reported, ' Oh . . . it's near impossible to speak . . . when that stuff hits you . . . but most people are retreating now . . . well, I don't know what sort of gas that was . . . but it was particularly effective . . . this huge crowd of ten to fifteen thousand's been scattered by it . . . and coming back for fresh air . . . many people are rolling on the ground and being sick . . . other people still blinded can't see . . . and er . . . it's vicious stuff this gas.'

General Ford was sure the gas had been thrown from the crowd. 'You know, at this stage I'd be quite within my rights to open fire,' he was overheard to say.

After the gas had cleared, the crowd came back to the barrier and resumed stoning. Only the hard-core rioters were left now. The RUC reported on the police radio link: 'The usual hooligan element is back now at Chamberlain Street (William Street) stoning the military. Gas is being used in Waterloo Street. There's been some stoning there.'

As the crowd surged back to Barrier 14, the lieutenant ordered his troops to load their baton guns. The snub-nosed riot guns which fired the bullets made a loud, distinctive thump accompanied by a bright flash. The bullets could be fatal if fired at close range. They were made of hard black rubber, five and three quarter inches long, one and a half inches in diameter and weighed five and a half ounces. Since their introduction in Northern Ireland, as part of the army's 'minimum force' arsenal, at least three people had been killed and several others blinded. The bullets left the barrel at 160 mph, much faster than any hurtling cricket ball, and were meant to be aimed to bounce off the ground and strike the target on the legs or the genitals, or, as the army manual said, 'the lower torso'. But soldiers had been known to aim them directly at targets.

By the beginning of 1972, surgeons at the Royal Victoria Hospital in Belfast, by then the world's leading authority on street-fighting injuries, had concluded the rubber bullet was a lethal round. Some soldiers have admitted to 'customizing' or 'doctoring' the bullets. One soldier remembered that by cutting off the end of the bullet it was possible to increase the explosive charge and make the bullet hit the target harder.

Rubber bullets had become the weapon of choice in the daily rioting at aggro corner (more than 15,000 rubber bullets were fired in Ulster between 1971 and 1972) and the youth of the Bogside had become skilled in picking them up as they bounced along. Rubber bullets as trophies could be found in many Catholic homes in the Bogside and Creggan, often mounted on a stand with the date when they were picked up and the name of the proud owner. The bullets were also sold to visiting journalists for five pounds five each – a lot of money to a Bogside schoolboy.

As they saw the soldiers preparing to fire, the crowd retreated, but only for a moment, then surged forward again. The lieutenant ordered his troops to fire in volleys of four, as Ford had demanded. The first volley hit two male marchers, one in the stomach and one in the chest. The lieutenant repeated the order to reload and fire several times. In the next fifteen minutes the Green Jackets at Barrier 14 would discharge a total of 137 rubber bullets. Each time the volleys were fired the crowd retreated and advanced again.

Given the range, those hit were lucky to escape with bad bruises.

After the water cannon's driver had recovered from the gas, it was brought into action again, dousing the crowd. They fell back again, moving further up William Street towards aggro corner.

The water cannon, not the rubber bullets, seemed to have the most effect. Lieutenant Colonel Welsh in the army helicopter radioed MacLellan: 'Your large water pistol seems to have removed all the crowd on to aggro corner and there is a general move down Rossville Street . . . apart from the hooligan fringe, the vast majority of the people now in the area of the waste ground by the flats and on aggro corner. They look as if they are not quite certain what they are going to do next.'

The Green Jackets at Barrier 14 confirmed with a message: 'Neptune [the code name for the water cannon] has been used with considerable effect.'

The time in the Brigade log was 3.44 p.m.

Although the Green Jackets were clearly prepared to use every weapon in the riot control arsenal, few of the marchers at this stage thought the violence would escalate.

Several onlookers stayed on to watch. Willy Barber was there because he wanted two rubber bullets as souvenirs to send to friends in America and Australia. But the main body of the marchers seemed to be drifting slowly down to Free Derry Corner, and the youths were turning their attention to the army barriers at Little James Street and Sackville Street. A group of them ran towards the barrier in Little James Street, hurling chunks of paving stone. Others joined them and a great cheer went up.

The soldiers replied with salvos of rubber bullets and volleys of CS gas. At Little James Street they also fired two smoke grenades, which spewed out a dense purple-blue smoke that rose about forty feet in the air and totally obscured the barrier and the troops. The youths picked up the grenades and lobbed them back, adding to the confusion and the rising fear among the marchers that the situation was getting out of control. One policeman, a Detective

Sergeant, who was behind the Little James Street barrier, saw the smoke grenades being thrown back at the soldiers and reported over his radio: 'Unable to see anything now.'

The smoke grenades were not mentioned on the open military radio net, nor on the log later written up by MacLellan's headquarters staff.

Several people had been hit by rubber bullets, on the chin, the ear and in the chest. One man was hit twice. But at aggro corner it was the CS gas that took a higher toll. Volley after volley was fired by the troops at Barrier 12, filling the air with white clouds of the gas, adding to gas that was drifting up on the wind from William Street. An elderly man named John O'Kane collapsed and had to be treated by first aid volunteers. Young Hugh Hegarty, hit in the face by a gas canister, was knocked unconscious and was bleeding from the lips and nose. Makeshift gas masks, a six-inch square of lint first-aid dressing, were being handed out by the Knights of Malta, some of whom were also overcome. The paramedics' commander, Leo Day, and Tom McKinney, a seventy-year-old volunteer, were choking and spitting, and clinging to each other for support. 'I remember feeling a bit silly, but we were really in a bad way,' recalled Leo Day. 'All we had were the squares of lint and they weren't much help.' Several old people were overcome by the gas. The Knights of Malta treated them as best they could and sent them home.

It struck some of the civil rights veterans among the marchers that the army and the police could be losing control and they feared what might happen next.

Dr McClean and his friends had been with the crowd in William Street and received a heavy dose of gas, which left them coughing violently. McClean felt he was going to throw up; he knew better than anyone on the march what the peppery white cloud was doing to his lungs – and what it might do if he inhaled too much. Two and a half years earlier, McClean, then a local GP, had thrust himself into the forefront of the Derry civil rights movement by making a fuss about the use of CS gas in the Bogside. He had become something of a local hero, as well as a much sought-after community physician.

The first time CS gas had been used in the city was during the Battle of the Bogside in August 1969. Dr McClean had set up an emergency dressing station in the Candy Corner shop. Shortly after midnight on the first night the first gas casualties came in, coughing and spitting. The victims complained of intense eye irritation and some could hardly breathe. One of them had been hit in the face by a canister of gas apparently fired from a gun rather than being lobbed by the soldiers and his nose had been almost severed from the bone. McClean stitched the flesh up as best he could – without anaesthetic or running water. He advised any old people suffering from bronchitis to move out of the area for the night.

The next day, the Rossville Street–William Street area was saturated with gas and women were standing at their doors with buckets of water so that passers-by could soak their handkerchiefs as a protection against the constant irritation. They quickly learned that a rag soaked in vinegar was the quickest antidote. One old woman offered McClean a half-filled bottle of brown vinegar. 'Here, son,' she said, 'put a drop of that on your hanky. It helps to keep the gas out.' McClean marvelled at the resilience of the old woman in her new and impossible situation.

In the early hours of the second night, 13 August, as the police were working their way further into the Bogside, the fusillade of gas bombs became so intense that the gas penetrated the Candy Store and McClean had to abandon his efforts. The doctor and his handful of young first aiders, including some off-duty nurses, gathered up their rudimentary medical equipment and set up shop again in a nearby Boys Club. The next day British troops marched into the city – to be welcomed more as conquering heroes with cups of tea. Relative calm was restored – for a while.

After the riots McClean started to give serious thought to the problem of the use of CS gas and its effects on the Bogsiders. Over a period of thirty-six hours, according to official police figures, 1105 cartridges had been used, some people had been very sick and McClean didn't even know the formula for CS.

Over the next few days he made statements to the media about his experience with gas and one report appeared on the front page of *The Times*. Next day, he received a call from Elizabeth Compton, a veteran campaigner against chemical weapons and herbicides who lived in Devon. She told him that CS was a chemical compound known as ortho-chlorobenzal-malonutrile.

At the DuPont synthetics factory where he worked, McClean discussed the formula with the company's chemists; chlorobenzene was a well-known industrial poison with known harmful effects on the brain, the liver and the kidneys, and malonic acid had caused fatalities in American industrial plants. What he didn't know was what happened when the two were combined.

A few days later McClean received through the post (from a reporter in London) a plain envelope containing a secret report on CS trials carried out by Britain's chemical and biological warfare laboratories at Porton Down in Wiltshire. The Porton research showed liver damage had been found in rats following exposure to CS and that liver or kidney damage could be a possible side effect. McClean made further statements to the press about the possible effects of CS on the livers and kidneys of Bogsiders.

Harold Wilson's Labour government was sufficiently concerned about the RUC's massive use of gas during the August Bogside riots to appoint an inquiry under Sir Harold Himsworth, Britain's chief medical officer. Sir Harold quickly assembled a team of medical and scientific experts, and arrived in Derry at the beginning of September. After seeing several people who had been exposed to the gas, he met local doctors, including McClean.

Sir Harold asked McClean why he had been making statements

in the press about liver and kidney damage, and McClean explained that he was simply quoting directly from an official Porton report.

'And where did you obtain this information,' asked Himsworth, surprised.

'I am not at liberty to say,' replied McClean, adding that he wondered if the British government had carried out CS gas tests on humans for traces of harmful by-products.

Himsworth was taken aback and had to admit such tests had not been made. A few weeks later, he published his report, which attempted to reassure the public that nothing of a serious medical nature had happened on those two August nights in the Bogside. But Himsworth did recommend that chemical agents used in civil disturbances were treated like any other pharmaceuticals; they should be thoroughly tested before use.

In the past, concluded the Himsworth report, there had been only a 'tacit understanding' that such tests were carried out. Now there should be an 'explicit requirement'. The report stated quite clearly that when inhaled in huge amounts by experimental animals, CS produces serious lesions on the lungs and, as a result, respiratory and circulatory failure may develop, 'and lead to death in the course of the next few days'. McClean had scored a victory. Although the army continued to use CS gas, by 1972 operational orders were issued that it was to be used only in certain circumstances. When Ford told MacLellan to draw up his plans for this Sunday he had stressed that CS gas was to be used as a last resort. Yet almost as soon as the young rioters started pounding Barrier 12 in Little James Street, the army retaliated with volleys of CS gas – and would continue to pump gas into the Bogside. Within half an hour the 'last resort' had been exhausted.

VI

How Could Anyone Pick on Me as a Gunman?

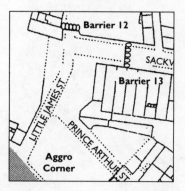

I was walking away with my back to the troops,
they were just shooting at anything, like herrings
in a barrel

*John Johnston, aged fifty-two, one of the
first wounded on Bloody Sunday*

IN WILLIAM STREET the rioting had now moved to Barriers 12 and 13 in Little James Street and Sackville Street, the roof of the GPO Sorting Office, the Presbyterian church and the nearby derelict building where the Paras were concealed. It was here that the first live rounds would be fired.

At 3.16 p.m., before the marchers had entered William Street, Major 236 had received an order from Colonel Wilford to move his company of 103 men forward from its base location in Clarence Avenue to the junction of Queen Street and Great James Street, opposite the Presbyterian church.

Support Company was made up of a mortar platoon, a machine-gun platoon and a composite platoon. The mortar and machine-gun platoons were in six Pigs, the Composite Platoon in two four-ton canvas-covered trucks. Company HQ, including Major 236, was in another Pig escorted by a Ferret Scout car.

All but fifteen of the paratroopers were armed with SLRs. Three of the soldiers in the composite platoon carried sub-machine guns because, the army would say afterwards, there was a shortage of rifles. The soldiers were clearly expecting a fight. Each paratrooper was issued with fifty rounds of live ammunition, twenty in a magazine loaded in the rifle, a spare magazine and ten rounds in a bandolier in a pocket of his camouflaged jumping smock.

A radio operator for Support Company recalled being filled with

an indescribable feeling as I heard the awesome roar of hatred

111

and defiance which a riotous crowd of 15,000 can summon. We took up a position in a churchyard listening to the din which was out of sight beyond the rooftops.

As I was carrying the radio, I listened to the exasperated comments from 22nd Light Regiment. They were clearly at their wits' end and trying to contain the violence . . . Looking around me our faces were blackened and we were wearing helmets. Adrenalin was running. Excitement was in the air. I know I speak for the majority when I say that the common feeling amongst us [was], please let us be called in – we'll go nuts if we miss a chance like this.

Some of the Paras had returned from Cyprus only that morning and had to be briefed on the way to Derry. One of them missed the general ammunition handout and only had one magazine of twenty rounds.

The paratroopers had been told to plan for two possible routes into the Bogside where the marchers would be congregating. One was through, or over, the twelve-foot wall beside the Presbyterian church. The nineteenth-century church, built in the style of a neo-classical temple, was out of sight of the marchers. The back of the church was visible and the adjoining twelve-foot wall could also be seen from waste ground on William Street. The wall had barbed wire on top that would have to be cut in full view of the marchers.

Wilford's choice of this route was therefore puzzling, for not only would the wire cutters be exposed to the crowd, but also to any snipers looking across William Street. Even if the assault was achieved without casualties, MacLellan's orders had made clear to his officers that they should expect 'the hooligan element to accompany the marchers', and a 'high degree of violence through-out the city'. Wilford knew that as soon as his men showed their faces, they would be stoned or shot at.

The Paras would have to climb the wall laden with gear, again in full view of snipers. And they could only come out one at a time, giving the youths plenty of time to disappear into the Bogside. The choice of route provided any IRA gunman with a tempting target.

Major 236 quickly came to the conclusion that the way through the wall, even if it could easily be demolished by the Pigs or climbed by his men, was 'narrow and exposed, and was not suitable for deploying men quickly'. There was an alternative.

Beside the church the derelict building had its windows boarded up with corrugated iron, but this could easily be removed from the inside to give the Paras a second route into William Street for the arrest operation. Major 236 ordered his machine-gun platoon to occupy the house – which presented them with another obstacle course, including two twelve-foot walls and more barbed wire at ground-floor level. One of the six soldiers of the machine-gun platoon clambered over the walls, then fell and hurt his back, putting him out of action – the first, and most serious, Para casualty of the day. His five colleagues took up firing positions, four on the ground floor and one, a corporal, managed to climb to the first-floor level (above the ground floor) and balanced himself precariously on a partition wall. It was 3.40 p.m.

From the marchers' viewpoint the soldiers of the machine-gun platoon were more threatening than the Paras on the Post Office roof because they were at such close quarters – almost on William Street itself. As they poked their rifles through the corrugated iron over the windows they were pelted with stones and bottles. Most of the missiles bounced off the walls of the house; a few came through the windows but none of the soldiers was hit. For several minutes the youths threw stones and the soldiers fired six rubber bullets in return. This was still not a serious riot in Derry terms.

By ten minutes to four, the stragglers in the march were arriving at the waste ground opposite the Presbyterian church. Among them were Damien Donaghy, a fifteen-year-old youth and John Johnston, the fifty-nine-year-old manager of a Derry drapery store.

Donaghy, who was known to his mates as 'Bubbles', had just left school to begin an apprenticeship in plumbing. He was also a talented football player with a realistic ambition of one day turning professional.

Johnston was a quiet, serious man with thin, greying hair. He had never been on a civil rights march and had no intention of joining this one because he had a bad chest and had to avoid the gas. He was on his way to Glenfada Park to visit his friend, Tommy Duddy, who was ninety and unable to look after himself. Each day, either Johnston or his wife would drop into Duddy's flat to check up on him, especially when there was likely to be trouble, making sure his windows were shut tight to keep out the gas. Johnston left home his home as the marchers were passing by. Like many of them he was dressed in his Sunday best, an overcoat, tweed jacket, grey trousers, white shirt and tie, and a thick woolly cardigan. In an effort to avoid the violence he intended to bypass aggro corner and cut across the waste ground opposite the old Stevenson bakery and the derelict house now occupied by the paratroopers of the machine-gun platoon.

At this moment, one of the rioters decided on an insane gesture of defiance. He broke off from the march and crawled up the side of the derelict house, out of view of the paratroopers. In his hand he was clutching an empty lemonade bottle which he had bought earlier and which he and his friends had drunk as they marched along. His plan was to hurl the bottle through the window in the hope of hitting a paratrooper at close quarters.

Across William Street on the waste ground, Charlie Meehan, a former policeman in the RUC, stood with a friend, Pat O'Carolan. Meehan spotted one of the paratroopers in the window of the derelict house with his rifle pointing at himself and O'Carolan. He was worried that they were too exposed. 'We're in a very bad position if something starts,' he said. 'Come on, we'd better go.'

According to the Para corporal in the derelict house, two objects shaped like cans of beans then flew past his window. Smoke was coming out of one of them. The corporal had not seen the objects thrown and did not see them land, but heard two bangs. He shouted out to his colleagues, 'Nail bombs.' The platoon commander, a sergeant, was on the ground floor and he ordered the corporal to open fire if he saw any nail bombers. Meanwhile, the rioter with the lemonade bottle was edging closer to the window in the derelict house, getting ready to chuck it in.

On the waste ground, Donaghy was just rounding the corner of the Nook Bar, where Duffy's the bookmaker used to be, when the Paras in the derelict house fired a volley of rubber bullets. Micky McGuiness, who had become separated from his brother-in-law, Dr McClean, picked up one of them as it bounced off a wall and put it in his pocket for a souvenir.

Donaghy chased another of the bullets. As he bent over to pick it up the distinctive sharp crack from a high-velocity SLR rang out across William Street from the derelict house. The bang was deafening to the daring bottle-thrower, now directly underneath the rifle barrel sticking out of the window; he thought the soldier must have fired at him. He immediately tossed his bottle through the window. He claimed that he hit one of the paratroopers in the chest and raced back to William Street, lucky to be alive.

The shot struck Donaghy in his right hip. The boy's head twitched, his hands went up as in surrender, his legs gave way and he fell to the ground on his back crying, 'I've been shot, I've been shot.' Charlie Meehan heard his screams and saw him writhing on the ground. There was nothing in his hands, no explosion and no nail bomb at his side, only rubble and stones. Blood spurted through a hole in his trousers just above the right knee.

The corporal of the machine-gun platoon would later claim that he had seen a man coming out from the corner of a building on the waste ground and striking what seemed to be a match against the wall as though he were about to light a bomb. With his other hand the man was holding an object ' a little bigger than his fist', the corporal said. He assumed this was a nail bomb and he fired one aimed shot at the centre of the man's body from his SLR. It missed and he immediately fired again. The man was knocked backwards and fell down. Two civilians came out from behind the same building and dragged him out of sight. The corporal did not see what happened to the object he was holding and did not hear any explosions from that direction.

A private of the machine-gun platoon who was in the same derelict building but at the ground-floor window nearest to William Street had already cocked his rifle. Seconds after the corporal fired, he would say that he spotted the same man with a black cylindrical object in one hand strike what appeared to be a match against a wall. The private fired an aimed shot – with difficulty because he was wearing his gas mask. The shot apparently missed as the man was still there, so the private fired two more shots and he saw the man fall to the ground. There was no explosion.

Johnston was standing a few feet from Donaghy. One of the three shots sliced through his right thigh. Another bullet made a hole in his right shoulder. Johnston fell to the ground startled, thinking that he had been whacked by a rubber bullet.

A woman shouted, 'Jesus, there's two men shot' and everyone started to run back up the alley into Columbcille Court away from William Street, a group of them carrying Donaghy to safety. Another woman who was in a state of confusion as a result of the shots, came up to Pat O'Carolan and pleaded, 'Mister, what do I do?' He took her arm and guided her out of the waste ground. 'They are not rubber bullets they're firing, they are real bullets,' he told her.

As Johnston hobbled across the open ground towards the cover of Columbcille Court, no one could believe he had been hit. But then a man shouted out, 'Christ, Mr Johnston, you're shot, your trousers are soaking in blood.' Johnston looked down and saw that his trousers were wet through. He was carried away.

Dr McClean was further down William Street when he heard the high-velocity shots, three or four in quick succession, he thought. He turned to his brother-in-law, Danny, saying, 'That sounds different, doesn't it?' Danny replied, 'I'm afraid it was.'

Sean Duffy, the manager of the Rocking Chair pub on Waterloo Road, was standing nearby talking to David Capper of the BBC. 'Those were live shots,' he said

Capper answered, 'I know that.'

Just then, a man came running down William Street calling for Dr McClean to hurry to the flat of Mrs Bridget Shields in Columbcille Court, where Donaghy and Johnston had been taken. 'For God's sake come quick, there's two men shot.'

'What with, rubber bullets?'

'No, it's real guns they're using.'

Dr McClean, Danny McGuiness and Sean Duffy pushed their way through the crowd back up William Street. The Shields' house was in a low-rise complex of maisonettes, honeycombed with pedestrian ways and small, intimate squares. The paramedics from the Knights of Malta, Leo Day and Tom McKinney, were also heading away from Barrier 14, still suffering from the effects of gas, when they heard a man shouting, 'Someone's been shot over here.' They shoved through the crowd to the Shields' flat.

Inside, Dr McClean was already treating young Donaghy on the low settee and Mr Johnston was on the floor, with a Knights of Malta man kneeling over him. Eibhlin Lafferty, an eighteen-year-old student who was also a member of Leo Day's contingent, was putting a dressing on Mr Johnston's leg.

Dr McClean found that Donaghy had a neat, small entry wound, about 7mm in diameter (matching the SLR round) on the upper third of the inner surface of his right thigh. The bullet had tossed and tumbled on impact, smashing the thigh bone and leaving a jagged exit wound. Donaghy was pale and shocked, but wasn't losing much blood.

Johnston had a gunshot wound to his inner right thigh and a

peculiar jagged wound in the region of his left shoulder, which McClean thought could have been caused by a ricochet. They tried to cheer him up by telling him that his big grey overcoat, tweed jacket and a woolly cardigan had probably saved his life. 'The bullet must have been slowed down,' they said, but they didn't really believe it.

They placed Johnston on a sofa and applied a tourniquet. He kept on saying, 'My legs are burning up,' but as they were dressing the wound, he perked up, announcing, 'I'll be all right' and told them that he was ready to go home. Dr McClean told him he would have to go to hospital just as soon as they could get an ambulance.

'How could anyone pick on me as a gunman?' Johnston asked. 'There I was, walking away with my back to the troops. They were just shooting at anything; like herrings in a barrel.'

Reporters were rushing to the Shields' flat, wanting to find out who had been shot. A BBC television crew, with cameraman Cyril Cave and soundman Jim Deeney, were on the waste ground at Rossville Street when they heard the firing. They ran into William Street where people offered to take them in to the Shields' home and they were joined by David Capper of BBC radio. They got to the Shields' front door, but the men inside wouldn't let them in for fear that Donaghy and Johnston would later be identified on film and prosecuted for being on an illegal march.

'Get those bastards out of here, they'll only show his face,' shouted one man. A couple of punches were thrown. Cave was hit and Deeney was kicked. The front of Cave's TV camera was slightly damaged. A young marcher, Peter Mullan, calmed everyone down. 'Don't harm these men, they're only doing their job,' he said.

Someone said if the BBC would give assurances they wouldn't show the faces they should be allowed to film them. More punches were thrown.

'Look, I know you're upset and angry, but I'll give you

categorical assurances that we will just show his injury and not show his face,' said Cave. 'If you want to cover his face, that's all right.' So they covered Johnston's face and filmed his wounded leg.

Outside, there was a shout from the back of Columbcille Court 'Get clear, someone wants to go into action.'

Two volunteers from the Officials' Bogside unit had marched with the crowd from the Creggan but had peeled off just before the waste ground on William Street and walked through Columbcille Court into Glenfada Park, where one of their mobile armouries was parked in the square. In the boot of a stolen dark-blue Avenger were a Sten gun, a carbine, two old Lee Enfield .303s and a .22 automatic. The Officials, like the Provisionals, were under strict orders not to use their weapons, unless the army fired first – and then only to fire in self-defence and away from the crowd. But in case of emergency, the two volunteers had arranged their own sniping positions – in one of the maisonettes in Columbcille Court. These houses had balconies at the back – the side facing the paratroopers across the waste ground at Williams Street. The balconies were used to hang out laundry to dry and were covered with white wooden slats, providing a good line of sight to the Presbyterian church and the top of the GPO Sorting Office. The volunteers had arranged with the woman in one of the flats to leave open the gate to her balcony.

Waiting in Glenfada, they heard that 'two boys' had been shot by the army on the waste ground. One of them grabbed a .303 out of the Avenger, slid it underneath a coat and raced to the balcony. He was striding forward, obviously in a rage. 'Those bastards can't get away with that . . . a young boy, a little boy and an old man, shot down, doing nothing. They were doing nothing. You all know they were doing nothing. And they were shot down.'

To most of the onlookers the men were unknown; it was the first time they had ever seen an armed IRA man. Peter Mullan had never seen anyone with a gun – except someone shooting crows with a shotgun. He could see the muzzle of the .303 sticking out under the gunman's coat.

'They can't be allowed to get away with it,' the Official with the gun was yelling. 'I'll get one of them. It was that bastard on the roof there. I know it was him.'

It seemed to Mullan that he had lost control of himself. His comrades were saying, 'You can't do it. There are too many people around. You know you're not supposed to. If you shoot now far too many people are going to get hurt.'

The gunman's comrades closed around him, as if to overcome him, but he brushed them aside and raced up on to the balcony.

Fearing a firefight, Mullan decide to leave quickly. 'For God's sake come on out of William Street,' he shouted to the others.

Once in position on the balcony of Columbcille Court, the Official gunman took aim at the soldiers on the right of the church, where one of the paratroopers kept peering over the top. He fired a single shot from the .303 and thought he hit the soldier, but the bullet missed.

The paratroopers on the roof of the Sorting Office and the wall by the church would say later that a single high-velocity round hit a drainpipe on the East wall of the church just above the heads of the wire-cutting party. Major 236 timed the shot at 'about 3.55'.

The paratroopers would testify that a shot was fired before the machine-gun platoon opened up on Donaghy and Johnston. The preponderance of the civilian testimony, however, indicated that the army fired first. There is no record of the shot in any of the military or police radio logs; nor does the log note the paratroopers' shots that hit Donaghy and Johnson. This is strange because other shots fired at other army units, and returned, were meticulously recorded.

The distinctive thump of the .303 – compared with the sharper crack of the high-velocity SLR – filled the waste ground and Columbcille Court. David Capper of the BBC was standing right beside the flats and heard 'a very loud report'. His impression was that 'someone very close to me had fired a shot, presumably at the soldiers about sixty yards away [on top of the wall by the Presbyterian church]'. Tony Martin, the secretary of the Catholic Ex-Servicemen's Club (who was one of the first to join the Ulster army reserve in 1969) had been one of the stewards trying to turn the march at aggro corner, also heard the sound of the .303. It was a 'racing cert', he would say later, that the Para shots came first. After the confrontation at the William Street barricade, Martin had walked down Chamberlain and Eden Street into the car park in front of the flats, where he chatted with Peter Lancaster. He then went with Lancaster to a friend's flat in Kells Walk to use the toilet. As he came out of the flat at the corner of Columbcille Court he heard the SLR shots from the machine-gun platoon that wounded Donaghy and Johnston. A few moments later he heard the .303. '[It was] right beside us on the corner of Columbcille Court – one round was fired.'

When a group of Provisional IRA men on the march heard the same report, they rushed towards the balcony and found the volunteers coming down the stairwell. The Provos tackled one of them, hitting and pushing him, and accusing him of disobeying orders not to fire and of putting the marchers in danger. Tony Martin saw this, so did people on the balconies of the flats in Kells Walk. Martin told them all to go indoors because he also feared a firefight, perhaps between Provos and the Officials.

One of the Provos tried to grab the Officials' .303, but the volunteer turned it on him. 'I'll fucking shoot you,' he said and the Provo backed away. Then they calmed down and he agreed not to fire again and to return his weapon to the boot of the Avenger.

Minutes later, at 4.10 p.m., the first of the Pigs carrying Support Company burst through Barricade 14 into Rossville Street. The gunman shouted to his Official IRA comrades to get the car out of Glenfada, or they would be caught red-handed. But it was too late;

the soldiers were roaring up Rossville Street, and the army helicopter was hovering overhead. They grabbed the weapons and ran out of the Bogside, heading up the hill to the Creggan.

Inside the Shields' flat, Dr McClean and the Knights of Malta had done all they could to patch up Donaghy's and Johnston's wounds, and were waiting for a car to take them to hospital. Leo Day and Eibhlin Lafferty thought they could probably be of more help elsewhere. But as Day opened the door, two long bursts of fire came from the direction of Rossville Street. He and Lafferty ducked back into the porch. Someone was banging on a window opposite and Day saw two women waving frantically and pointing towards Glenfada Park. One of them opened the window and shouted, 'There's bodies lying behind this block . . . for God's sake be careful, you'll be shot if you're seen.'

VII

Move! Move! Move!

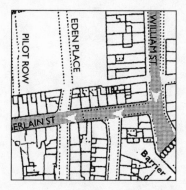

The scoop-up operation depended for its success
on pinching out the rioters before they could
escape down into the Rossville complex

Lt Col Wilford, CO 1 Para

I was anxious to confirm that there was absolute
separation of the hooligans from the bulk of the
marchers, as this was a pre-requisite of the arrest
plan

Brigadier Maclellan

WILFORD WANTED ACTION. He had seen the rioting at the William Street barrier, he had been on the roof of the Embassy building in the Strand Road and had watched the stoning at Little James Street. By 3.45 p.m., the crowd at those barriers had been doused by the water cannon, peppered by volleys of rubber bullets and covered with clouds of CS gas. Most of them had drifted back up William Street towards the meeting at Free Derry Corner, or were going home. A handful of regular rioters – perhaps 200 in total – were still throwing stones. It must have been obvious to Wilford that if the Paras were not sent in now even the regulars would begin to tire and he would lose the opportunity to pick up more than a handful of them.

But Brigadier MacLellan was not yet ready to launch the arrest operation. He was sticking rigidly to his own orders that required a clear separation – however illusory – between the stone throwers and the majority of the marchers before authorising the scoop-up.

MacLellan's problem was that while the youths closest to the barrier were doing most of the stoning, there were other people milling about, apparently more interested in watching the riot than moving on to the meeting at Free Derry Corner where about 500 marchers had gathered to hear speeches.

Wilford was left waiting. The delay mirrored an earlier frustration caused by the failure of his radio communications. The radio that had conked out on the way from Belfast was apparently still giving trouble as the launch operation grew closer. In the early afternoon the Paras had been out of touch with Brigade headquarters.

Wilford was supposed to be linked by radio on three separate nets. The main link with 8th Infantry Brigade Command net was 'open' and could therefore be heard, like police radio links, by anyone tuning to the correct frequency. The second was the Paras's own battalion net and the third was a so-called 'secure link', which either used a frequency not normally available on domestic radios, or a land line telephone.

Shortly after two o'clock, before the march had left Bishop's Field, MacLellan's headquarters could make no contact at all with Wilford.

The voice of a Brigade officer, could be heard over the open link from Ebrington Barracks: '81 [Wilford's call sign] is paying no attention. I have been calling on other [secure] means. Make sure that information coming over on this means is relayed to call signs on other means, over.'

Wilford himself was even having trouble contacting his own men on the battalion net. At one point he told them, over the open Brigade link, that all stations had been trying to reach their call sign, 65, for ten minutes without any answer.

65 this is 81. Get that other means working as quickly as possible. I cannot tolerate it not working, out.
65 this is 81, over. 65 this is 81, over. 65 this is 81,over.
81. What on earth is going on with your communications?
I have been calling on other means. I have been calling for three minutes on this means and I am getting no answer, for Christ's sake get the communications sorted out, out.

Listening to this outburst, and somewhat bemused by it, was the Bogside's chief amateur radio enthusiast, Jim Porter. He owned an electrical and TV repair shop at 38 William Street, not a hundred yards from Barrier 14. It was his custom to record army radio traffic, especially on march days, and at one o'clock that afternoon he had started to tape the brigade net. He had also set up a second tape recorder to record police messages.

The 'other means' mentioned by the army signallers was their jargon for the Brigade's 'secure net'. For Porter, there was no problem in picking it up on his receivers, which he had designed himself and which covered frequencies between 40Mhz and 1000Mhz. The Brigade net frequency was normally found at around 82Mhz. He usually located the secure net at 250Mhz, but on this Sunday, after constant scanning, he could find nothing at the high end. Then the Paras' signaller gave a clue as to what might be happening.

Over the brigade net call sign 65 (the Paras' signaller) was trying to explain why he had not answered headquarters' and Wilford's urgent requests. 'We were under the impression that someone was on permanent way. We can't get anybody at this end.'

Porter interpreted 'on permanent way' as signaller's language for saying the secure net was stuck on 'send' in the headquarters at Ebrington Barracks. Thus, Brigadier MacLellan, or whoever was in the operations room, could send messages over the secure net and they would be received. But messages could not be transmitted back to him.

Quite by chance, Porter later obtained evidence supporting his thesis. He used to teach electronics at a local technical college and every now and then the army garrison would pass on pieces of radio equipment which had become obsolete, or didn't work properly. Three months after Bloody Sunday, Porter was given an AR43 Mk2 transceiver, the same type as the secure net transceiver used on Bloody Sunday. When he tried it out, Porter discovered that the AR43 had a sticking relay that meant it was on permanent 'send'. This had occurred after an electrical arc, or spark, within the electrical circuit inside the transceiver had welded two platinum contacts together in the 'send' position. The sticking relay concerned was located inside a sealed metal box. Porter broke the seal and looked inside. Someone had tried to mend it but failed and, in the process, had pulled other bits apart and put the AR43 out of action. Porter got it going again. In 1997, on the twenty-fifth anniversary of Bloody Sunday, a former major from the Anglians visited Porter in his home and confirmed that an AR43 had been issued for use with the secure net on Bloody Sunday.

How long the problem with the secure net continued has never been made clear by the army, but there is evidence to suggest that the net never functioned properly throughout the day.

At 3.15 p.m. the army helicopter reported the head of the procession was at Lecky Road, at least fifteen minutes from the barriers at Little James Street and William Street. One minute later Wilford ordered Support Company over the Para radio net (now working, apparently) to be prepared to move up in fifteen minutes from their assembly point in Clarence Avenue to Queen Street behind the Presbyterian church. At 3.30 they moved and began to explore the assault route over the wall by the church. At the same time, 'A' Company had moved forward from Clarence Avenue to form up behind the Coldstream Guards outside St Eugene's Cathedral. They were to move through Barrier 11 to block marchers coming back up William Street, and to push stragglers down the street and into the arresting forces of Support Company. 'C' Company was waiting just round the corner from the William Street barrier to chase the stone throwers up William Street, into Chamberlain Street and out on to the open ground in front of the flats.

According to the Brigade log, MacLellan knew nothing of Wilford's preparations until 3.55 p.m. when Wilford told his signaller to request permission over the open radio link to deploy 'C' Company through the William Street barrier.

The impatient voice was loud and clear over the open frequency: '65 from my Sunray [commander], I would like to deploy one of his sub-units through barrier 14 [William Street)] around the back into the area of William Street, Little James Street. He reckons if he does he should be able to pick up quite a number of yobbos, over.'

The request was acknowledged, but ignored. The reply from headquarters was simply: Zero, Out.

Why did Wilford send this highly sensitive message about the scoop-up over the open net? Anyone listening could have been alerted that the Paras were about to storm into the Bogside. Porter's theory of the disabled AR43 provides a credible explanation.

Perhaps in part because of the lack of communication with Wilford, MacLellan was still not to be hurried into making a decision. He would recall, 'At this time I was anxious to confirm that there was absolute separation of the hooligans from the main bulk of the marchers, as this was a prerequisite of the arrest plan. I therefore did not give permission at this stage for the arrest operation to be launched.'

The army helicopter now reported that the general crowd movement was down into the Lecky Road area, around the Bogside Inn, away from the Rossville flats. 'It seems as though a lot of people feel they have made their protest and are now returning back to their homes,' reported Welsh.

Still MacLellan would not give the order. The impatient Wilford sought a second opinion from the soldiers at Barrier 14. Again over the open net, he told his radio operator to get hold of the Barrier 14 commander to confirm rioting was still taking place.

Hello 90, this is 65, is there still a hooligan element in the area of Barrier 14, over. Hello 90, this is 65, over?

90 Alpha, send, over.

65, is there still a hooligan element in the area of William Street, Little James Street and around Barrier 14, over?

90 Alpha, yes, over.

65 roger. Would you mind informing Zero [MacLellan], they don't appear to believe us on this point, over.

90 Alpha, wait now.

The Coldstream Guards, who were manning Barrier 11 at Lower Road beside St Eugene's Cathedral, reported that the crowd were dispersing in a northerly direction up Creggan Road, suffering from the effects of CS gas.

At 4.03 p.m., Barrier 14 informed MacLellan that youths were advancing on them using a corrugated-iron shield they had ripped off an abandoned dwelling. The officer's message ended with the question, 'Have you any idea what time 65 [the Paras] are going in, over.'

MacLellan was still not ready. 'Zero, roger. I will tell you all I can. We will leave it for the moment, out.'

The Coldstream Guards at the cathedral then reported that most of those making their way home to the Creggan were children, women and old people – leaving the men and the youths on the street.

This appeared to be what MacLellan had been waiting to hear. He immediately ordered Wilford – over the secure net – to send in 'C' Company from Barrier 14. His instructions would appear in the typed version of the Brigade log at 1609 hours from 'BH' (Brigade Headquarters): 'Orders given to 1 Para at 1607 hrs for 1 subunit (Company C) to do scoop-up OP through Barrier 14. Not to conduct running battle down Rossville Street.'

No confirmation of this order appears in the Brigade log, again lending support to Porter's theory that Wilford could not send messages back over the secure net.

In MacLellan's office at Ebrington Barracks Chief Superintendent Lagan was picking up snippets of the army's radio traffic from the adjoining operations room. The messages were sometimes difficult for him to comprehend because they were in unfamiliar military jargon, but he got the gist of it.

MacLellan was in the Ops room when Wilford made his request to launch the arrest operation. He came back into his office and told Lagan, 'The Paras want to go in.'

Lagan had a gut feeling, from overhearing the radio traffic and from his own experience of marches and riots, that there were still too many people around. 'For heaven's sake hold them until we're satisfied the marchers and the rioters are well separated,' he told MacLellan.

MacLellan went back into the Ops room, returning shortly afterwards. ' I'm sorry, the Paras have gone in,' Lagan recalled him saying, and without waiting for a reply he continued into his inner office.

Lagan has always been adamant that MacLellan said the word 'sorry'. He took it to mean either that MacLellan was not personally responsible for the Paras going in, or that someone else had despatched them. MacLellan is emphatic that he did give the order for the Paras to go in and then told Lagan. He cannot remember the exact words he used, but thought that Lagan replied, 'Well, I hope they are separated enough.'

MacLellan says his reply was, 'I am assured that they are, but anyway it is too late to stop them now.' He says he might have used the word 'sorry', but if he did, it was not meant to express regret that he had just given the orders to launch the arrest operation. (Under cross-examination at the Widgery inquiry, Lagan's interpretation that MacLellan was not responsible for the order was never put to the Brigadier. It is certain to be a contentious issue at the Saville hearings.)

Throughout the day it appears there was a steady devolution of operational control for the conduct of the scoop-up from MacLellan at HQ to Wilford on the spot. According to the radio log, the Para commander, not MacLellan, had moved his men from their original stand-by positions up to the front lines of the confrontation at the barriers in William Street and Little James Street. Now he would develop MacLellan's original plan to conduct the arrest operation on foot and send at least seven armoured Pigs into the open ground south of aggro corner. One minute after receiving his initial order from MacLellan, according to the Para log, Wilford told Major 236 to prepare to send his Support Company through the Little James Street barrier.

The mortar platoon returned to its vehicles in Queen Street, but the sergeant in command of the machine-gun platoon couldn't get his men back over the twelve-foot-high wall which they had scaled to reach the derelict bakery house on William Street – and there was no time to fetch the ladders the mortar platoon had used to climb the wall by the Presbyterian church. Major 236 instructed his sergeant to stay where he was; he was told his vehicles would be brought to Little James Street after Support Company had gone through Barrier 12.

At 1610 hours, three minutes after MacLellan's order for one company to go through Barrier 14, Wilford ordered Major 236 to deploy Support Company down Little James Street.

The paratroopers would penetrate deeper into the Bogside than had originally been envisaged.

Op order 2/72 said the arrest operation was 'likely to be launched' on two axes, one directed towards hooligan activity in the area of William Street–Little Diamond (the top of William Street by St Eugene's Cathedral) and one towards the area of William Street/Little James Street. But the Paras would now charge down Rossville Street almost as far as they could go – right up to the rubble barricade. MacLellan's order about 'no running battles down Rossville Street' was open to interpretation, of course. He would claim that he had not known the Paras would go in that far.

According to Wilford, 'The breakout [as described in the original order] was intended to be on foot. It was obvious there was going to be no way of getting vehicles through by the Presbyterian church. I told OC Support Company that if we were ordered to move to effect arrests we should probably have to use the Little James Street route.'

MacLellan would insist, after the event,

The purpose of my order was to ensure that the arresting force only scooped up those actively engaged in riotous behaviour in the William Street–Rossville Street area, and NOT [sic] those other persons engaged in a non-violent meeting which had already started at Foxes Corner [Free Derry Corner]. To achieve this scoop-up it was necessary for the troops to get beyond the rioters and place themselves between the rioters and those already at the meeting place at Foxes Corner. The company therefore that moved rapidly in their vehicles to the area north of the Rossville flats acted in accordance with my instructions in that such action would effectively place the troops between the rioters and the marchers.

General Ford knew Wilford had been ordered in. He was standing at Barrier 14 talking to a high-ranking security official, who reported the following conversation. 'Now, you're going to see something,' said Ford.

'What do you mean?' asked the observer.

'They're going to put the Paras in,' replied Ford.

'What are you going to do with them?'

'Don't ask me, I'm only an onlooker here,' Ford said, adding, 'But the local commander has a plan.'

Wilford immediately requested Barrier 14 to be lifted to let his troops into William Street: 'Hello 90 this is 65 can you lift Barrier 14, one of our four trucks is coming through, over.'

'Barrier 14 being lifted now,' came the reply.

'C' Company of 1 Para had been waiting in their armoured cars, out of sight of the rioters at the corner of William Street and Waterloo Street. Hooting and whistling, the paratroopers jumped into the Pigs and raced up the Strand Road. They arrived at the William Street barrier before the Green Jackets had time to remove the water cannon and two of their own Pigs. The Paras yelled at the Green Jackets to move their vehicles.

Operation Forecast was under way.

VIII

Shoot Me! Shoot Me!

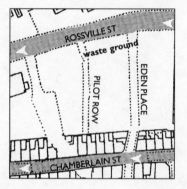

For God's sake watch out, that one's going to fire

Peggy Deery just before she is shot

Tell the world . . . bastards just killing my people

Woman in Rossville Flats

AT TEN MINUTES past four by the Guildhall clock, 'C' Company charged on foot through the opening in Barrier 14 at the bottom of William Street, scattering what was left of the crowd before them. General Ford urged them on, 'Go on, 1 Para, go and get them.'

One section in riot gear ran up William Street to aggro corner, arresting anybody they could catch; they soon returned with a handful of prisoners who were put up against a wall at the corner of Chamberlain Street and searched. Another party with SLRs at the ready took up firing positions.

The marchers still at Barrier 14 rushed down tiny Chamberlain Street, which was narrower than William Street, and many stumbled and fell. Paddy Walsh was there. For a moment, he and others thought of making a stand; if the army would not let them go to the Guildhall, then they would not let the army come up Chamberlain Street and into Free Derry. There was a lot of shouting and yelling from both sides . . . 'English bastards', 'Irish pigs'.

Michael Bridge, an unemployed labourer from the Creggan, also ran into Chamberlain Street. He had volunteered to be a march steward, wearing a white armband with the letters NICRA on it. At Barrier 14, in an effort to prevent a clash, he had taken sticks away from some youths, then linked arms with other stewards to try to stop the crowd reaching the barrier. As the water cannon doused the marchers he was drenched and the foul smell made him vomit. When the troops at the barrier opened up with rubber bullets, one hit him on the foot.

Somewhere in the mêlée in William Street was Jackie Duddy, a seventeen-year-old apprentice weaver. Duddy came from a typically large Catholic family of fifteen children, nine girls and six boys. His hobby was also one common in the enclave; he loved to box. He was a regular at St Mary's Club and his trophies filled the family maisonette in Central Drive, Creggan. He had boxed in England and he was good enough to be a hopeful for the Olympics, or at least the European games. When he left school he had worked for a local garage, before becoming an apprentice at the weaving mill of Thomas French.

Since then he had been in regular training, which meant a lot of roadwork before breakfast. One of his sparring partners at the club was Charlie Nash, and in their way Charlie and Jackie were idols of middle-aged Creggan parents yearning to see their children achieve something against the background of the ghetto.

On this Sunday, after mass, Jackie had planned to spend the afternoon playing records – he was a member of the record club and used to have friends in for sessions most Sundays. But his pals were going on the march and, as it was a nice day and the assembly point was literally outside his front door, Jackie went along. He wasn't a stone thrower; if anything, he resented the rioting because it had forced him to give up road training. Each time he went anywhere with his sports bag he was stopped by the army; he was toying with the idea of joining the merchant navy to get away from it all.

Duddy had chatted with friends for a while. As the confrontation escalated, one of Duddy's friends said, 'This is getting hot,' and they parted. His friends would not see Duddy alive again.

Among the last to leave Barrier 14 were the photographers and TV crews. To Jeffrey Morris, a photographer for the *Daily Mail*, seeing the paratroopers come in was 'just like watching an old war film, a sort of bayonet charge without bayonets'. As the marchers fled, Morris followed a group of them down a small alley into what used to be Eden Place but was now open ground in front of the Rossville flats. Two paratroopers caught him, pinned him against a wall and jammed a rifle across his neck. Shouting 'Press, Daily Mail,' he fumbled in his pocket for his press card and one of the Paras lifted a knee to kick him in the crutch. He moved just in time and the Para caught him on the thigh instead.

At that moment a man ran out from a nearby doorway and the paratrooper holding Morris against the wall shouted to his mate, 'Get that bastard.' The man was arrested.

Morris raised his camera to take a picture of the arrest, but the paratrooper holding him threw him to the ground. Then he saw a youth, about sixteen or seventeen, running across the open ground, looking from side to side, obviously confused and wondering which way to go. A paratrooper stood up and levelled a pistol at the boy and shouted, 'Stop, you bastard, or I'll shoot.' Another Para came up behind the youth and slammed him across the head with a rifle, then he was arrested.

Three minutes after C Company went through Barrier 14, the ten armoured personnel carriers of the Paras' Support Company, with their engines whining at full throttle, prepared to burst through Barrier 12. But it was not an instant charge. There were 103 men in Support Company travelling in a convoy of seven armoured Pigs, two four-ton trucks and a Ferret Scout car. It took two minutes to bring them up to the barrier, where there was a delay of at least half a minute while it was cleared to let them through. A cloud of CS gas hung on either side of the barrier, causing Support Company soldiers to don their gas masks.

The delay was crucial. Seeing the convoy lined up, with engines revving, the stone throwers on the other side of the barrier in Little James Street took off down Rossville Street towards the flats.

As the wooden knife rests and the barbed wire were lifted, the army helicopter reported from overhead, 'The crowd, as I see it now, is about seventy on Chamberlain Street. The people at aggro corner have been driven away by the last fusillade of gas cartridges moving down towards the meeting which is now gathering strength. So far, I suppose about 200 people on the corner by the flats.'

Wilford's concerns about the success of his own operation had been realized: only 'about 200 people' remained in the area of the flats and as soon as they saw Support Company's vehicles lined up, preparing to come in, they fled.

The convoy raced after them across William Street and up Rossville Street towards the rubble barricade. They drove fast, trying to split up the crowd, which had now divided into three groups, one into the narrow passages between the flats, another over the rubble barricade towards the meeting at Free Derry Corner and a third into the warren of courtyards and alleys of Glenfada Park and Abbey Park. Behind the armoured cars came two four-ton trucks, packed with paratroopers.

The two lead Pigs of the mortar platoon roared into the open space before the flats, bumping across the uneven ground and sloshing through icy water in the potholes. In front of the flats, they swung into the car park. They were going too fast to avoid stragglers. By a wire fence on the waste ground, eighteen-year-old Alana Burke was hit in the back by one of the vehicles and sent flying into the air. Burke had been at the William Street barrier and had run in a panic with others down Chamberlain Street, but she was wearing a corduroy maxi-coat that had been soaked by the water cannon; it was heavy and she was having difficulty running. She was also sick from the gas. A man helped her, pulling her along, but he let her go as the sound of the Pig grew louder behind her. When she was knocked down, her legs went numb and she was unable to get up. She crawled to an alleyway between the Rossville flats.

Derrick Tucker, who had served in the Royal Navy during World War Two and then spent thirteen years in the RAF, was looking down from his flat in Garvan Place as the Paras came in. He saw Burke 'flung up into the air like an old coat'.

Each of the lead Pigs contained eight soldiers. As the vehicles came to a halt, they burst out of the back doors, four of them armed with baton guns, the rest with SLRs and fifty rounds of ammunition.

In his briefing on 29 January, Major 236 had told his men to beware of snipers, particularly from Rossville flats. Two immediately took up firing positions to cover their colleagues trying to arrest stragglers from the march, but the young stone throwers were mostly too quick for the soldiers.

The lead Pig was under the command of Lieutenant N, who was in charge of the eighteen soldiers of Support Company's mortar platoon. He had joined 1 Battalion, Parachute Regiment at Christmas 1969 and had taken over the company in May 1971.

Once through Barrier 12, Lieutenant N paused for a second to get his bearings. He could see a crowd some fifty metres away from him who had started running up Rossville Street, and he told his driver to follow them and then overtake them in order to cut them off and make arrests. His Pig turned left on to the car park in front of the flats and stopped between Eden Place and Pilot Row. The second Pig, following standing orders, overtook and turned to the right before coming to a halt. In it was Sergeant O. Then came Major 236, the Support Company commander in his own headquarters vehicle with a Ferret Scout car following.

Behind them were two empty Pigs belonging to the machine-gun platoon and, bringing up the rear, two four-ton lorries carrying the thirty-six members of the composite platoon, commanded by Captain SA8.

A few youths still foolhardy enough to confront the paratroopers were hurling stones. The soldiers would later claim they were fired on from the flats, and that they saw and heard a Thompson sub-machine gun, nail bombs and petrol bombs, but none of these was recorded in army radio messages sent back to

Brigadier MacLellan. Two privates from Sergeant O's platoon would claim they were hit with acid bombs – bottles thrown at them from the verandas of the flats by a man wearing a white shirt, a dark suit and a tie. One of the privates fired two shots at this man; one shot 'hit the wall a few feet above his head. As a result of this he disappeared.'

Civilian eyewitnesses are sure there was no firing from the flats and no nail bombs or petrol bombs were thrown. The Paras' radio log recorded only one civilian gunman, with a pistol, at fifteen minutes past four. The log says simply, 'Gunman. Pistol. Returned fire.'

The soldiers' recollections afterwards were inconsistent and confused – as might have been expected in the din; each time a shot was fired the distinctive crack of the SLR echoed round the U-shaped flats, which trapped the sound.

The army helicopter was circling overhead and John Chartres, a reporter for *The Times*, had noticed earlier that when the pilot altered the pitch of the blades it had made a noise that closely resembled machine-gun fire. At one point he turned to a colleague and said nervously, 'I wish those choppers did not make that noise.' At the time the Paras went in, Chartres was with Colonel Wilford and his adjutant, Captain Michael Jackson, at the battalion headquarters in Great James Street. Chartres recalled later that he had heard a message over the battalion net which said, 'We are under fire from the Rossville flats and are returning fire.' No such message appears in the typed-up version of the battalion radio log; the only mention of hostile fire is the pistol.

Soldier S, in the lead Pig, said he came under immediate fire from single repeated shots, as he jumped out. Later he said it might have been the sound of nail bombs. Soldier V said he heard two bombs go off while still inside the Pig and as he jumped out and was moving to cover a snatch squad he heard single rifle shots – certainly high-velocity – from the area of the passageway between blocks 1 and 2 of the flats. Soldier Q, in the same Pig, did not hear any bombs go off; he and another soldier with a rubber bullet gun ran towards the car park but had to take cover from heavy stoning behind the northern end of block 1. Only then did he hear four or five shots.

The paratroopers were dashing about on the waste ground, fully exposed to sniper fire from the flats. If the soldiers did come under a hail of automatic fire, nail bombs and petrol bombs, it is indeed remarkable that none was hit.

Sergeant O jumped out to cover his men; he would claim that a bottle had been thrown at him, and that he chased and arrested the culprit. Then he said he heard low- and high-velocity shots from four or five positions in the flats. Soldier R heard two explosions first, then shots, including pistol shots, all coming from the flats. Finally, Soldier T said firing began almost immediately he jumped out – probably from a single rifleman in the centre of the flats.

Major 236 halted his Pig at the end of Pilot Row – the now demolished terrace on the waste ground in front of the flats – and his soldiers immediately made two arrests. At the same time, they say that they were shot at. Major 236's signaller warned him that they were under fire and would claim later that he had seen rounds strike the ground in front of them. Major 236 told his crew to get back into the Pig and moved to a position just north of the first block of flats.

None of the civilians – in the car park or in the flats – witnessed what the soldiers described. All are quite clear that no petrol bombs or nail bombs exploded at any time during the afternoon, not only in front of the flats, but anywhere in the Bogside. Several witnesses saw the gunman in the flats car park, a man with a pistol who fired two or three shots from behind the gable end wall of Chamberlain Street.

In the space of the next ten minutes the Paras fired 108 rounds of 7.62 live ammunition, an average of one every six seconds, from different positions in a confined space little larger than a football pitch. In addition, sixty-four rounds of rubber bullets were discharged. Gunmen did shoot back; in addition to the man with a pistol at the end of Chamberlain Street, another pistol man was seen firing from Kells Walk. Later in the afternoon the IRA arrived in cars from the Creggan and took several pot-shots at the troops.

As the Paras opened fire, there was tremendous noise and confusion, with echoes of the shots bouncing round the Bogside. It was very hard to be certain where they were coming from.

The first shots from the soldiers appear to have been fired by Lieutenant N, the only officer known to have used his weapon during the scoop-up operation.

When he and his men got out of their Pig people were still running past them up Rossville Street. According to N, a youth with a handkerchief tied round his neck threw a lump of concrete, but he dodged it and gave chase. The youth turned, threw another chunk and ran on. As Lieutenant N was about to catch him, the youth lifted his arm to throw again and the lieutenant put up his rifle in self-defence, but the strap of his helmet broke off and fell across his gas mask, obscuring his vision. By the time he had his helmet back on the youth had fled.

Lieutenant N was then joined by one of his men with a riot gun and by his signaller, carrying a radio on his back. They chased people down Eden Place into Chamberlain Street. There, the crowd stopped on the corner and, according to Lieutenant N used the cover of the gable end, and resumed throwing stones. Seeing only the three soldiers, the rioters gained confidence and began advancing.

Lieutenant N would later recall that he feared the mob might overpower his group of three and, against the rules of the Yellow Card, he decided to fire two warning shots down Eden Place above the heads of the crowd. They slammed into the front wall of a house in Chamberlain Street, about eight feet off the ground.

Paddy Walsh was standing nearby and heard the 'whoosh' of the bullet. A woman opened the door of her house, wondering what was happening and Walsh told her, 'Get down out of the road.'

The crowd now moved back around the corner into Chamberlain Street. The next bullet from Lieutenant N's magazine stuck in the breech, so he quickly ejected it and cocked his rifle again. The crowd came back and he fired a third warning shot, at about head height, into the gable end of a house on Chamberlain Street. After that, the crowd moved back around the corner.

Lieutenant N's shots narrowly missed Gilles Peress, a young French photographer who had been one of the last to leave the William Street barrier after the Paras of 'C' Company charged in. He followed the crowd up Chamberlain Street and as he came to the Eden Street junction he peeked round the corner and saw a soldier, about fifteen yards away, kneeling with his rifle pointing at him; he turned towards him. Peress raised his cameras and called out, 'Press.' Then he walked slowly across Eden Place. As he set his foot on the pavement on the south side of the street, Lieutenant N fired and Peress saw the bullet smack into the wall of a house in Chamberlain Street immediately above a window. (Lieutenant N agreed he was kneeling.) The bullet hole was about five inches above his head. Peress ran on down Chamberlain Street towards the flats.

Father Daly, from St Eugene's, witnessed the first killing. In the car park of the Rossville flats, one youth would be shot dead and four other people would be wounded. After conducting a funeral service for Mrs Organ of Columbcille Court, Daly had returned to the parochial house for lunch. He came out again around three o'clock and joined the march, which was still passing by the cathedral. It was his custom on days when there might be trouble in the Bogside to visit older parishioners in Kells Walk,

Columbcille Court and Glenfada Park, to check if they needed any assistance, especially when there was a lot of CS gas.

Daly stayed with the marchers as they went down William Street but he stopped at aggro corner. He could hear the commotion at Barrier 14 and there was a handful of youths throwing stones at the soldiers at the Little James Street barrier.

He saw Kevin McCorry trying to coax the crowd to go to Free Derry Corner for the meeting. He also saw Peggy Deery with her sister, Mrs Nichol, on their way to their mother's house in Limewood Street and suggested that they should move on as it looked as though there might be trouble.

Daly had chatted earlier with Stephen McGonigle, vice-chairman of the Derry Development Commission, and Patrick Duffy, one of the stewards on the march. They had both remarked how peaceful it had been so far and hoped that it would stay that way.

Father Daly himself was worried about vandalism. He had spotted some youths behaving suspiciously at the back of the shops on the ground floor of the High Flats. There had been so much vandalism that he was concerned they might take advantage of the riots and break in.

After about fifteen minutes, above the shouting, the rubber bullet guns and the CS grenades, Daly heard the sharp cracks of the shots that had wounded Donaghy and Johnston. They were single shots with a split-second pause in between, maybe two or three. People in Kells Walk opened their windows and called out to ask him what had happened. A man came rushing up and told him two people had been shot by the Nook Bar. He was going to go and investigate this when a second man told him two priests were already attending the wounded.

Daly stayed on the corner of Rossville Street until 4.10 p.m. when the first of the paratroopers, from 'C' Company, charged through the William Street barrier. Everyone started running across Rossville Street towards the cover of the flats. Daly did not

146

see anything unusual about the Paras' sudden advance; it often happened like that during regular stoning at aggro corner. But in the past the soldiers had usually stopped their vehicles at Eden Place.

Now Major 236's Pigs were charging across Eden Place into the car park in front of the flats. As people scattered in panic, Daly ran with the crowd up Rossville Street. So did Willy Barber, his two rubber bullets safely in his jacket pocket.

A determined if somewhat ungainly runner, Daly sprinted past a young lad whom he recognized as one of his parishioners, Jackie Duddy, who had earlier been at Barrier 14.

Duddy was running and looking back at the advancing paratroopers. So was Daly as he ran past Duddy. The lad was chuckling at him. Daly imagined he was amused to see a cleric in a dog collar going at such a lick.

Seconds later, Daly heard a single shot from behind him where the soldiers were and simultaneously Duddy let out a gasp and a grunt. He looked back and saw Duddy falling forward on his face, hitting the tarmac hard. Daly ran on, assuming Duddy had been struck by a rubber bullet.

Willy Barber had also run on to the waste ground by Eden Place, trying to keep in front of the armoured cars of Support Company. He was beside Duddy when he was shot.

'Suddenly he just fell, a dead man's fall. His knees didn't even buckle, he just toppled forward. I thought he must have been hit by a rubber bullet on the back of the head. His face hit the ground and I looked down and saw a trickle of blood on the ground coming, I thought, from his face.'

There was another youth beside Duddy, and he and Barber tried to lift him and drag him along, but he was awfully heavy. They turned him over and blood was gushing from his nose and mouth. They dropped him and his head hit the ground. Barber ran around in circles in a panic, knowing he had to get Duddy to hospital immediately. He shouted up to two women on the first-floor balcony of the flats to telephone for an ambulance, but they threw up their hands in a gesture of despair, as if to say, 'There are no phones here.' Barber wandered in a daze for several moments before returning to Duddy, where a man in a cloth cap was supporting his head and trying to lift him up. This was Liam Bradley, another amateur boxer. He knelt down beside him and said the Act of Contrition in his ear. Bradley noticed that Duddy was wearing a Pioneer pin on his coat. It was from the Total Abstinence Association. Jackie Duddy never took a drink and he didn't smoke.

Father Daly had sought what little cover he could find by a low three foot wall in front of the flats near the passage between blocks 2 and 3, and was lying flat on the ground. He saw the lead Pigs of Lieutenant N and his sergeant come into the car park, and watched one strike Alana Burke, hurling her into the air.

The Pig of Sergeant O stopped barely thirty feet from where Daly was taking cover. Panicked people were now fleeing from the open area of the car park into the narrow passages between the flats. Some were trying to rip down a shop door that had been boarded up so that they could take shelter inside. A woman was screaming.

Several people had been looking out of their windows, or had been on the balconies of their flats watching the convoy race in. Derrick Tucker saw one paratrooper standing upright, leaning on the bonnet of his Pig as he fired. Then Tucker saw Duddy hit and fall headlong to the ground.

Mary Bonner was at home on the second floor of block 2. She had just had lunch with her mother and father, one of her sisters and her brother, Hugh Gilmore. From her open balcony, with a view of Chamberlain Street and William Street, she saw the Pigs of the mortar platoon skid to a halt at the car park. Two paratroopers jumped out of the back of the first vehicle. One soldier went down on his knee and aimed his rifle; the other was immediately behind him, holding his gun at waist level as he opened fire.

148

Bonner saw a young boy and Father Daly running through the car park and when the youth turned slightly to the left, she heard a bang and he fell to the ground. It was Duddy. She shouted down to people hiding behind the low wall, 'That young fella's been hit by a rubber bullet.' She watched as Father Daly came to the aid of the dying youth. She screamed until a man came and took her off the balcony back into her flat.

Isabella Duffy was visiting her brother on the first floor of block 2. She was coming out of the door to the block when the Pigs came in. From the balcony, she saw Duddy shot, his hands straight out, falling to the ground. She also saw an old grey-haired man being beaten to the ground with batons and rifles. She yelled at the soldiers, 'You have murdered that little boy, are you going to murder that old man, too?' One of the soldiers then shot up at her where she was standing. The bullet took a chunk out of the iron of the balcony. She did not know if the soldier was aiming at her, but it felt like it.

When Duddy was shot, Peggy Deery and several others had arrived at the end of Chamberlain Street just as one of the Pigs come racing across the waste ground in front of the flats. Deery saw a paratrooper get out and immediately take aim in her direction. He was about twenty-five yards away and she could see his features; he had a round, fat face covered with dark streaks of camouflage paint. 'For God's sake watch out, that one's going to shoot,' she yelled to a man standing next to her, and she moved towards him for protection.

The paratrooper fired and Deery felt a hard blow in her left thigh.

She stumbled, tried to get up but couldn't and fell forwards, cutting her eyebrow open.

The wound in her left leg was bleeding badly. The bullet had pierced the front of her thigh, shattered the femur and sliced through the back muscle. It was an appalling injury.

Deery looked up as she was lying on the ground and saw the paratrooper who had just shot her still aiming in her direction. 'Mister, don't shoot,' she begged. 'I've fourteen children and I'm all they have.'

The paratrooper ran off.

Several men, including James McDermott and Patrick McDaid carried Deery into Chamberlain Street and to the first house at the gable end, Number 33, the home of Mrs Brigid Nelis, her son and two daughters. Mrs Deery's wounded leg was sagging in her black stocking, and when they lifted the leg the knee bent sickeningly in the wrong direction.

McDaid was a plumber with the Londonderry Development Commission. He decided to go back outside and joined a small group who were waiting for a lull in the shooting to make a dash across the car park. Just ahead of McDaid a man ran, dropping his camera as he went. He stopped to pick it up and then ran on, making it to the cover of the flats. It was now McDaid's turn. He ran bent over and near the alleyway there was a low wall. He dived over it and as he did a paratrooper opened fire. If it was an aimed shot, it was meant to kill, but McDaid's body was bent, in a dive, and the bullet merely grazed his back; a glancing blow from the 7.62mm round that opened a nasty flesh wound over the upper part of his left shoulder blade but did not penetrate. Paddy Walsh fell beside him behind the wall and McDaid said, 'Mister, I'm shot, I'm shot.'

Walsh ran his hands over McDaid's body, looking for the wound. It was not on his head. Then he felt his back and found the rent in his jacket. He lifted up the jacket and the shirt beneath and saw the wound in McDaid's back. It looked as though a knife had scooped away a chunk of flesh; it wasn't bleeding much, just oozing.

McDaid was terrified. He begged Walsh not to leave him. A girl in the flats shouted to them that it was all right to run – and they half walked, half ran to Joseph Place. McDaid would recall, 'This

Above: The procession winds its way through the Bogside in a carnival atmosphere. Aboard McGlinchey's coal lorry are the march organisers. Most stewards used a white handkerchief for an armband. (Copyright Robert White)

Following spread: At Barrier 14, the army water cannon sprays rioters and peaceful marchers alike with purple dye. The protester sitting masked against CS gas fumes is Jim Wray. A few minutes later, Wray would be shot dead by paratroopers in Glenfada Park. (Copyright Gilles Peress/Magnum Photos)

Top: Paratroopers with rifles and batons leave their armoured troop carrier to launch the arrest operation, driving marchers towards the Rossville flats. One man lies at the feet of a soldier. (Copyright Colman Doyle)

Bottom: Two paras wearing gas masks advance to cut off the crowd's retreat with SLR rifles at the ready. A member of the Knights of Malta paramedic team lies in a crumpled heap behind them after being assaulted. (Copyright Colman Doyle)

Top: Lt Col Derek Wilford, the Para commander (wearing beret) crouches behind the wall at Kell's Walk as his men fire in the direction of Free Derry Corner. Three young men were killed on the rubble directly in front of them. (Copyright Jeff Morris/ Associated Newspapers)

Bottom: Michael Kelly lying mortally wounded at the rubble barricade after the first volley of shots.(Copyright Robert White)

Paddy Doherty tries to crawl away from the gun fire in the Rossville flats car park area, where the French photographer Gilles Peress had already been shot at. The hankerchief Doherty used as a steward's armband was around his face for protection against gas. (Copyright Gilles Peress/Magnum Photos)

Top: Seconds later Doherty was shot from behind and lay prostrate, crying for help. (Copyright Gilles Peress/Magnum Photos)

Bottom: Paddy Walsh tried to pull him to safety but gunfire forced him to retreat. (Copyright Gilles Peress/Magnum Photos)

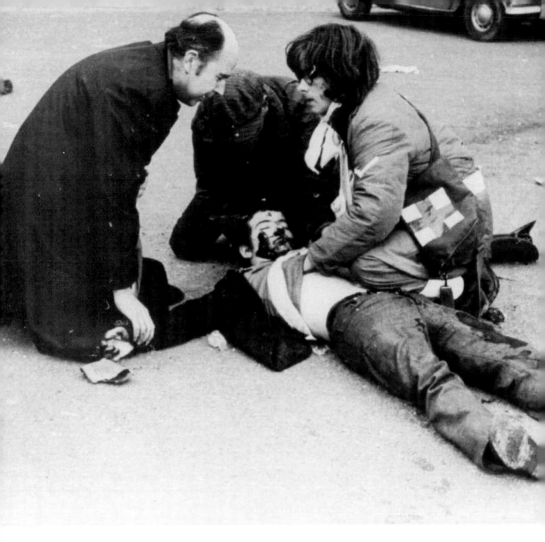

Jack Duddy lies dying outside the Rossville flats with Father Edward Daly and Charlie Glenn, a Knights of Malta paramedic, helpless to aid him. Glenn was subsequently arrested and roughed up by the Paras. The picture was taken by Fulvio Grimaldi, who was later trapped in a flat as six bullets were pumped through a window. (Copyright Fulvio Grimaldi.)

man pushed me into the first house ... we went in through the back door, through the kitchen and into the hall. There was a whole crowd of people in the house taking cover. Someone said that I should be taken upstairs into one of the bedrooms. I was laid down on a bedroom floor and someone pulled off my coat and jumper ... A woman with a basin of water came into the room and knelt down beside me. The only thing she had with her was some TCP and she started to bathe the wound. All I could think about was how bad I had been hit and whether I was going to live or die.'

An Italian photographer, Fulvio Grimaldi, took the only picture of the wounded Mrs Deery. She had been shot in front of him going down Chamberlain Street and Grimaldi followed her into number 33, taking pictures of her as she was placed on the settee. Then he left, accompanied by his wife, Susan, and took more pictures of people cowering behind the low wall in front of block 2 and in the passages between the blocks. He went to make a phone call in the flat of a woman he knew on the second floor of block 1, facing out on to Rossville Street. He had been in Northern Ireland several times and had written a book, published in Italy, entitled *Ulster: Britain's Lost Empire Outpost*. He had been in Derry since 5 January and was well acquainted with the local IRA. Grimaldi and his wife had been at Barrier 14 and had fled with the crowd down Chamberlain Street. He had gone to the flat to make a call to Italy. When he was on the phone there was more shooting in the street below; he went to the window and started taking pictures, and almost immediately a shot came through the window above his head. He, his wife and the woman in the flat threw themselves to the floor as five more shots were pumped through the window in quick succession.

Grimaldi had a tape recorder running. What follows is the heated exchange between him and the people in the flat as the shooting began.

151

A woman in the flat yelled at him, 'That's at you for taking those photos. That's what that is, that was at you.'

Grimaldi said he wouldn't take any more pictures.

'Get down, no stay there . . . down . . . down . . . down flat, down flat . . . ' said the woman. 'Get on the floor, they're firing at our windows.'

'Are they out of their minds?' asked Grimaldi.

The woman started screaming. 'Shut, up will yous?' she yelled. 'Don't you go out with that camera near our windows again please . . . you can phone and say you were trying to make a picture . . . lie down on your stomach.'

They crawled on their bellies away from the window and into the bathroom.

'Not there . . . not near the window . . . other side of the house . . . Go on, just lie down on your stomach, get to your belly.'

The television was on in the living room and was just then airing a recruiting ad to join the British army.

The woman of the house moved to another window and called out that she had seen a man shot. 'They shot him, they shot him like a dog . . . he was running to get in the alleyway and he was shot and fell and he moved his hand and they shot another bullet into him . . . and the fella called for help . . . oh them savage Pigs.'

A man's voice said, 'Mercy, there's eight dead.'

The woman of the house started screaming again: 'Kill all the British, the murdering bastards . . . tell the world . . . tell them . . . bastards just killing my people.'

The woman's daughter intervened: 'Mummy, you're doing no one no good talking like this.'

But the woman continued shrieking. 'Mister,' she yelled at Grimaldi, 'Tell the Dublin government who stand there watching their people get slaughtered . . . they're watching their own Irish people get slaughtered . . . Dublin's no good.

152

Tell them, we've had eight hundred years of them and we want them out . . . '

The daughter said, 'Mummy, don't now . . . she's got to stop.'

But the woman yelled again, 'Christ and suffering, God's curse on them and the curse of the dead generations of Irish . . . quote me.'

Grimaldi tried to calm her: 'Don't get excited, you'll do yourself harm.'

The woman shrieked, 'Curse of the dead generations of Irish men, every Irish man that ever laid down his life . . . Dublin's no good . . . '

'You'll do yourself harm,' said Grimaldi again.

'Get the brandy,' shouted a man's voice.

'Look, give gran a drink here,' another woman added. 'Give her a drink.'

The woman yelled again: 'Tell the Pope.'

'Mum, don't be saying anything against the Pope, now,' her daughter said.

'I am not saying anything about the Pope . . . tell them they need to stop the killing.'

Seconds after the Paras came in, the flats' car park was empty of people and Father Daly looked back at Duddy lying motionless on the ground. It was then that he realized the youth had been hit by a real bullet, not a rubber one. Daly was with others behind the low wall at the north end of block 2 and did not see or hear any shots coming from the flats. If there had been firing from that direction, the crowd would never have sought cover there.

Daly decided he had to go to Duddy. He took a white handkerchief out of his pocket and, crouching, almost crawling, he started to move slowly out from his cover, waving his little flag of truce.

He could not know that Duddy was dying. The bullet had entered his right shoulder, passed behind the upper part of the right arm bone and shoulder blade, before bursting through the inner end of the second right rib and second thoracic vertebra. It was deflected off the bone, fracturing the left collarbone, leaving the body through the upper part of the left chest.

The bullet had caused immense internal damage. It cut blood vessels in each lung and severed the windpipe and carotid arteries. Duddy was bleeding to death. By the time Daly reached him, all he could see was blood oozing from wounds on to Duddy's red shirt and pinstriped jacket. The priest mopped it up as best he could with his hanky, and then a first aid man named Charles Glenn from the Knights of Malta joined him and put a dressing on the wound, trying to staunch the flow.

There was a fusillade of shots, more sharp cracks of high-velocity bullets. Daly and Glenn were very frightened. Glenn started to weep and asked Father Daly if they were all going to be killed. Daly wept with him. Willy Barber was also at Duddy's side, so was Liam Bradley.

Not knowing how long the boy might live, Father Daly was telling everyone to get out of the way because he wanted to administer the last rites, but then the gunfire started again and once more they threw themselves flat on the ground.

Others came out from cover to see if they could help, but Daly and Glenn pleaded with them to go back because they were afraid the group would attract more shots from the Paras. A photographer came up and Barber, now very angry, told him to 'fuck off'. While Daly was giving the last rites, Barber was keeping people away. He thought Duddy might be conscious and making a confession.

Then Father Daly said, 'We'll try to take him away.' Barber, Glenn, Bradley and another man agreed to carry the body if Father Daly would go ahead of them waving his white handkerchief. Barber wanted to take Duddy to the paratroopers in the nearest Pig, hoping that would be the quickest way to get him to hospital.

As they were getting up off the ground a tall fair-haired man broke from the group, taking cover by the flats, and ran towards the soldiers, prancing and waving his arms, and crying out, 'They're killing, they're killing. They're shooting.' Father Daly shouted to him to get back, but he kept on yelling at the soldiers.

This was Michael Bridge, a twenty-five-year-old unemployed labourer from the Creggan. He was one of the stewards at the William Street barrier. He had been hit by a rubber bullet on the foot and was then overpowered by the gas, which made him throw up. Bridge was sitting on the kerb in Chamberlain Street, recovering and smoking a cigarette, when a youth shouted, 'The army's coming in, the Saracens are coming.'

The crowd raced down Chamberlain Street towards the flats and Bridge was carried along with them. He turned right into Eden Place and when he arrived at the waste ground he saw a Pig pull up, and three soldiers get out and start firing. It was Lieutenant N, his signaller and another soldier. With the crowd, Bridge retreated back into Chamberlain Street.

When Lieutenant N fired over the heads of the crowd down Eden Place into Chamberlain Street, an elderly man standing next to Bridge collapsed and Bridge thought he had been shot. He helped the man to his feet and the man walked off. As Bridge headed up Chamberlain Street towards the flats, a youth came down the street shouting, 'There's a boy shot in the car park.' Bridge moved out of cover, alone, and ran towards Duddy. He could see there was blood pouring from his mouth and nose.

The sight of Duddy lying there, dead or dying, consumed him with rage. He lost control. Bridge saw a soldier directly in front of him, standing just out from the wall at the back of Chamberlain Street. He was aiming his rifle, just as Lieutenant N said he had done. Bridge saw another soldier, kneeling at the end of block 1 of the flats and faced him. This soldier was also aiming at him. Bridge yelled, 'Shoot me, shoot me.'

Daly was still attending Duddy's now lifeless body and saw a soldier step out from a Pig, go down on one knee and fire in Bridge's direction.

Bridge staggered and clutched his left leg. He felt a thud in his left thigh as a 7.62 round passed straight through the outer muscle, spinning him round with its impact. He was lucky; it was a relatively minor wound compared with others that day. Bridge was even able to keep prancing about, still screaming at the soldiers.

Like the other wounded, he thought that he had been hit by a rubber bullet until he felt the blood on his thigh. He never knew which of the soldiers had fired at him, but the track of the bullet suggests it was Lieutenant N. After firing above the heads of the crowd in Eden Place, he had gone back to the wall of Chamberlain Street when he said he saw a young man come out with his hands in the air. Lieutenant N would claim later that he thought the youth was going to throw a nail bomb and he saw a smoking object in his hand. He raised his rifle to his shoulder and fired one aimed shot while standing up. He saw that he had hit the man in the thigh because his other hand grasped the wound. There was no sign of the bomb and no explosion.

Two youths dashed out from the crowd in Chamberlain Street to help Bridge and they half carried, half dragged him into the first house in Chamberlain Street, which was number 33.

Michael Bradley, a 22-year-old unemployed painter from Creggan (where he was a member of St Mary's Accordion Band, playing the accordion and bass drum), had reached the relative safety of the flats' forecourt when he heard that Jackie Duddy, his neighbour and a personal friend, had been shot. Like Michael Bridge, Bradley lost control of himself. He rushed back into the forecourt and ran towards the soldiers, screaming and swearing. Suddenly, he felt a dull thud and his whole body shook. He realized he had been hit. There was a clean hole through his left arm, two in his upper abdomen and the muscle of his right arm was ripped open. He staggered across the car park, through the passage between the flats and into the first house on the corner of

Joseph Place. The house belonged to Mr O'Neill, and there Bradley was helped by Father Tom O'Gara and McClone of the Knights of Malta.

According to the Porter tapes, during these opening shots Brigadier MacLellan did not know exactly what the paratroopers were doing – or how many had been deployed. Callsign 65 (the Paras) informed Brigade headquarters that C Company had gone through Barrier 14, and that Support Company had 'moved south from the [Presbyterian] church' to aggro corner, but MacLellan then asked, 'Did you, in fact, conduct any sort of scoop-up?' Callsign 65 replied that he would get the information. But MacLellan was impatient. He then issued an order: '65 this is Zero, if you have not conducted any scoop-up, then you should withdraw your callsign Bravo 3 (C Company) back to its original position for any further operations, over.'

There was no immediate reply from Wilford, causing MacLellan to ask urgently, a second time, for the 'current deployment of Bravo 3'. With no satisfactory reply, MacLellan repeated his order: 'Hello 65 this is Zero, you were given instructions some time ago to move Bravo 3 from the area of William Street/Rossville Street back to its original location, is this now complete over?' Wilford then signalled that he had been 'telling you on other means, the secure means ... exactly what we are doing'. Evidently, MacLellan did not receive the message. At the height of the battle the secure means appears to have been still stuck on send.

IX

The Rubble Barricade

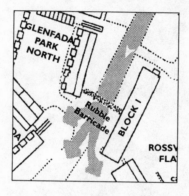

I saw about three people behind the barricade and I could also see smoke coming from their rifles

Lance Corporal J, anti-tank platoon,
Support Company, 1 Para

I saw heads. One was popping up and down; one was crouching much lower . . . I said to myself, 'Aye, aye, we have got gunmen behind the barricade.' This was an assumption

Captain SA8, composite platoon,
Support Company, 1 Para

THE SECOND WAVE of paratroopers jumped from their armoured cars and four-tonners just south of aggro corner and zigzagged up the west side of Rossville Street. They worked in pairs, one advancing while the other covered against sniper fire. Lance Corporal F and Private G took cover behind a wall jutting out from the low-rise flats at Kells Walk, where they were joined by several other paratroopers, including Lieutenant 119 and Lieutenant Colonel Wilford. He was still wearing his red beret.

By this time the fleeing marchers had reached the flats or the rubble barricade one hundred and fifty yards up Rossville Street. The barricade was the central point of the killing field, bounded to the north by aggro corner and the south by Free Derry Corner. To the east of the barricade were the three blocks of the Rossville flats. To the west was Glenfada Park – two sets of four three-storey blocks of brick and stucco maisonettes, each with a central courtyard for parking cars, and Abbey Park. As few people owned cars the car parks were almost always empty. Between Glenfada Park and aggro corner was Kells Walk, another complex of brick and stucco maisonettes. When they were built in the early 60s, young saplings were planted along Rossville Street, and in the courtyards, but only one or two had survived the rioting and vandalism. The paving stones had long since been torn up by the rioters to make missiles. It was a desolate, grubby and unfriendly place. The barricade, which stretched from the entrance to block 1 of the flats to Glenfada Park, afforded only partial cover. It was in disrepair, barely three feet high in some places, and there was a gap in the middle to allow a single line of traffic. Made of 'liberated' wooden knife rests, an oil drum, slabs of concrete, gravel, iron bars topped with coils of barbed wire and months of accumulated rubbish, the barricade was a good source of missiles, but only a brazen few now attempted to defy the paratroopers.

With insane bravado, one youth ran right up to the nearest Pig hurling stones and was immediately arrested. His mates rushed forward to help him, but when they saw F and G take up firing positions behind the low wall at Kells Walk, they dashed back to the barricade.

Twenty-five-year-old Danny Craig was one of them. He found himself running next to Michael Kelly, who was eighteen and on his first march. Craig knew Michael's older brother, John, and so decided to look after him, telling Michael when to run to avoid the rubber bullets and when to throw stones. As long as Michael stuck by his side, Craig told him, the worst that could happen was that he would be hit by a rubber bullet.

But the paratroopers were on full alert for snipers and nail bombers; they had already cocked their SLRs and loaded one round in the breech, with the safety catches on. They had been told by their commanders to expect the IRA to start shooting once the crowd had dispersed and there was a clear line of fire. The no man's land between the barricade and the crowd was now about fifty yards, plenty of room for the IRA to fire without endangering civilian lives.

Lance Corporal F would say later that when he looked towards the barricade he saw a man about to throw something fizzing that he thought must be a bomb. He went down on one knee and took aim.

At that moment, Craig and Michael Kelly jumped back over the barricade. Craig bent to pick up a stone and told Kelly to get down. Kelly also picked up a stone and as he stood up there was a sharp crack of an SLR shot and he fell back, crying, 'Danny I'm shot.'

Soldier F had hit Kelly in the stomach and he was bleeding to death. No bomb exploded.

The others at the barricade could not believe the army was firing real bullets. They scattered in confusion. A fusillade of shots then came from the Paras at the wall. Some stayed behind the barricade, lying flat on the ground. Three youths came to lift Kelly's body out of the line of fire and they were shot at. Bullets were bouncing off the rubble.

Liam Griffin was beside Kelly when he was hit. Griffin ran on for a few paces and then crawled back to Kelly, who had been knocked backwards by the shot and was lying on his back, his head towards Free Derry Corner. Kelly's hands were clutching his stomach. Griffin felt around his body, under his light-blue jacket and his mustard pullover, looking for a wound but couldn't find anything. Griffin couldn't see any blood, so said to Kelly, 'It's OK, you're fine, you're not hit.'

But the bullet, which might have been a ricochet off the rubble, had made a one-inch hole in the front of his jacket, ripped into his stomach and lacerated his intestines, an artery and a vein before embedding itself in a vertebra. The bullet was later matched to F's rifle.

None of the people at the barricade, watching from the flats or from Glenfada Park, saw Kelly with a bomb. Forensic tests found no trace of gelignite on his clothing. If F shot Kelly because he thought he had a bomb, then he was mistaken; it was a stone.

Could F have shot Kelly while aiming at someone else who had a bomb, or a rifle? The civilians at the barricade and nearby are adamant that no nail bombs or petrol bombs were thrown that afternoon. And the soldiers who fired would produce conflicting stories of what they saw of the men behind the barricade; some had nail bombs, some had rifles, they said.

One paratrooper with F and G said he saw three people with rifles with smoke coming out of the barrels. Another said he saw two men crawling on their bellies from the barricade to the entrance to block 1 of the flats and they appeared to be trailing rifles.

A Para radio operator would later write that he was 'amazed' at the action taken by his comrades. He was in the leading group of half a dozen soldiers as they reached the low wall; he reckoned that the barricade was about a hundred yards away. He would recall that one of the Paras dropped into a kneeling position and fired into the centre of the crowd; another soldier dropped beside him and also opened fire, so did a third standing on the pavement just beyond the wall.

The radio operator saw two bodies fall and prepared to fire himself. 'But on tracking across the people in front of me [I] could see women and children, although the majority were men, all wildly shouting, but [I] could see no one with a weapon.' He then lowered his rifle.

I remember thinking, looking at my friends who had now grown to half a dozen in a line side by side, do they know something I don't know? What are they firing at?

Opposite us I could see members of the Machine-Guns, helmeted and blacked-faced, in a standing position also pumping off rounds at quite a rapid rate . . .

In the initial thirty seconds I would say that one hundred rounds were fired at the crowd. A thing that struck me was the time that elapsed from the commencement of the firing to the time when the crowd began to realize what was happening.

But no civilian eyewitnesses around the barricade saw rifles, and no weapons were ever found. Accounts from the soldiers were inconsistent.

After F had shot Kelly, a Para captain who commanded the composite platoon of Support Company and was in Rossville Street, looked over at the barricade to see what F had shot at. Under cross-examination at the Widgery inquiry the captain was asked,

Q: Did you see these people behind the barricade?
A: I saw heads. One head was popping up and down; one was crouching much lower.
Q: Could you see what they were doing apart from popping up and down or what they had got with them?
A: I still had my gas mask on at the time. I did make an assumption. I said to myself, 'Aye, aye, we have got gunmen behind the barricade.' This was an assumption.
Q: What was your assumption based on?
A: The action they were or seemed to be taking.

Under further questioning, the captain admitted that he had not, in fact, seen rifles.

Q: You talked when you were giving evidence, captain, about seeing men firing from the barricade, that is the barricade in Rossville Street?
A: Earlier on, yes, sir.
Q: And, of course, as you have already said, you did not see any shots, or hear any shots coming from the barricade?
A: There was a lot of shooting at the time. I certainly didn't hear it.
Q: You did not see any weapon in the hands of the people at the barricade?
A: This was just a glance, as I said before.
Q: Whatever it was, you did not see any weapons at the barricade?
A: I did not see any weapons at the barricade.

Another army captain, an engineer from the Royal Electrical and Mechanical Engineers who was attached to 22 LAD, was directing official army photographers from OP Echo, the observation post on top of the Embassy building in the Strand Road. He had a good view of the barricade 'using very powerful binoculars'. As he would say himself, it was a much better, if still incomplete, view than the paratroopers had from the low wall in Kells Walk. He was sixty to seventy feet higher up than they were. He did not mention seeing any men with rifles behind the barricade.

An even better view was to be had from the army positions on the city walls.

Lieutenant 227, of 22 LAD, was at an observation post known as Charlie between the Royal Bastion and the Platform. He was in charge of several snipers whose job was to spot any gunmen and to 'engage' them. He heard over the army radio that the Paras were coming in and saw them fan out over the waste ground in front of the flats. At that moment he also heard two bursts of automatic fire, which he thought had come from a Thompson sub-machine gun in Glenfada Park.

He then heard an explosion on the William Street side of the flats, which he thought was a nail bomb, and then he heard three deliberate shots from an SLR.

At the sound of those shots about a hundred people at the barricade turned and ran towards Free Derry Corner; another group moved out of the line of fire behind the gable end of Glenfada Park. Lieutenant 227 did not see any of those at the barricade with a gun and would say later, 'If they had been carrying weapons I think I would have seen them.'

At the same OP, one of Lieutenant 227's snipers, Soldier 025, was looking through binoculars at the barrier at the time Kelly was shot and claimed to have seen a male civilian being handed 'what seemed to me to be a nail bomb, or another type of bomb' by another man. Soldier 025 said the person holding the object was aged about twenty, about five foot eight with black hair, he was dressed in a slate-grey coat and dark trousers. Kelly was wearing a blue coat.

Kelly's mates would have been surprised if he had thrown a bomb. He had never been in trouble – never even been interviewed by the police or the army. In fact, he was nervous of the soldiers after they had shouted at him one time on the Craigavon Bridge. At the sewing-machine factory, where he was an apprentice, Kelly was a hard worker, sometimes putting in twelve-hour days. He had got the job after taking a City and Guilds course, which he passed well enough to be asked to take an advanced one. He was earning £13 a week, with a pay rise due the next day, Monday. His hobbies included the odd bit of football and his flock of sixteen racing pigeons. He had built a house for the pigeons in his back garden. He was good at electronics and at St Mary's Club he used to fix the record player when it broke down. He'd just started dating his first girlfriend.

He was a sheltered child, his mother's favourite after a childhood illness. She didn't want him to go on the march, but he went anyway, joining it at the Bishop's Field with his friends from across the road. His mother went after him on the march. 'She followed him everywhere,' his uncle, Barry Liddy, used to say. Mrs Kelly caught up with the march in Lone Moor Road, but didn't find Michael, so she headed down to Kells Walk, where her sister had a flat. She saw him standing behind the barricade. Then she saw him shot.

As the Paras took up their positions at the low wall, they came under fire from a man with a pistol at Glenfada Park. Father Thomas O'Gara, of St Columb's College, had been watching the crowd fleeing down Rossville Street from the corner of block 1 of the flats when he saw a young man in a longish coat and completely separate from the rest of the crowd around the barricade. He drew a pistol from his pocket, leaned over a wall somewhere in the Kells Walk and fired three shots rapidly. O'Gara later recalled that the soldiers didn't even see the gunman, who disappeared as quickly as he had come. O'Gara was certain that the man fired after the troops had opened fire.

Lieutenant 119, who was with Lance Corporal F and Private G at Kells Walk, said he saw distinct muzzle flashes from a pistol at the corner of Glenfada Park; he did not see the actual weapon, nor the person firing.

'He was obviously aiming quickly around the corner of this building without exposing himself,' the lieutenant said later.

Private G said as the paratroopers were moving up Rossville Street towards the barricade he saw a gunman in an alleyway that led into Glenfada Park. He fired 'two quick rounds' at the gunman who 'went to ground'. Whoever this man was, and whatever he fired, the paratroopers were not hit.

In a lull in the shooting, Griffin and three or four others helped to carry Kelly's body to the cover of the gable end of Glenfada where they found Father Bradley. He had been by Kells Walk when Support Company charged through Barrier 12 in Little James Street. He fled with others into Glenfada Park and now joined the small group at the gable end huddled around Kelly's body. Kelly was very pale. There was blood on his right hand and more blood coming through his vest around his stomach. Father Bradley gave him absolution, just in case, and said an act of contrition in his ear, which Kelly repeated back.

Then he asked the group to carry Kelly to the safety of a house and get him first aid. Among the group were Joe Donnelly, a chemical operator, and Pearce McCaul. They carried Kelly on their shoulders to Peter Kerr's house at 8 Abbey Park.

Father Bradley was going to follow the group with Kelly when someone told him to look behind him at the barricade where three or four people were lying on the ground, almost piled on top of one another, their bodies contorted as though they were dead. Father Bradley could see that at least one of them was alive because he was putting his hand in the air for help. Bradley began to crawl out from the safety of the gable end in Glenfada; the bodies were only about five yards away. But as he started out, Barry Liddy, Kelly's uncle, pulled him back, because shots were still being fired at the barricade.

Four others had been shot behind the barricade. Three of them, William Nash, a nineteen-year-old docker, John Young, seventeen, a shop salesman, and Michael McDaid, a twenty-one-year-old barman, were dying from their wounds. The fourth, Alexander Nash, the fifty-two-year-old father of William, had gone to the aid of his son and was shot in the arm.

Willie Nash had turned nineteen on 23 December. He was the seventh son in a family of twelve in the Creggan. Willie had a traditional Creggan education at St Joseph's. A large, well-built boy, he had left school at fifteen and worked as a docker on the potato exports, which ran from September to March. He gave his mother £15 a week from his wages. He joined St Mary's Youth Club and used to spar with his brother Charlie, a lightweight of great promise who went on to represent Ireland in the Munich Olympic Games. The Nash house was filled with Charlie's cups.

The weekend had started with the wedding at St Mary's Church in the Creggan of the fifth Nash son, John, to Margaret Friel. Unfortunately, Mrs Nash could not be there; she had just suffered a heart attack and was in hospital, but by all accounts it was a fine event with singing and dancing into the small hours.

Willie was known for his high spirits and his practical jokes – but he was not among the regular Derry hooligans. He had been in trouble with the law and been in prison twice in 1971, once for three months and the second time for two months, of which he only served three weeks. The first arose from a punch-up at the Select Bar in Foyle Street. When the RUC came to break it up, Willie thumped one of the policemen. The latter incident was another squabble at a dance hall. In neither case was the army involved.

On this Sunday Willie had joined the march with a couple of friends. In fact, most of the Nash family went along and those who did not went to Altnagelvin Hospital to visit Mrs Nash. Willie was wearing a new brown suit, which he had bought for his younger brother's wedding. He was also wearing his sister's graduation ring – which she had been given by her American boyfriend; Willie had borrowed it for the day because he liked the look of it. Round his neck he wore a chain and cross.

Willie was running away from the paratroopers, crossing the barricade, when he was shot in the chest. Denis McLaughlin saw him turn towards the soldiers, the sharp crack of SLRs rang out and he fell backwards and rolled on to his face. Matthew Connolly was standing next to him when he fell. He saw him go down hard, like a dead man. The autopsy report would track the path of the high-velocity bullet through his body:

> A bullet entered the right side of the chest about one and a half inches above and two and a half inches to the left of the nipple. It grazed the upper border of the fourth right rib as it entered the right chest cavity. It then passed through the front margin of the upper part of the right lung, through the right atrium of the heart, the heart sac, before entering the abdominal cavity through the diaphragm, lacerating the inferior vena cava, the largest vein in the body, as it did so. It then lacerated the liver, the right suprarenal gland and the right kidney before leaving the body through the right side of the back wall of the abdomen. The combined effect of these injuries would have caused his rapid death.

The bullet travelled at an angle of forty-five degrees down through the body, meaning that it was fired from above. It was never recovered so could not be matched to the rifling on an SLR, as the bullet that killed Kelly had been. If Willie Nash was shot by a paratrooper at Kells Walk, he would have had to be facing the soldiers and crouched over. The other possibility is that he was shot by a soldier from another unit on the city walls. There were army snipers in observation posts on the walls and also in a derelict house in Nailor's Row, just below the walls. Any of them could have had a line of sight to Willie Nash as he ran back to the barricade.

Nash was not alone when he died. Others had dived for cover behind the barricade where he had fallen. James Begley and George Roberts were there, lying beside him as he screamed. Denis McLaughlin crawled up to his side as the screams turned to a low moan. McLaughlin was only sixteen and terrified but, scared as he was, he began telling Willie, 'Don't worry, you'll be all right. We'll get you in.' McLaughlin looked up at his friend Roberts for support, but Roberts shook his head. Willie was already dead.

The firing stopped and another youth, John Young, was crawling out from Glenfada with his head down and calling out to Begley, 'Are you all right?' John was a salesman in a men's clothing shop in Waterloo Place, with good prospects for management. He was a snappy dresser himself and was said to own nineteen suits, useful for the pursuit of his hobbies: girls and dancing. On this afternoon he was wearing a black-and-white check shirt, brown sweater and blue zip-up jacket, green trousers and brown suede shoes. Young walked to work every day from the Creggan, a route which would have taken him past aggro corner, but he had never been even in oblique contact with the police or the army; he had never received a warning of the 'friendly chat' variety.

He was a yard away from Willie Nash's body when there was another SLR shot. Young was hit in the left eye and he fell on top of Begley. The bullet tore into Young's body at forty-five degrees, the same angle as the one that hit Kelly. It bruised his brain, fractured the base of his skull and severed the spinal cord. Death was almost instantaneous.

The paratroopers were still firing from Kells Walk, pinning down the group taking cover behind the gable wall in Glenfada

Park, while others were cowering in the doorway of the flats and clustered around the telephone.

Alex Nash, Willie's father, was among the group at the flats. He saw his son had fallen and pushed himself to the front of the group. 'My son Willie is dead as a maggot,' he cried. 'They shot him.'

Ignoring the danger of going out into Rossville Street and, by his own account, fortified by Dutch courage, Alex Nash walked alone to his dying son at the barricade, waving his hands with his fingers spread to show he was not carrying a gun, or a nail bomb. Again, shots rang out. Nash fell down, shot through the left arm. He reached over and put his right hand on the back of his dying son, raising his left arm in the air to summon help. There was more firing.

Much would be made in the media of the father braving the bullets to go to the aid of his son. He was quoted in the *Irish Independent*: 'I knew my son was dead. He was murdered. He had nothing with him. The soldiers were shouting and laughing – like mad bulls.'

The army would say Alex Nash had been shot by a gunman firing blindly with a pistol from the main entrance to block 1 of the flats. Soldier 031 later told the Military Police:

A man of about forty-five years came across to give assistance to one of the bodies. He had come out of the flats. I saw this man sit one of the bodies up behind the barricade and wave for assistance. I could now see that the body he had propped up was a youth of about sixteen-seventeen years; this youth had a wound in the stomach. I was approximately fifty metres from the barricade. The main doors at the bottom of the flats facing Rossville Street were open and I saw an arm holding a pistol extended from behind the door. I saw the pistol jerk, observed the strike of the bullet. It hit about fifty metres short on the other side of the barricade, ricocheted and hit a man who had gone over to the youth, in the right arm. Immediately after this shot, another was fired by the gunman at the doors. I saw the youth's head jerk and he slumped into the man's arms. Previous to this the youth had been looking round. The man had been shouting, 'Come and help me, he's dying.' He also said, 'He's been shot.' After the youth was hit in the head, the man said, 'He's dead.' And he got up on his feet and wandered off away from the barricade, apparently in a daze.

The surgeon who later treated Alex Nash at Altnagelvin, Mr H. M. Bennett, concluded from the limited tissue damage that he was probably hit by a low-velocity round (from a pistol, for instance). Such evidence was inconclusive and did not take account of a possible ricochet from a high-velocity round, of which there were many at the barricade. None of the civilians actually in or near the entrance saw a gunman with a pistol.

After Nash was hit, he lay on the ground next to his dead son for several minutes until a Para lieutenant came up to the barricade with his pistol drawn. Nash complained to the officer that he had been shot in the shoulder. The lieutenant would say later, 'I briefly examined him but found no external sign of injury. He left the barricade on my instructions.'

Nash thought the end had come. 'I thought he was going to finish me off.'

'There's dead men,' people were shouting from the flats and pointing to the group lying at the barricade. McLaughlin had been on his stomach and now he turned over on his back to show he was still alive. As he did so another young man behind the barricade was shot.

Michael McDaid, whom everyone knew as the twenty-year-old apprentice barman in the Celtic Bar beside the grocery shop in Stanley's Walk, had been at the front of the crowd at Barrier 14.

He was wearing his Sunday best: a green sports jacket, a blue shirt with cufflinks and metal armband and a blue and orange tie. McDaid had never been in trouble with the police or the army. He was hard-working and had one hobby – the Cortina car which his mother had bought and given him a half-share in when her endowment insurance policy matured a year earlier. He used to think nothing of running people anywhere in it, and was always being put upon for car trips. He was just 'car crazy'.

The SLR bullet that killed McDaid entered his left cheek and again followed a forty-five degree track downwards through his body, fracturing his lower jaw, breaking three vertebrae and severing the spinal cord. It tumbled on through his chest, fracturing two ribs, and sliced through the upper part of his lung before leaving his body through his back. As with John Young, the injury to the spinal cord caused rapid death.

The horrified Denis McLaughlin saw McDaid's head burst open and blood start to pour out. His face was covered with blood. His body fell beside McLaughlin and the blood splashed over his hands. He had no idea where McDaid had suddenly come from. He started screaming at his friend Roberts, 'Look at the blood.'

'There's nothing we can do now, we'll get in out of the road,' said Roberts, trying to calm him down, even though shots were still being fired.

Roberts started to crawl backwards towards the gable end of Glenfada. A youth known as 'Smiler' was crouching behind the wall and he grabbed Roberts's feet and started to pull him in, then Roberts clutched McLaughlin's hands and slowly they inched to cover.

On the other side of the barricade, by the flats, another youth had been defying the army, facing the paratroopers at Kells Walk. He was Hugh Gilmore, who lived in the Rossville flats, on the second floor. He was a regular at aggro corner. He was also one the keenest of the Rossville flats car park football players and used to play ferociously energetic free-for-alls. Gilmore had a minor police record. In 1967 he was charged with others for stealing lead to the value of £2 7s 6d and given a conditional discharge for twelve months. He was also 'known to the army', as the saying went. One evening in 1971 he was going home with friends from the cinema when he was stopped by soldiers and taken to the barracks on the Strand Road, then to the Bligh's Lane army post. After a chat he was told to go home. Nobody was charged and it seemed like a routine check-up.

After leaving school, Gilmore had worked on building sites making tea, but when he turned sixteen – and the contractors had to pay reasonable rates – they wouldn't keep him on, so he got a job as a tyre fitter at the Northern Ireland Tyre Services in Strand Road.

He had joined the march from the Creggan and at aggro corner he had met up with Geraldine Richmond, a machinist at, Hogg & Mitchell's shirt factory off Little James Street. She had gone on the march with her boyfriend, Hugo McBride, whom she would later marry. It was her first march, but she was not expecting more than usual rioting because she had heard on the grapevine that the IRA had given assurances to NICRA that they would not be operating that day.

At aggro corner she met up with Gilmore and when the Saracens came in she ran with him down Rossville Street towards the rubble barricade. About halfway down they paused, and Gilmore and another youth with him picked up stones. They threw one each towards the oncoming Pigs.

When the paratroopers started shooting Gilmore cried, 'They're firing live ammunition.'

Richmond and Gilmore quickly realized that this was not the normal snatch squad, but something very different. They ran as fast as they could on down Rossville Street. People were screaming and crying, and shouting, 'Live bullets – get down.'

As they ran past block 1 of the flats, Gilmore was close to the

175

wall and Richmond was to his right, slightly behind him. He was cursing, 'The bastards are killing us.'

They were among the last to reach the barricade where others were throwing stones. Gilmore and Richmond stumbled over it as best they could; Gilmore was ahead and Richmond kept falling over.

After the barricade they kept running along the side of block 1. Geraldine Richmond recalled, 'I was still to his right and slightly behind him, about six feet away from block 1. I was running on the cobbles between the road and the pavement. I do not know whether Hugh was still holding one of the stones he had picked up . . . I heard two shots from my right. I felt the bullets rush past in front of me. I heard Hugh gasp.'

Gilmore jumped up in the air, clutched his stomach and cried out, 'I'm hit, I'm hit.' And he started running towards the entrance of the flats.

Richmond thought he must have been hit by a rubber bullet. They ran on, Gilmore crouched over, taking deep breaths and gasping. Just past the entrance to block 1 he stumbled forward and his legs went from under him.

Sean McDermott and Frank Mellan had been running with him; they also assumed that he must have been hit by a rubber bullet. All three of them – McDermott, Mellan and Richmond – helped him round the corner of the flats, where Gilmore collapsed. They turned him on his back and blood was pouring out of his side. Mellan was a student nurse and he opened Gilmore's brown anorak and bared his body.

There was a hole on the left side and a gaping exit wound on the right side from which his innards were protruding. Mellan pulled off Gilmore's sweater and used it to try to staunch the flow of blood, but as he placed the sweater on the wound, more of Gilmore's bowel came out.

Richmond, who was helping and had also done some first aid, would recall, 'There was a small entry wound to the left side of the upper abdomen and a massive exit wound . . . where his organs were exposed. The smell was very noticeable. I knew there was nothing I could do for him. I knew he was dying. I started praying. I couldn't believe what was happening. I was terrified.'

Mellan tried to give him the kiss of life, but blood was coming from Gilmore's mouth. And each time he pushed air down into Gilmore's lungs he heard a sound which he took to be the air escaping from a punctured lung. Gilmore's left lung had been torn. He was still conscious.

Richmond looked at his wounds and could not believe how he had managed to run on after he had been shot. He was talking to her. 'He told me his address and that he wanted his mother. I moved round so that his head was resting on my knee and one of the young men in the small crowd that had gathered took off his jacket and put it under Hugh's head. There was a shocked look on Hugh's face. Just before he died his face changed – it sort of relaxed and he knew he was dying. His head then went forward and he died.'

Richmond checked his pulse and stayed with him. 'I thought that if I stayed there everything would be all right. I didn't want him to be on his own.'

Gilmore's sister, Mary Bonner, was in her mother's flat on the second floor of block 2 when there was a knock at the door. A stranger told her, 'Your Hugh's been shot but he's all right.' She was told he was going to the hospital in an ambulance.

There were four bullet wounds on Gilmore's body. The bullet, or bullets, had made a typical entrance wound in his left upper arm and a slightly bigger hole in his left forearm, a gaping wound on his left side and a smaller wound on his right side. By bending the left forearm at the elbow and bringing the upper arm almost alongside the body all four wounds could be brought into line, suggesting a single round had done all the damage.

No bullet was ever found in Gilmore's body, but the track of the bullet and the fact that he was facing the paratroopers when shot suggested the soldiers who killed him must have been at Kells Walk.

It was strange, however, that the hole on the left was bigger than that on the right side of his body. Normally, the entrance wound is smaller than the exit wound. This oddity suggested that two bullets, one from the left, or Kells Walk area, hit Gilmore's upper arm and exited through his forearm, and another from the right – perhaps from the walls – had caused a separate wound. People at the flats were shouting that there was firing from the walls.

Yet if there were two bullets, they must have been fired simultaneously from two different directions, a highly unlikely event, and no one saw Gilmore hit twice.

Mellan, McDermott and Green couldn't move his body to safety, so they ran to take cover with others by the telephone box, leaving Gilmore on the pavement.

Across the barricade the small group with Father Bradley was still cowering at the gable end of Glenfada Park. Among them was Father Terence O'Keeffe, Dean of Humanities at the University of Ulster at Coleraine. Like Father Bradley, he had wanted to go to the aid of the youths dying behind the barricade but others had pulled him away, saying, 'You're mad, you'll get killed if you move from here.' In the lulls from the shooting, Father O'Keeffe would peer round the gable end and each time he would see a paratrooper aiming his rifle at him. Bullets were hitting the gable end above his head.

Father O'Keeffe then witnessed the killing of seventeen-year-old Kevin McElhinney. He was the only one shot that day who did not live in the Bogside or the Creggan. His home was in a Catholic street, Philip Street, by the Buncrana Road where he lived with his parents, one brother and three sisters.

When Kevin left school at fifteen, he wanted to be a mechanic, so he got a job on the petrol pumps in the Waterside. When the

Troubles worsened, the Waterside was not an easy place for a young Catholic to work, so he took a job as a shop assistant with Lipton's in the Strand Road and had been there for two years. He was known by the management as quiet, punctual and with no political views. Lipton's is right opposite the army barracks in the old market, and also opposite John Temple's, the clothing store where John Young worked.

Part of Kevin's routine, especially on a Saturday, was to guard the door and frisk people for guns and other weapons. He didn't go to dances and didn't drink, preferring to listen to his favourite band, T. Rex, and play with his slot racing cars. He had a large layout in the loft of his two-up, two-down home. He was a DIY enthusiast, had built bookshelves in the living room and had fixed up the mantel-shelf on which stood his one athletic trophy from the annual mile race round Derry Walls two years before. He loved to work on his father's ageing grey Vauxhall Victor and he was going to learn to drive. His provisional driving licence had arrived on the Friday.

That Sunday, as always, he asked permission from his mother to go on the march and she couldn't say no because all his friends from Philip Street were going. She simply urged him to look after his new brown boots.

Kevin was throwing stones at the paratroopers from the barricade when the shots began to bounce off the rubble and he half ran, half crawled to the entrance to the flats. On the Glenfada side they were egging him on: 'Come on, lad, you're nearly there.' They were also shouting to those in the entrance way to help him.

From the low wall at Kells Walk, Sergeant K of the Paras' composite platoon, whose SLR had a telescopic sight, saw two men

doing a leopard crawl [which he described as using your elbows and knees and toes to move along] and I could see the rear man was carrying what I could see clearly was a rifle. I

179

then cocked my rifle and fired one round at this man. I could not see this man too clearly except to say that he was wearing a dark suit. It is difficult to say whether I hit the man . . . he appeared to lurch and then carried on crawling.

Kevin McElhinney was wearing a brown suit and the new brown zip-up boots.

Private L, also of the Paras, said he fired at the man who was crawling in front of Sergeant K's target.

One shot whined past McElhinney and hit the door to the flats. As he reached the first metal pole supporting the canopy over the door, he grabbed at it to haul himself inside, there was another shot and his body jerked once and then half fell into the entrance.

McElhinney was hit in his left buttock, an inch from the anus. The bullet tore up the muscle of the pelvic cavity, fractured the bone and ripped the bladder. It divided a segment of the large intestine, cut through the artery supplying the left leg and tore open two segments of the small intestine before entering the left side of the abdominal wall. Here, it broke up into metal fragments, one large piece and three small ones emerging separately. The larger piece fractured the ninth left rib. Death was caused by bleeding from the cut artery. There was also a graze on the outer side of McElhinney's left thigh, which could have been made by a second bullet.

Volunteer Jim Norris, of the Knights of Malta, had been in the flats with Bernard Feeney, another volunteer, treating the youth who had been hit in the face with a gas canister, and he was leaving as McElhinney was shot. He passed people huddled on the stairway and as he reached the entrance, the doors suddenly flew open and McElhinney crashed through and skidded to a halt in the hallway. He was limp, like a drunk. Norris tried to catch him to stop him falling. When Norris opened his jacket his left side was covered with blood; in seconds the floor was also slick with it.

With the help of a photographer Norris carried McElhinney up the stairs; his legs were shaking violently and his eyes were rolling back into his head. His face was a yellowish white. Norris knew the youth was dying. He ripped off his coat and shirt which were soaked with blood. Helped by the photographer, he turned McElhinney on his stomach and saw the wound on his side. It was turning black. His pulse was weak. Norris took out a gunshot dressing from his first-aid bag and pressed it on the wound, and then turned McElhinney on his back again.

At that moment, a man with a red beard and wearing glasses shouted to Norris to go to the second floor of the flats where someone had been shot in the head. He left the photographer and another man named Liam Mailey with McElhinney and went back upstairs, passing people who were crying and praying. As he came out on to a balcony – he was the only one moving about; everyone else was lying on the floor – he yelled at the paratroopers, 'First aid, first aid.' And one of them yelled back, 'You better start fucking running.'

Norris ran along the balcony and saw the soldiers pointing their guns in his direction and, he thought, firing.

When he reached the flat where the man had been injured his colleague Bernard Feeney was already there. The man had apparently been hit in the head by flying glass when his window was smashed by a rubber bullet and he was unconscious. Feeney had already applied a gunshot dressing to the man's head. (The man was Patrick Brolly. The round that broke the window was later thought to have been a real bullet, not a rubber one.)

In the same flat was a woman suffering from angina and Norris gave her one of her heart pills, and left Feeney to take care of her and the man with the head injury. He made his way down the stairs to where he had left McElhinney, but he had just died. His pulse had quickened and become very fast just before death. Norris and the photographer whispered an act of contrition in his ear and he was given the last rites by Father John Irwin, who had

181

arrived by his side. McElhinney's eyes wouldn't close, and they covered his body with a blanket and waited for the ambulance to arrive.

From Kells Walk, Lieutenant 119 ordered Lance Corporal F and Private G to move into the courtyard of Glenfada Park to 'cut off the retreat of three men they saw leave the barricade'.

X

Don't Move, Pretend You're Dead

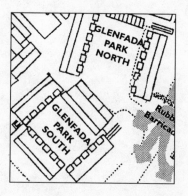

Don't move, pretend you're dead

Advice from a sixteen-year-old schoolboy, Malachy Coyle, to Jim Wray, who had just been shot in the back by the paratroopers in Glenfada Park

As Michael Kelly lay dying on the pavement at the gable wall of Glenfada courtyard there was nothing Father Bradley, Father O'Keeffe and a small group of terrified citizens around his body could do to help. They were pinned down by gunfire from the paratroopers. A few feet away, bullets were bouncing off the rubble barricade and chipping the stucco walls. Across the street, people in the flats were shouting warnings that the paratroopers were moving up into Glenfada; the twenty or so men and one woman would soon be surrounded.

It was a diverse group of priests, professional types, workers and youths out for some aggro. Some were bound to be arrested because they had been in the mêlée at William Street and were drenched with purple dye from the water cannon. One of those was Jim Wray, the tall twenty-two-year-old with the dark woolly hat who had protested peacefully at Barrier 14 by sitting down in the middle of the road. Another was Michael Quinn, who had just turned seventeen and was still in school; his back was soaked with dye.

At least one youth was apparently running the risk of being shot on sight. He was carrying a biscuit tin lid on which lay a number of bomb-like objects. The youth was crying his eyes out. 'Mister, what do I do with these?' he sobbed.

'Get your arse out of here,' an onlooker told the youth, kicking the tray out of his hands.

(It was never clear what the objects were. 'They looked like fireworks [but] whatever was on that tray never got used,' said the onlooker.)

One member of the group was already known to the security forces, not as a troublemaker but because he worked for the government. Joseph Friel was a twenty-year-old tax officer with the Inland Revenue. He worked in the Embassy building in the Strand Road where the army had an observation post on the top floor and he needed an official security clearance to get into the building.

In fact, Friel came of a family who had long served the Crown. His father, who had been in the British army, now worked in Ebrington Barracks as a civilian maintenance man. His grandfather had fought in the First World War and his great-grandfather had also served with the British forces.

Friel was on his way to the meeting at Free Derry Corner when he was caught in the gunfire. After lunch at home on the eighth floor of the Rossville flats he had decided to go to Free Derry Corner for the meeting. His father told him to look after himself.

None of the lifts in the flats would come to the eighth floor so he ran down the stairs, leaving block 1 at the entrance by the rubble barricade, and headed across Rossville Street.

He could hear shouting from the crowd there and loud bangs coming from Little James Street, which he took to be rubber bullets and CS gas. He could also hear Bernadette Devlin's distinctive voice over the loudspeaker, but he could not see her because of the crowd around the lorry.

As Friel reached the speakers at the corner, the shooting broke out and shots came down Rossville Street. 'The crowd was squealing, crying, roaring and shouting,' he would recall. 'I saw sheer unadulterated terror on people's faces. I froze momentarily and thought where to go. From where I was standing I could have gone in any direction.'

Bernadette Devlin, standing on the back of the lorry, saw the Pigs drive up Rossville Street, and thought they were coming right to Free Derry Corner and everyone at the meeting would be arrested. As she was about to speak, there was a hail of fire and the shots went whizzing overhead. She threw herself flat on the lorry, looked up, covered in coal dust, and saw Lord Brockway, still on his way down, as if in slow motion. She pulled the old man's ankles from under him. Ivan Cooper was already curled up like a dormouse and she wedged herself in between him and Brockway.

Kathleen Meenan and Helen Young, whose brother John was shot dead at the barricade in that first fusillade of bullets, crouched down for cover beside the coal lorry. Someone said the soldiers were firing from the walls, and Eamonn McCann came up with another man and they covered the two women with their bodies.

When McCann said it was safe, they all began crawling away on their hands and knees. Meenan wore out the toes of her boots before she had reached the safety of her aunt's house in St Columb's Wells.

As the paratroopers opened fire, Dr Donal MacDermott, the Bogside GP, was walking down Rossville Street towards the meeting. He had been told there was a wounded man in the flats but had been unable to find him. Now he was worried because he had left one of his sons, Eamon, in his car near Free Derry Corner. Devlin was telling the crowd, 'Sit down. If you sit down they won't shoot you.'

Then MacDermott saw Eamon by his car, jumping up and down, crying 'Daddy, Daddy, they're firing real bullets.' MacDermott packed him into the car and drove home.

Friel ran back to the flats, thinking he would also go home but when he arrived at the entrance to block 1 the doorway was packed with people taking cover and he couldn't get in. The shots were coming faster and louder, it seemed, but he still had no real impression where they were coming from.

There was complete chaos on Rossville Street. People were running in every direction and bumping into each other, leaping over the barricade and stumbling as they did so. A woman with a child in a pram got stuck, but people ran on too panic-stricken to stop and help her.

Realizing he could not get through the door, Friel crossed over at the rubble barricade into Glenfada Park and reached the gable wall where Father Bradley and others had been attending to Michael Kelly.

In the group now was Gerry McKinney, a thirty-five-year-old businessman (among other things he had run the roller-skating rink in Strand Road), and William McKinney (no relation), a printer at the *Derry Journal*. The paratroopers were closing in and they knew they would be arrested, but of the thousands on the march that day the two McKinneys were among the least likely Bogsiders ever to cause the army any trouble.

Gerry had never had anything to do with the IRA, or even the civil rights organization, and he had never thrown a stone in his life. His only brushes with the law were tickets for parking and speeding.

Gerry had no intention of being on the march. He had left home after Sunday lunch to go over to his mother's house in Beechwood Street at the back of Glenfada. Like all Bogsiders, Gerry was bitter about the treatment of Catholics – because of his religion he had been turned down for several jobs for which he was well qualified, or so he had concluded, and he had found work outside Derry several times. At the start of the Troubles in 1969, he had sent the family south to Dublin for a spell, and since internment, he would not let his wife Ita go into the centre of town – he did all the shopping and ran the errands. But he did let her go to bingo once a week across the border in Buncrana.

He had never been unemployed and for the last six months had been working for John McLaughlin, a local builder, and was making a steady £35-40 a week, topped up by his management consultancy. Gerry was a generous man, always helping neighbours down on their luck by lending them a few quid and asking every day, as he left home, whether Ita was OK for cash.

That afternoon he was due to go into the office to meet his boss McLaughlin to discuss a few business matters and ideas he had for a job in Dublin. The papers were in his car, but he couldn't get out of the Bogside because the army had closed off the exits. Gerry's brother-in-law, John O'Kane, and some other friends were at his mother's and they were going on the march, so Gerry decided to join them.

Willie McKinney was twenty-seven, the eldest of ten children. He was a quiet young man who still lived in the family home in the Creggan, where he pursued his two obsessions of photography and the accordion. He had always been studious and, since a child, had worn thick glasses. The other children had teased him, calling him 'the professor', or sometimes 'four-eyes'. When he went to Friday night hops he used to take off his glasses to give himself a better chance to get a girl, and his brothers and sisters would watch him spin round the floor wondering how on earth he could see his partner.

Willie started work at the *Derry Journal* when he was fourteen, first as a tea boy and then as an odd job man. On *Journal* outings to Bundoran, a seaside resort in Donegal Bay across the border, Willie would play the accordion on the bus, mostly Irish folk songs. But his favourite from the hit parade was 'Where Would You Like to Be? Under the Bridges of Paris with Me.'

He wanted to be a printer but, in those days, first you had to be a member of the printers' union. McKinney badgered union officials, writing them letters, and they eventually gave in; if the other printers agreed, he could become a member. The others did, because they liked him.

When he got the job the family were very proud. He would come home for lunch each day on his bike, and his brothers and sisters would be sitting down at the table, waiting for him. He started dating Elizabeth O'Donnell from the Waterside and they got engaged, but they never married.

By chance, he had been arrested once by the army. It had happened late one evening after he had been out with his fiancée. She had gone home, but Willie had stayed to watch a few young lads stoning an army patrol. They were all arrested and held at the barracks until five in the morning. Anyone with dirty hands – showing they had been picking up stones – was charged with riotous behaviour. Willie's hands were clean and he was not charged with anything.

Recently, he had bought a good camera second-hand from the *Journal* because they had no use for it any more. He was mad about it and used to develop his own film at home, after the family had gone to bed. He kept all his chemicals in old lemonade bottles in the kitchen.

The week before he had been to the protest march at Magilligan and had taken pictures there, and this Sunday he was out again with his camera. He had left the house looking smartly turned out, as he always liked to be, with a shirt and tie, a black blazer, his corduroy cap and his dark-grey mohair three-quarter-length coat under his arm, and carrying his camera. He could have been mistaken for a reporter.

One of the last to seek refuge in Glenfada Park was Danny Gillespie, who lived in the Creggan, was thirty-two and unemployed. He had been with the march since the Bishop's Field and found himself standing next to a man who was hit in the mouth with a rubber bullet at Barrier 14 and had to have several stitches in his lip. Gillespie then made his way into Glenfada, warning a group of youths clutching broken-up bits of flagstones that they would be wise to clear off; the paratroopers were firing live rounds.

At Father Bradley's urging, three men in the Glenfada group at the gable agreed to carry Kelly's body across the courtyard and through a passageway into Abbey Park. As they were lifting Kelly, Gregory Wild, a fourteen-year-old schoolboy, was looking towards the garages at the north end of the courtyard and spotted the paratroopers coming in. 'Watch out,' he shouted, 'there's a limey.'

Joe Friel looked round to the north of Glenfada. He was without his glasses; that day they were being repaired. Even so, he could see paratroopers standing by the garages at the north end of Glenfada, three or four of them.

'The one in front was firing,' Friel would recall. 'He had his gun at just above waist height and was moving it from side to side, not swinging it, just moving it a few inches from left to right. The other soldiers were not firing their weapons. The soldier was not picking me out. The fire was random.'

Friel started to run towards the alley leading into Abbey Park. Suddenly, he felt a thump in his chest. He thought he had been hit by a rubber bullet; he couldn't believe it was a real bullet because he thought that must feel different – 'like a red-hot wire boring into you'. He looked down and saw the gash in his jacket and the blood starting to come through his clothing. There was also blood in his mouth. 'I'm hit, I'm hit,' he cried. He collapsed into the hands of three men taking cover in the alley.

One of them was Leo Young. He was looking for his brother John who was lying dead or dying behind the rubble barricade in Rossville Street. Friel was fully conscious and scared he was going to die, but he had been incredibly lucky. The bullet was 'an almost near miss', as the doctor at Altnagelvin would later say. It was a flesh wound; no vital organs or blood vessels had been hit. The bullet had gone clean through the front of his chest, entering on the right side, cracking the breastbone and exiting on the left.

If he had not turned slightly to see the paratrooper who shot him when Gregory Wild shouted his warning, the bullet would almost certainly have hit him in the back and probably would have killed him.

Young and others carried Friel into the Murrays' house in Lisfannon Park. He was treated by the young paramedic, Eibhlin Lafferty, who tore open his shirt and put a sterilized pad on the wound. There was a crowd in the house, mostly older women who knelt around him and started saying the rosary. Mrs Murray ran upstairs, unable to take the drama. Joe Friel was convinced he was going to die.

When Danny Gillespie first saw the paratroopers come into the courtyard, one of them was directly in front of him, aiming his gun at him from the shoulder. Gillespie turned and ran across the yard and there was a sharp crack. His head was stinging and burning. He fell forwards with his face down on the tarmac. Everything went black.

When he regained his senses Gillespie found two of the youths he had told off about carrying stones asking him if he was all right and trying to help him up. He had almost made it to the cover of the alley leading out of Glenfada into Abbey Park when there were more shots and one young man let out a grunt and fell on top of him, pinning his legs to the pavement. Gillespie managed to push him off and run through the alley into Abbey Park.

This was Jim Wray.

There were now four paratroopers from the anti-tank platoon of Support Company in Glenfada Park, led by Corporal E and including Lance Corporal F, and Private G and Private H. Their plan was to cut off those who had been on the barricade and were fleeing through the courtyard. Father Bradley's group was trapped.

Seventeen-year-old Martin Hegarty was scared stiff. 'How do I get out of this one?' he was asking himself. Several in the group had given up, accepting that they would be arrested, at best. They were squealing and some had their hands over their ears, trying to shut out the commotion and the reality of their plight. Hegarty proposed dashing south into the next courtyard of Glenfada; others were in favour of running across the yard into the alley that led into Abbey Park. 'Jesus, don't go out there,' someone said.

But Michael Quinn, a seventeen-year-old schoolboy, was ready to run. Ahead of him he saw a youth shot in the right thigh on the west side of the park. The next moment he looked up he had gone. He was wearing a black anorak and had brown hair. Quinn now ran towards the alley, doubled over. He had taken only a few paces before he was hit. The bullet ripped the right shoulder of his jacket before blowing away a chunk of his cheekbone and came out through his nose.

Quinn staggered through the alley into Abbey Park and saw the youth who had been shot in the leg lying on the ground. Someone helped Quinn towards Fahan Street and across open ground to Blucher Street, where he was treated by the paramedics, Pauline Lynch and Eibhlin Lafferty.

Others from Bradley's group now dashed for the alley into Abbey Park. One of them was John McLaughlin, supervisor at the National Coal Board's yard in the Waterside. Ahead of him was a young lad sprinting for the alley. One of the paratroopers spotted him and swivelled round, aimed at the boy and called out for him to stop, but the boy kept running. McLaughlin took his chance and ran for the alley. The same soldier shouted at him to stop and he saw him swing his rifle round to aim at him, but McLaughlin put his hands on his head, bent double, and just kept going. More people followed.

In a fusillade of bullets Joseph Mahon was hit in the thigh and fell, and behind him Willie McKinney, clutching his precious camera, was cut down by a bullet in his back.

The four paratroopers would later say they shot at gunmen, petrol bombers and nail bombers.

Corporal E said when the paratroopers arrived in Glenfada there were about forty or fifty people who started to throw missiles and he saw a man throwing a petrol bomb which landed ten yards from him. He then saw that the same man had a nail bomb and as he was lighting it he shouted to him to drop it, but as he had already lit it, Corporal E fired two shots. The second hit him and he fell down. According to Corporal E, the nail bomb exploded but no one was hurt, but none of the civilians saw or heard any explosion in the confined courtyard.

Lance Corporal F, who fired five rounds from Glenfada, would say that he spotted three men who had left the rubble barricade move into the courtyard. 'One of them turned and was about to throw what appeared to be a bomb (because it was fizzing) in our direction. Myself and "G" dropped down on one knee. I took an aimed shot. The first shot seemed to hit the man with the bomb in the shoulder, the second in the chest. The man fell to the ground.' The bomb did not explode, Lance Corporal F said.

His partner, Private G, said he fired three rounds at two gunmen who were standing on the same footpath leading to the alley into Abbey Park where Friel, Gillespie, Wray, Mahon and Willie McKinney were shot.

. . . We moved quickly into the alleyway and I remember looking round for F who was just behind me. There is an archway into the courtyard of Glenfada Park. There was a car parked close to the mouth of the archway and I went round to the right-hand side of the car with F close beside me. As I got round the end of the car two men attracted my attention in the opposite corner of Glenfada Park. These men were armed. I cannot identify their weapons exactly but I think they were short rifles like an M1 carbine. They both had weapons of this sort. I immediately dropped to one knee and fired three aimed shots at one of the men. F was firing beside me and I saw both men fall.

Private H fired a total of twenty-two rounds in Glenfada Park, more than any other paratrooper's total for any of the killing grounds. (Lance Corporal F fired the second highest total of thirteen, five of them from Glenfada.)

Private H's first target in Glenfada, he would say, was a youth who he thought was about to throw a nail bomb.

194

I saw a lad . . . he had an object like a Coca-Cola tin in his hand. He was drawn back in the throwing position. I fired two shots at him and he fell to the ground. The bomb just thudded to the ground without rolling or bouncing. I am still sure it was a bomb. It did not explode. There was an alleyway at the opposite corner of the square from which a youth ran. He picked up the bomb, I think with his right hand, and I thought he was about to throw it. I fired one round at him and think it hit him in the right shoulder or upper arm. He was able to stagger away. He did not drop the bomb.

Private H's next target, he said, was a gunman who was pointing a rifle from behind a frosted window-pane in a house on the north side of the courtyard. He said he pumped nineteen rounds into this bathroom window, but no window was found punctured with nineteen bullet holes and none of the other paratroopers saw or heard Private H firing nineteen shots at one target. The bullets that Private H fired clearly went somewhere else.

Sheltering in the doorway of 7 Abbey Park, the house of Mr and Mrs O'Reilly, was John William Porter, a quartermaster sergeant in the Irish army. He ran through the alley and a woman in number 8 said, 'Mister, quick. Come in here.' He slipped in and hid behind the door, keeping it slightly open so that he could see down the alley.

Porter saw Jim Wray fall and hit his head on the sidewalk. Then there was a volley of shots. He closed the door and went to the window. 'My God, there's a man been shot,' he told the people in the house. He went back to the door and opened it. He saw Wray lying half on, half off the pavement. His left arm was limp and there was blood on his wrist.

Wray raised his head up off the ground and looked towards where Porter was standing in the doorway. Wray then tried to press himself up with his right hand, but he couldn't move. Porter ran out of the door towards Wray and three bullets smacked into the wall in front of him. He ran back into the house and slammed the door.

Malachy Coyle, a sixteen-year-old schoolboy, also saw Jim Wray fall on to the pavement. Coyle had been running away from the paratroopers as they came into Glenfada and had almost reached the alley into Abbey Park when he was grabbed by a man who pulled him to safety into the backyard of a house. It had a slatted wooden fence through which Coyle could see the Paras moving into the courtyard. He was scared stiff. He thought of hiding in the dustbin but it was full of rubbish, so he just crouched down behind the fence.

Wray was looking directly at Coyle, raised his head off the pavement and said, 'I can't move my legs.' The bald man who had pulled Coyle to safety told Wray, ' Keep calm, keep calm.'

Coyle said, 'Don't move. Pretend you're dead.'

More shots rang out from the north end of the courtyard and the pavement around Wray exploded in sparks. Wray was still trying to raise himself up. From the house he was in, John Porter saw Wray's brown corduroy jacket jump twice four or five inches in the air and his head went down slowly on to the pavement. Wray had been shot in the back, for the second time.

The first bullet, which had apparently caused him to fall so that he couldn't move, entered Wray's back from the right and travelled to the left almost horizontally across his back – from the direction of the paratroopers. The bullet damaged the spine at the tenth and eleventh thoracic vertebrae, fractured the tenth and eleventh left ribs and bruised, but did not penetrate, the left lung. The spinal injury meant that Wray could not lift himself up.

The second bullet was the one that killed him. It entered Wray's back, just above the first bullet. Then it passed through muscle tissue, damaged the eighth thoracic vertebra, fractured parts of five left ribs by which time it was tumbling through the tissue of the left lung before leaving the body. The gaping exit wound exposed lacerated muscles. Death, which was not instantaneous, was caused by bleeding and the escape of air into the left chest cavity from the damaged lung.

The wounded Joe Mahon watched, terrified, as Wray was shot while on the ground. Mahon was lying behind Wray and saw his desperate efforts to get up. He heard him calling for help to Porter, Coyle and others sheltering in the alley.

After Wray was shot the second time, Mahon could hear the soldiers coming closer. He lay still, pretending he was dead. Behind him, Willie McKinney was moaning.

Mahon was seriously wounded, but he would live. The bullet had entered the right pelvic bone and tossed through the intestines, splitting up into tiny bits that bored twelve holes in the small intestine and made six separate perforations of the mesentery – the membranes that hold the intestines to the abdominal cavity – before embedding itself in the muscle beyond the bone. (The surgeon who operated on Mahon noted in his report, 'The bullet was a high-velocity one and such missiles when they penetrate the abdominal viscera, carry a notoriously bad prognosis.')

However, Mahon's medical report would give no accurate description of the entry wound, as was done for all the other dead and wounded and, although the bullet was found intact, the government forensic staff, while agreeing it had been fired from an army SLR, could not match it to any of the twenty-nine rifles the army would submit for examination. The mystery was why it had split up so readily into tiny fragments without hitting a bone.

Behind Mahon, lying face up on the pavement, Willie McKinney was still conscious after being shot, also in the back. One bullet had caused four surface wounds and multiple internal injuries. The entrance wound was on the right side of his back. As it travelled through his body, it fractured some ribs, lacerated the diaphragm, the right lung, the liver, colon, stomach and spleen and then made a hole in his left side big enough for his guts to be hanging out. The bullet then ripped holes in the back and front of his left forearm before leaving his body.

A paratrooper, whose footsteps Mahon could hear coming closer, left McKinney alone and walked forward towards the alley. He then fired three more rounds into the alley and Mahon heard him say, ' I've got another one.' Mahon did not dare move to see what he was firing at. Another soldier said, 'OK, we're pulling out.' Before they left, Mahon saw the first soldier remove his helmet to wipe his brow.

The paratroopers' last shots into the alley before leaving killed the businessman, Gerry McKinney, and a youth in blue jeans named Gerald Donaghy. The bullet that killed Donaghy came from Private G's rifle.

After the rush out of Glenfada through the alley into Abbey Park, people took shelter in and behind the houses there. John O'Kane had run through the alley with his brother-in-law, Gerry McKinney, and they had dived for cover. Through the alley they could see where Wray had fallen in Glenfada Park and wondered how they could reach him.

Donaghy was seventeen and an ardent Republican who had just completed six months in jail for rioting. He said he would be able to get to Wray if he crawled on his stomach but as he started out O'Kane and McKinney pulled him back saying it was too risky. There was more shooting and then all three started to move out across the mouth of the alley. People on the other side shouted, 'Get back, get back.'

O'Kane turned back, but McKinney and Donaghy kept edging out. O'Kane shouted, 'Come back, it's not worth it.' But it was too late.

The paratrooper spotted them.

Gerry McKinney's arm was stretched out across Donaghy's chest, holding him back. He said to Donaghy, 'Just a minute, son, 'til we see if it's clear.' As he turned his head into the alley to see if it was safe to cross, he spotted the paratrooper aiming at him, his hands shot up in the air and he cried out, 'No, no.'

Two shots rang out. McKinney and Donaghy fell to the ground. Donaghy was clutching his stomach.

A thirteen-year-old schoolboy, John Carr, saw Gerald McKinney shot. He lived with his family at 8 Abbey Park.

John's father, Peter, had let the group with Kelly's body inside the house, then herded all the children upstairs and put four or five of them, including John and the one-year-old baby, in an empty wardrobe, closed the door and told them to stay there.

After a minute, John's curiosity got the better of him, and he came out of the wardrobe and went into his brother's bedroom at the front of the house. As he looked out of the widow through the alleyway into Glenfada several shots rang out and he saw Jim Wray's head fall slowly on to the pavement.

Then he saw a soldier come through the alleyway and face a group of people who ran away – except for one man who threw his hands up in the air and looked directly at the soldier. The bedroom window was closed and John could not hear whether the man said anything, but as his hands went up, the soldier shot him and he fell on his back. John saw him bless himself with his right hand across his face. It was Gerry McKinney. John screamed out, 'They've shot a man and he had his hands up.'

His father ran into the room, saw John standing at the window, grabbed him and told him to get down on the bed and to stay there while he checked the other children.

When the shooting stopped people came out of the houses in Abbey Park and tried to get to the wounded. The first to go to Donaghy and Gerry McKinney were shot at. Eibhlin Lafferty came out of the Murrays' house, where she had been treating Joe Friel. Another paramedic, Robert Cadman, joined her.

Looking through the alley, Lafferty saw the bodies of Wray,

Mahon and Willie McKinney lying on the pavement. There was blood coming from McKinney's mouth.

Cadman saw the barrel of a rifle appear at the Glenfada end of the alley and shouted to Lafferty to stay still but she didn't hear him. She was bending over Gerry McKinney and Donaghy, and only had time to see they were still alive when there was a shot. The bullet, apparently, hit the cobblestones behind Leo Young and he ducked down on one knee. Lafferty lay flat and shouted, 'Don't shoot, don't shoot, Red Cross.' Cadman joined her and they moved towards the alley into Glenfada.

At the same moment Mahon, who was still pretending to be dead, turned his head to see if the paratroopers had gone and looked straight at one. The soldier got down on one knee and took aim. Just then Lafferty shouted again, 'Don't shoot, Red Cross.'

The soldier shouted back, 'Your white coats are great targets but your red hearts are even better.'

She shouted, 'Are you mad?'

He didn't fire and Mahon would later credit Lafferty's intervention with saving his life.

When Leo Young reached Donaghy's body he was lying on his back, with his right leg tucked up underneath him and his guts hanging out. He grabbed Donaghy by the legs and hauled him into the open door of Raymond Rogan's house.

More people came out to help carry in the wounded. Jim McLaughlin helped get Willie McKinney into 7 Abbey Park. There was a first-aid man with a deformed hand who treated him, and he was struggling with the oxygen equipment and couldn't put the rubber pipe into the cylinder.

They brought James Wray into Peter Carr's house and put him on the floor in the living room beside Kelly.

Malachy Coyle would later describe the actions of Corporal E, Lance Corporal F and Privates G and H. He did not know which regiment they were from – they were all dressed alike, except one who was without a helmet.

The soldier without a helmet acted differently from the rest. He entered the car park ahead of the other soldiers and I noticed him immediately because he stood out from the rest by his dress and his manner. He was bareheaded and I could see he had blackish-coloured hair. He was not particularly tall, but he had a wiry build and looked to be very fit and strong. I think he had black streaks on his face.

While the other soldiers adopted a defensive position . . . this soldier ran on ahead of them to the south gable end . . .

[There] he discovered between twenty and thirty people all hunched down for cover beside the wall . . . the crowd of people there started squealing. I saw the bareheaded soldier turn around to face the crowd . . . and I heard him shout, 'I'll shoot you, you Irish bastards. You Irish scum!' He shouted this three or four times, very loudly. All the time he was standing with his gun pointing towards the crowd at the south gable wall . . . I remember hearing a woman's, or young boy's, voice crying out, 'Please don't shoot us! Please don't shoot us!'

The bareheaded soldier's behaviour was weird . . . he was acting completely irrationally and he could not stand still. He kept jerking about in a strange manner. He was very angry. He was obviously totally out of control and he could not stop shouting and screaming and moving about. It was very, very frightening to see him so full of anger and pointing his rifle at innocent civilians . . .

I became deeply afraid of leaving the safety [of the backyard] . . . I said to the bald man, 'They'll see us soon. We'd better get out and give ourselves up before that happens.' I remember that the man stood up and went out of the backyard first and I followed him with my hands behind

201

my head. We tensed ourselves as we stood up because we were expecting to be shot.

The bareheaded soldier fired again and Coyle 'lost it'. He panicked and bolted through the alley to the south, ran across the old Bog Road and took refuge with others by a fence. When the others asked him what was going on in Glenfada, he was in such a state of shock he couldn't get the words out. He broke down and wept.

XI

I Can't Stand This Any Longer

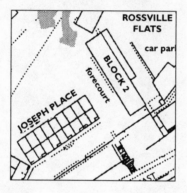

I can't stand this any longer

Barney McGuigan,
who refused to let Paddy Doherty die alone

THE FOURTH AND last killing ground was the forecourt of the Rossville flats, where Harley's fish and chip shop normally did a brisk trade. The forecourt was designed as a pedestrian walkway between block 2 of the flats and Joseph Place; it had fancy brickwork for a row of trees, but only one tree was still standing and there was rubbish scattered everywhere.

One strange fact separated these shootings from the earlier ones: no youths were hit. The two killed and the two wounded were all older family men.

Danny McGowan, aged thirty-eight, was a maintenance operator at the DuPont factory. He led a very stable family life; his wife Teresa was expecting their ninth child and he was not even on the march. As was his custom each Sunday, he had been visiting his brother-in-law who had a house near Free Derry Corner. They would have a chat and sometimes cut wood on the sawmill in the backyard.

The coal lorry with Lord Brockway, Bernadette Devlin and Eamonn McCann had arrived at Free Derry Corner and a crowd was gathering outside the house for the speeches. McGowan spotted his oldest boy, Danny, who was not supposed to be on the march, and he clipped him and told him to go home. McGowan himself was not interested in hanging around for the speeches and he walked off down the alley behind Joseph Place towards the centre of town.

He was halfway down the alley when he heard shots. He didn't really know the difference between a high-velocity round and a rubber bullet, so it didn't bother him and he kept walking. Then he heard four or five single shots, which were high-pitched cracks, plus a burst of what sounded like automatic fire. He ran to the end of the alley. Beyond the fish and chip shop he could see the group cowering by the telephone box. The body of Hugh Gilmore was lying there and Geraldine Richmond was screaming uncontrollably. He bent over Gilmore for a few minutes while others tried in vain to revive him with mouth-to-mouth resuscitation.

It was then that he saw Patrick Campbell, whom he knew, staggering and weaving 'like he'd had a few bottles'. 'Help, son, I'm shot, I'm hit,' he was moaning.

Campbell was a burly docker, aged fifty-three, who lived in the Creggan. He had been on the march since the Bishop's Field, had a bad whiff of gas at aggro corner and had left to come down Rossville Street.

When the paratroopers appeared he made a dash for the passage between blocks 1 and 2, and the relative safety of the alcove by the phone box. The next thing he knew he was shot in the buttock. The bullet punctured his colon and bladder, but he would live.

Now, McGowan saw him leaning against the wall of the shops in the forecourt trying to stop himself falling, then he was staggering towards the alley behind the Joseph Place maisonettes. McGowan thought he must have been shot in the car park of the flats or as he came through the passage.

McGowan could not see where Campbell had been hit because he was wearing a heavy coat. He went to help him, propping him up with difficulty because of his size – Campbell weighed close to fifteen stone – and half carried, half dragged him up the forecourt to the alley behind Joseph Place.

McGowan was on Campbell's right side. Behind him he saw two soldiers at the gable end of Glenfada, both in the aim position, one, he thought, kneeling and the other lying down on one elbow.

He was afraid that they might shoot and tried to hurry Campbell along, but the docker was so heavy that McGowan's arm quickly tired. The alley behind Joseph Place was now packed with people taking cover and McGowan decided to try to drag Campbell up some steps and on to the car park above the alley. As he reached the steps he was about to switch Campbell to his other side, when he was shot in his right leg. The leg buckled under him and he fell. The bullet had fractured the shin bone between the knee and the ankle.

As he fell down, he pushed Campbell away towards Abbey Place and then passed out.

Which soldier, or soldiers, wounded these two men is not clear. It is possible that Campbell was shot in the car park on the other side of the flats; there was still shooting from paratroopers at the end of Chamberlain Street, and from the gable end of block 1 on the waste ground.

It is also possible that he was shot from Glenfada. Lance Corporal F and Private G were in the southern part of the Glenfada courtyard and could see across Rossville Street into the forecourt and the shops. The former would say that he fired two shots in this direction. Corporal E and Private H were also still somewhere in Glenfada.

A third possibility is that soldiers of other units, who were in positions on the city walls, shot either or both men.

In Campbell's case that would mean he had his back to the walls at the time he was shot, which seems unlikely. When McGowan saw him he was leaning against the wall of the shops near the passage between blocks 1 and 2.

McGowan's wound presents a more convincing possibility of him being shot from the walls. He was propping up Campbell with his left arm, walking in the same direction to the alley with his back to Glenfada. The bullet entered the outside of his right lower leg and exited on the inside of the leg, slightly further down. At the time he did not know who shot him or from which direction the bullet had come. As he was taking a step towards the city walls and the bullet was travelling downwards he assumed he had been shot from the walls. It is also possible that the bullet came from Glenfada and either he turned at the moment it hit, or it was a weird ricochet.

In the panic and the confusion at Joseph Place, and the shooting earlier at the rubble barricade, several people had the impression that at least some of the shots had come from the city walls. Those running down Rossville Street heard people in the flats warning that the army was shooting from the walls.

Denis McLaughlin thought he saw Willie Nash running over the rubble barricade towards Free Derry Corner when he was shot and fell back. If that was so, he could not have been shot by paratroopers in Rossville Street or at Kells Walk. But he could have been shot from the walls.

Teresa Cassidy, a thirty-one-year-old factory worker, was at Free Derry Corner when shots she thought were coming from the walls forced her to lie flat on the ground, and crawl on her hands and knees to her aunt's house in St Columb's Wells.

Agnes McGuiness, a nineteen-year-old clerk, was in the shops' forecourt and was convinced there was firing from the walls.

Joe Carlin, a thirty-three-year-old wine trader, had run with the initial crowd through the passage between blocks 2 and 3 of the flats, and continued across the forecourt into the alley behind Abbey Place. He was running along when someone from the alley shouted, 'Get down, they're shooting from the walls.'

At that moment a sod of earth tore up in front of Carlin. 'It literally lifted up in front me,' he would say later. He dropped his keys because he stopped so quickly and did not recover them until the next day. He threw himself down into the alley and landed right on top of a man whom he badly winded. Together they crawled along the alley and out towards Free Derry Corner and on to St Columb's Wells. As they were sitting in shelter, someone said, 'They've been shooting from up there [the walls] for ages . . .

I've been watching them . . . it's a wonder nobody has got the sense to get out of the way.'

Sean Canney, a twenty-two-year-old engineer and freelance photographer, went along the same route as Carlin a few minutes later when there were shots and 'a piece of turf about eighteen inches in front of me disintegrated and bits of dirt flew into the air. A fraction of a second later I heard the first of about six to eight single rifle shots. Some of these hit the walls at the rear of Joseph Place behind me. I have no doubt that these shots were fired from the city walls.'

In fact, the army's plan to contain the marchers included a ring of at least fifteen observers and snipers from the 22 LAD and the 1st Battalion, Royal Anglians in sandbagged positions on the city walls, or in derelict buildings nearby. The snipers had views into the flats' car park, the barricade and Joseph Place, and the army says these soldiers fired a total of nineteen rounds that afternoon.

The snipers' rifles, either SLRs, or the older .303s preferred by military marksmen for their accuracy, were fitted with telescopic sights. Their positions formed a semicircle looking down into the Bogside from beside the Sackville Street Barrier 13 in the north and along the walls to Barrack Street in the south. Their job was to look for gunmen or nail bombers and to shoot to kill, if they could positively identify one who was sufficiently separated from the main body of the crowd not to endanger innocent lives.

This was a most improbable situation even on a normal day patrolling through the Bogside or in Belfast, as veteran army snipers already knew. The most likely event of the day for them – as always for the British soldier on active duty in Northern Ireland – was to be shot at by the IRA and not have an opportunity to respond. Fortunately for the soldiers, the IRA bullets, fired mostly (in the case of the Bogside and Creggan units) from old weapons of questionable accuracy, rarely found their target. The IRA gunmen were hardly ever seen; they took pot-shots on the run and immediately disappeared from view; most of the time the soldiers did not return the fire.

In the case of this day's civil rights march, the difficulty of identifying a gunman in a crowd and then finding him sufficiently isolated to be shot without endangering the lives of others was well appreciated by the soldiers of the other regiments not involved in the arrest operation. There was so much panic, confusion and noise when the Paras came in that what the soldiers saw, or thought they saw, and what they heard, or thought they heard, during the ten minutes of the killings often conflicted – even when they were side by side in the same post.

Sergeant 040 and Gunner 134 of 22 LAD were in the attic of an abandoned typewriter factory near Butcher's Gate. The gunner, who was nineteen, had an SLR with a telescopic sight and a good field of view to the north of the flats. He heard a burst of about eight shots of automatic fire, which he thought came from a Thompson sub-machine gun, as the crowd were coming down William Street – before the Paras launched their arrest operation.

Sergeant 040, older and more experienced, had a different field of view that also overlooked the flats. He heard bangs that he thought were rubber bullets being fired and also thought he heard the sound of automatic fire after the Paras went in, but he was not sure.

The two snipers were in the house from 1.30 p.m. to dusk, changing positions every so often to keep them alert, but neither of them fired a shot.

Nearby, on the wall itself at what is called the Platform, were two gunners 030 and 001, also from the 22 LAD. They were five yards apart looking down on the flats. After the Paras came in, 030 would say that he heard low-velocity shots and saw a youth standing firing a pistol between Blocks 1 and 2 of the flats. He could even see what the gunman was wearing: a brown jacket and faded blue jeans. He had long, dark, well-kept hair. There were up to fifteen people crowding around him and 030 did not shoot for fear of hitting them. He also heard a burst of slow automatic fire, which he thought came from a Thompson sub-machine gun.

Gunner 001 did not see the pistol man, but heard two low-velocity shots that might have come from a pistol, and also what he thought was a Thompson being fired. He was looking over at Glenfada Park, where he heard two bursts of automatic fire. He also saw the muzzle flashes from a gun being fired behind a wooden fence. He called over to 030 and together they watched a paratrooper fire in the direction of the muzzle flashes. Neither of them fired his weapon because at that moment a paratrooper arrived in Glenfada and started firing.

Further south along the wall, near the Walker Monument, four gunners and a lieutenant from 22 LAD manned 'OP Charlie'. Shortly after the Paras began to make arrests, the lieutenant heard two distinct bursts of automatic fire, four rounds and then five or six rounds, which he thought came from a Thompson being fired from the Glenfada Park area. Immediately afterwards he heard the sound of a nail bomb exploding and what sounded like three aimed shots from an SLR.

Gunner 025 was a sniper armed with a .303 fitted with a telescopic sight. Five minutes after the Paras came in he also heard a burst of automatic fire, which he thought came from the Rossville flats, then he heard shots from a low velocity weapon, which he thought was being fired from Glenfada Park. Through his binoculars he thought he saw a man being handed a nail bomb at the Rossville Street barricade and went to grab his rifle, but it had already been taken by the lieutenant who was looking over the wall. Gunner 012, whose job was to watch the Rossville flats through binoculars, thought he saw one of the youths at the Rossville Street barricade with a pistol. Then he heard a burst of low-velocity automatic fire, he thought from Columbcille Court, or Glenfada Park. None of the soldiers at OP Charlie says he fired a shot.

The final observation post manned by 22 LAD on the walls was at Roaring Meg, the great cannon which had been on the City Walls since the 1689 Jacobite siege of Derry. At 4.15, according to Gunner 156, two shots were fired at the post but struck the wall beneath. Ten minutes later he heard a burst of machine-gun fire, which sounded like a Thompson, coming, he thought, from the Rossville flats and at 4.34 two more shots were fired at his post, he thought from St Columb's Wells in the area of the Bogside Inn.

None of the fire directed at 22 LAD posts was returned. But Gunner 156 recorded later, 'A military sniper who was situated about fifty metres away on my left in the attic of a building outside the city walls returned three shots.'

This incident was recorded in the Porter tapes version of the Brigade log as follows: '1615 . . . we just had two shots at one of our patrols on the city wall, 1614.' This was recorded in the Brigade log at 1617 – '4HV shots fired at call sign Q21, 2 shots returned.'

A subsequent message on the tapes read: 'Reference two shots returned at gunman near Bogside Inn, man seen to fall at 1620 hours. One further shot was fired from that area of the Bogside Inn towards Oscar patrol on the wall.'

Zero then asked, 'Reference your report of a man being seen to fall near the Bogside Inn, why was this man fired at?'

The Anglians replied, 'This man was fired at because he fired four shots at us.'

The Bogside Inn was on the corner of Westland Street. It was opposite the Joseph Place houses on the other side of Rossville Street from the flats and the phone box – and about fifty yards from the spot where McGowan and Campbell were shot. If the soldier on the wall had accurately reported where he shot, then his target could not have been either of the two wounded men.

We now come to the last two killings. Paddy Doherty, the DuPont worker who had started the day as a steward at the Bishop's Field, was caught up in the crush in the flats' car park and was doing his best to escape. When the paratroopers started firing he ran from Chamberlain Street to the cover of the low wall, where Father Daly and others were sheltering. Doherty had taken off the white handkerchief he had put round his arm to show he was a steward and tied it over his nose and mouth to help filter out the gas.

The best hope of staying alive, it seemed to this group, was to crawl into the passage between blocks 2 and 3, and either go up the stairs into the flats or out into the forecourt with the shops, and eventually across the forecourt to the alley behind Abbey Place. Joe Carlin, the wine trader, was one of many who had already made their escape.

In the car park the shots were coming in bursts and each time there was a lull more people would leave the wall to go that route – at first along a concrete wall on which someone had written in white paint, 'Join Your Local IRA Unit.' Residents in Joseph Place had left their front doors open, inviting the fleeing marchers inside.

Instead of running along the wall as though he were a fugitive or a gunman, Doherty decided it would be better to crawl. He would be less of a target.

Gilles Peress, the French photographer who had been shot at by Lieutenant N in Eden Place, was now at the low wall as Doherty set out. He photographed him going down into a crawling position and then, in the next frame of Peress's film, Doherty appears to have been shot; Peress thought he might have been hit at this moment because he appeared to be having difficulty crawling. Even so, Peress was not sure if he had been hit.

Peress himself then moved through the passage and started taking pictures again outside Harley's fish and chip shop.

On the second floor of the flats above, Charles McLaughlin, a workmate of Doherty's at DuPont, spotted Doherty 'lying parallel with the front of the flats, facing Fahan Street; in other words, with his feet towards Glenfada Park. He started to crawl on his stomach heading for the alley behind Joseph Place. He was trailing his left leg.'

From his window, McLaughlin yelled, 'For God's sake don't go across, or they'll shoot you.'

But Doherty ignored the warning and continued to crawl.

Two shots rang out. McLaughlin saw the first bullet chip the concrete wall at the end of the forecourt; the second hit Doherty in the buttock. McLaughlin was quite precise: the bullet had struck him high up on the right side of his body. (The entrance wound was on his right buttock.) He put his hand to his side and said in a loud voice, 'They shot me again.' And his head fell to the ground. He dragged himself forward a few feet and then lay motionless, moaning and crying out for help.

The bullet – and only one hit Doherty – had ripped through his body, severing the main artery to the heart, the aorta, and exited below the left nipple. He was bleeding to death.

Donna Friel, a sixteen-year-old technical student, had been in the car park area when the paratroopers opened fire. She ran through the passage and up the stairs on to the balcony, where she was pulled into a flat. From one of the windows overlooking the forecourt she saw a group of men crouched 'at the edge of the Joseph Place flats . . . trying to make their way to the alley at the back of Joseph Place . . . As the group ran forward an elderly man was shot in the leg and fell.' This was Danny McGowan. Friel said the shot came from Glenfada. 'Two of the men crawled back to get him and two ran forward. One of the men got behind his feet and the other at his head. They were crouched down and started to push him in.'

Danny McGowan had regained consciousness and remembered being helped. 'Willy Murray and Tom Hipsley had helped [the wounded] Campbell into a house and they turned me on my back and each took an arm and dragged me along the ground towards the end of the alley. I remember thinking it would ruin my good jacket, which it did; a terrible mess.'

The man at McGowan's feet was left behind. It was Doherty. He seemed to have fainted. Donna Friel called out to him, asking if he was all right. He said he was. 'He then asked me to tell him when he could crawl away to safety and what direction to [go].'

Friel would recall, 'As [Doherty] raised on his left knee as if to crawl a shot came from Glenfada Park area and got him in the hip or back.'

Derrick Tucker, the former British serviceman, was in block 2 of the flats and was able to see into the car park and also across the forecourt towards Abbey Place. He saw Doherty crawl out towards the alley and, when a shot rang out, he gave a kick with his right leg and then lay still.

None of the soldiers in the flats car park say they fired at a man who was crawling through the passage between blocks 1 and 2. The only paratrooper who admits to firing in the direction of the forecourt at a time which coincides with Doherty's shooting is Lance Corporal F. He says he fired two rounds from Glenfada Park at a man in the forecourt who had been firing a pistol. All eye-witnesses say Doherty was unarmed.

The medical question is whether Doherty could have been shot from the car park and, with such a fatal wound, have continued to crawl through to the forecourt and then on to Abbey Place, a distance of perhaps thirty yards? Humans have a remarkable capacity for survival and to keep moving despite fatal injuries; Hugh Gilmore kept running after he had been hit near the rubble barricade. But wherever Paddy Doherty was shot – and by whichever paratrooper – local eyewitnesses agree that a slightly bald man of between forty and fifty came out from the alley and tried to pull Doherty in. He was Paddy Walsh.

He didn't recognize Doherty, even though he knew him well enough and used to see him waiting for his lift to work, but he hadn't seen him in a year and Doherty had grown a droopy moustache. More shots rang out and Walsh had to retreat. Some other men came out, but they too had to go back. Others who had been with him looked on, too terrified to go to his aid.

Walsh crawled out from Joseph Place, waving a handkerchief. He tried to pull Doherty in by the arm, but couldn't manage it. So he turned him over and tried to pull him by the collar of his car coat. The paratroopers opened fire again. Donna Friel yelled at Walsh to get back into the house and he crawled back to Joseph Place.

At the telephone box by the entrance to block 1 of the flats, Barney McGuigan from the Creggan saw Doherty lying there, moaning. McGuigan's instinct was to brave the shots and go to Doherty's aid. He could hear Doherty crying out for help and told the others huddled around the phone box that he couldn't bear to let him die alone. Geraldine Richmond could also hear a man's voice calling. 'I don't want to die alone – somebody help me. God help me.'

The others told McGuigan it was too dangerous to leave the cover of the phone box. But McGuigan said that he could not stand the sound of the man calling any longer and if he went out waving a white hanky they would not shoot him.

He took out his handkerchief and, holding it high above his head and waving it, he moved out towards Doherty's motionless body. He walked out sideways, always looking at the people by the phone box who were calling for him to come back. Richmond could hear bullets whizzing past him.

Then there were two distinct shots. After the first McGuigan turned his body back towards the phone box. Richmond remembered, 'I think he turned his whole body and not just his face. I did not see the bullet hit anything, I just heard it. The second shot hit him and blew his head up like a tomato exploding. I saw his eye come out. I did not see the back of his head.'

He had taken only a few steps when a paratrooper in the Glenfada courtyard opened fire. McGuigan was hit in the back of the head. His body spun round and he fell to the ground, on his back, one leg folded unnaturally under the other, his blood and brains oozing from a large hole beside his right eye and pouring out on to the pavement. Death had been instantaneous.

Soldier F was the only one to have claimed that he fired from the southeast corner of Glenfada Park into the forecourt. This is how he described his shots:

> I then asked 'G' to cover me as I heard pistol shots in the direction of Rossville flats. I approached the south-east corner of Glenfada Park. I got down on one knee. I observed a man with a pistol at the far end of the Rossville flats. I think he was wearing darkish clothes. He had a black object which looked like a pistol in his hand. I then shouted to 'G', 'There's a gunman down here', and took two aimed shots and he fell to the ground. He was in a half-crouching position moving to the right as I shot him.

Lance Corporal F had not mentioned his final shots from Glenfada in his first statement to the military police. Asked why, at the Widgery inquiry, he replied:

> A: At the present time, sir , it slipped my mind what with the other events that happened.
> Q: What other events?
> A: Shooting the other two bombers.

Lance Corporal F had apparently described shooting Paddy Doherty, who was indeed 'crouching moving to the right' when he was shot. If he also shot McGuigan, he did not describe anyone coming out from cover waving a hanky. Other soldiers came close to such a description.

Sergeant 040 of 22 LAD was watching these events with Gunner 134 from the top floor of a derelict building in Magazine Street

Upper on the city walls. They had telescopic sights fitted to the rifles. Sergeant 040 said:

> I then saw a paratrooper on the south-west corner of Glenfada Park. The paratrooper knelt and had his rifle in the aimed position. He was pointing the rifle in my general direction [towards the walls]. I glanced down below along the line of the paratrooper's sight and saw a man who was facing the paratrooper . . .

In three separate statements, Sergeant 040 describes the man facing the paratrooper as either 'waving his arms', 'holding his arms above his shoulders with his fists clenched', or simply 'holding his arms above his shoulders'.

Gunner 134 summed up his day in the derelict house with Sergeant 040:

> From my position I could see down the south side of block 2 [the forecourt], across Rossville Street and the southern side of the courtyard of Glenfada Park. My duty was to look out for snipers or armed civilians and nail bombers. During the day I saw no armed civilians and nail bombers. I did, however, hear a Thompson and explosions like nail bombs.

Lieutenant 227 of 22 LAD, who was in command of OP Charlie on the city walls, also saw a paratrooper in a kneeling position in the south-east corner of Glenfada Park. He then heard two or three pistol shots 'from the area of the Rossville flats' – but not from the south-east corner of block 1. He then saw the kneeling soldier fire two shots into the forecourt.

He saw Barney McGuigan (whom he identified from photographs) fall 'a few paces out from the end of block 1'. He did not mention seeing any weapons on McGuigan. He also saw 'a man, apparently shot in the lower part of his body, dragging himself along by his arms' in the forecourt between the flats and Joseph Place. This could have been Paddy Doherty. Lieutenant 227 looked at this man through his telescopic rifle sight but could see no firearms.

Under cross-examination Lieutenant 227 mentioned that the paratrooper had fired at 'the man with the rifle low and to my right'. But Lance Corporal F never shot at a target with a rifle in the forecourt.

At 4.35 p.m., Major 236 ordered his platoon commanders to cease firing. He gave the order, he would say, 'because the rate of fire at us had generally diminished and the gunmen had generally withdrawn'. The Paras had been shooting live rounds for approximately twenty minutes.

After McGuigan fell, the group by the phone box cried out in horror. Geraldine Richmond saw the blood pumping from McGuigan's head. She screamed and fainted – or 'slumped', as she herself would say later. Sean Canney, the engineer and freelance photographer who was twenty-two years old, was in the group huddled by the phone box. He remembered McGuigan had taken only a few steps before his head exploded and he fell on his back. 'There was a large pool of blood around his head. I have a vivid memory of steam rising from the blood.'

At Free Derry Corner, they could see a Bogside drunk known colloquially as 'Gacko Wacka' walking all on his own in the middle of Rossville Street. He seemed quite oblivious to what was going on around him.

XII

A Token Retaliation

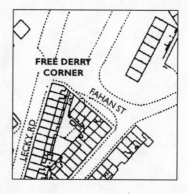

Zero this is 54 Alpha. Call sign Quebec 23 has had
one low-velocity shot fired at him from Fahan
Street, hit one of our soldiers in the flak jacket.
We don't believe he is a casualty. One round was
returned. No hit

8 Brigade radio log, 4.41 p.m.

THROUGHOUT THE AFTERNOON, according to the Brigade radio log, gunmen had fired about a dozen shots at the soldiers on the Derry walls from various positions in the Creggan or the Bogside gas works – favourite sniping positions for the IRA, but far from the action at the Rossville flats. The rounds thudded harmlessly into the ground in front of the posts on the walls. No fire was returned.

At 4.17 p.m., as the Paras were opening fire in the Rossville car park, four high-velocity rounds were reported by Anglians at their call sign Quebec 21 at Long Tower Street. Two shots were returned and one man was seen to fall in the 'area of ' the Bogside Inn.

One minute later, at 4.18 p.m., 22 LAD reported two more shots at their positions on the walls and at 4.21 p.m. another shot was returned. At 4.27 p.m. more shots – the Brigade log does not say how many – were fired at the Anglians from a prefab building. The gunman was not seen. At 4.30 p.m., shots were again fired at this post and one round was returned. At 4.35 p.m., two more shots were fired at the Anglians manning the post in Long Tower Street, and one was returned. At 4.41 p.m., one low-velocity shot was fired at a soldier.

If these shots at the army were accurately recorded, it appears that the IRA commanders, now receiving rumours of killings, were reluctant to put up more than a token resistance.

But after the paratroopers had stopped firing and the stunned marchers were going home, spreading word of what had really happened, the IRA commanders felt that they had to retaliate.

In anger and frustration, both wings of the IRA engaged soldiers from the first battalion of the Royal Anglians manning roadblocks, and snipers south of the city walls – on the periphery of the killing ground – and fired one shot only at the departing paratroopers.

The Officials moved first. In the Creggan, where they had been expecting an army invasion, an Official staff officer and four men jumped into one of their 'liberated' cars – a dark-blue Avenger – that had been parked at the roundabout outside the church at the top of New Road, and now roared down the hill into Westland Street where they were slowed by the crowds going home. At the bottom of Westland Street they turned right into Lecky Road and right again into the small car park behind a block of shops just south of Free Derry Corner.

Three men jumped from the car; one was carrying an M1 carbine with two 'banana' clips with about twenty-five rounds in each and a box of ten rounds. The magazines were not fully loaded as the gun was new and the spring so strong that it had been jamming rounds into the breech. The other two men carried .303 Lee Enfield No.4 rifles. People in the street cheered them on; women shouted at them to be careful.

The man with the M1 concealed beneath a coat went round the back of the Bogside Inn, taking the chance of being spotted from the walls. He immediately took up a firing position on the first-floor balcony of a block of maisonettes just to the west of Free Derry Corner. He had a clear field of fire towards the rubble barricade in Rossville Street, but his M1 jammed. The gunman wrestled with the weapon but could not free it, so he pulled out. He was taken back up the Creggan in an Official IRA car.

A second gunman, possibly one of the Officials armed with a .303, moved into St Columb's Wells towards Long Tower Street, where he came face to face with a soldier from the Royal Anglians who was walking down Barrack Street, investigating an earlier shot at the unit's road block. The gunman and the soldier

224

apparently surprised each other, only a few yards apart. They fired simultaneously, but neither bullet found its mark. The gunman's bullet hit the wall above the soldier's head.

The soldier recocked his weapon and continued down Barrack Street where he came under fire from the third Official gunman. He had slipped into a derelict house in Long Tower Street, near St Columb's Church where, according to one of the many fables about Derry's patron St Columbcille, Jesus once appeared to the saint in the guise of a beggar.

The houses had fallen into disrepair and the doors and windows were bricked up, but over the six months since internment the IRA had knocked holes in the brickwork to use as gunports from which to snipe at army patrols. The Official fired two shots at the Anglian. He missed, but one of his bullets struck the flak jacket of another Anglian soldier positioned further up Barrack Street. The bullet caused no injury. It was the only IRA hit of the day.

The first Anglian soldier saw the muzzle flashes from the IRA position and fired three shots at the gunport. He thought he saw the gunman's body slump over his weapon. He then fired two more shots at two different gunports in the same derelict building to deter the IRA gunman from further sniping.

The IRA man was hit in his right thigh and the right side of his back, but they were only flesh wounds, and possibly caused by ricochets. He lay still, the firing stopped and the Anglians withdrew. The gunman stayed in the house for a few minutes, taking cover from the army helicopter circling overhead, and then retreated back into the Bogside. He was the only known IRA casualty of the day.

The entry in the Brigade log that corresponds to this encounter was at 4.41 p.m., from 1 RANG. It read: '1 LV shot at sldr of 023 from Charlotte Street [at Long Tower and St Columb's Church]. Hit flak jacket. 1 shot returned, no hit claimed, later two shots fired at gunman, no hits recorded.'

In a lull after the first burst of shooting from the Paras, the Provisionals also sent gunmen into the Bogside. Two of their cars – a battered Ford Zephyr and an old Humber – which had been patrolling the Creggan came speeding down Westland Street, the only cars on the road at this time. There were four men in the first car and two in the second. They were dressed in green combat jackets and jeans, and most of them were wearing black berets and armed with rifles and pistols. One of them may have been carrying a Thompson sub-machine gun. They screeched to a stop in the parking area by the Bogside Inn and the driver of the first car burst out of the car with a rifle in his hand. People started saying, 'The Provos are here,' and 'Where have they been all this time?'

In full view of the 'Charlie' observation post and of the army helicopter circling overhead, the Provos opened the boot of the second car and handed out more rifles to a group of young volunteers. The cars roared back up to the Creggan, and returned with reinforcements. The gunmen moved off in the direction of Free Derry Corner.

One of them fired a machine-gun burst at troops on the walls from a position near the Bogside Inn, according to the Brigade log. This was reported by the Royal Anglians at 4.47 p.m.: '1 burst of fire from MG from GR 42531589 at 1645 hrs. 1 round returned, no hit.'

But no more shots were recorded by the army in the area of the Bogside Inn.

One Provo from the first carload, a burly, balding man in his mid-forties, came out of a community hall on the other side of Westland Street. He told his men to withdraw and they started running back, crouched over and went into the hall.

They all reached the hall entrance except for one youth with a .22 rifle who panicked when the army helicopter, which had been circling high above the Bogside, suddenly swooped low over the street. The youth hesitated and people began shouting for him to make a dash for it across the street. One of the residents in the flats opened his front door and beckoned him inside. At the same time a group of people ran over and gathered round the youth, shielding him across the road and into the hall.

Watching the arrival of the IRA were the terrified organizers of the march who had taken refuge in Meenan Square, just beside the Bogside Inn.

People were saying, 'There's the boys.' One man saw three or four with M1 carbines. It seemed terribly inadequate. He saw one gunman fire two or three shots, then dash across Westland Street and disappear. He heard another fire six shots – a pathetic number compared with the army's fusillade, he thought.

The lull from the Paras did not last long. Lance Corporal F and Private G were back in their Pig opposite the end of block 1 and about to move out of the Bogside when their driver, Lance Corporal 036, spotted what he took to be a gunman in a second-floor flat about forty yards away. He had seen the window open at the same time as he heard a shot and although he did not see a weapon, or a muzzle flash, he assumed there was a gunman behind the window. F and G jumped out of the back of the Pig and took up firing positions. F, G and the driver saw the window move again as another shot was fired. In the next few seconds, F fired eight shots at three different windows; in one, he 'saw a movement', in the second he spotted a man with a rifle, and in the third he 'saw a gunman appearing'. G fired a single shot at one window through which he saw 'someone standing slightly back'. No hits were claimed by the soldiers.

At the same time Fulvio Grimaldi was taking pictures from a second-floor flat in block 1 that faced on to Rossville Street. Six shots were pumped through the window.

The army's last shot of the day, according to the Brigade log, was one 7.62 round fired by Soldier Z of 22 LAD who was on duty at Barrier 13 in Sackville Street. Soldier Z said that a shot which came from a gunman in a derelict factory on William Street had struck the wall above his head, sending brick chippings down. Z saw a man on the top floor of the factory, standing at a window with a long straight object in one hand. The man appeared to kneel down and looked in the direction of the barrier. Z took aim and fired one tracer round – dusk was falling – from his SLR. He watched the round and it hit the man somewhere about the middle of his chest. Z would later state that the man 'fell from sight except for a hand hanging from the window'. No one came to help him and he did not move. Z was redeployed five minutes later.

XIII

I'll Never Turn My Back on a Para

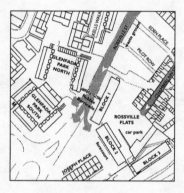

This Para said, 'Get up against the fucking fence'
. . . I said, no, I'll never turn my back on a Para, or
he'll shoot me. He told me, 'I'll fucking shoot you
where you stand', and I said, okay, go ahead. But
you'll have to do it from the front

Winifred O'Brien, on being arrested in Glenfada Park

THE FIRST PERSON to fall into the paratroopers' hands as they stormed across the waste ground in front of the flats was William Doherty, a sturdy grey-haired man of fifty-five who was a dustbin collector. He had been watching the march as it arrived at the William Street barrier and was badly affected when a CS gas canister exploded at his feet. He stumbled round the corner into Rossville Street to recover. Shouts of alarm alerted him to the onrushing troops, 'They're coming in, they're coming in,' and he began running towards the flats.

'I was not so fast on my feet any more and this little Para grabbed me,' Doherty recalled. 'He was certainly Scottish, I knew that well enough for he was abusing me all the time.' Before the eyes of horrified onlookers, the soldier struck Doherty repeatedly round the head with the barrel of his rifle, badly lacerating his scalp.

Charlie Glenn of the Knights of Malta was wearing his grey peaked cap and had a white bag with a big red cross on it when he saw the paratroopers jump out of their armoured cars, hyped up and shouting abuse at the crowd. They raced across the waste ground. Glenn saw Doherty being beaten up. He felt he ought to do something and he yelled at the Para, 'I order you to stop,' whereupon the Para threw Doherty to one side and turned his rifle on Glenn. Then another Para, who seemed to be in charge, came out of the same vehicle and hit Glenn in the chest with the butt of his rifle. He fell to the ground, dazed.

Doherty was kicked and shoved back to the nearest Pig, and hurled in through the rear doors. As he tried to rise, the soldier crashed a rifle butt full into his face, shouting, 'You Irish bastard.'

Alana Burke saw him being hit and lifted off his feet by the force of the blow; seconds later she was knocked flying by one of the armoured cars.

Then Doherty collapsed, blood streaming down his face. As he lay prostrate, a rubber bullet was fired at him from point-blank range, smashing into his left arm.

It happened so quickly that he could not be sure whether the Scottish paratrooper was responsible. The pain was excruciating, but he was afraid to protest 'because if I had, I would surely have been murdered'.

This incident was apparently witnessed by Captain SA8, the commander of the Paras' composite platoon, known as 'Guinness Force', attached to Support Company and consisting of clerks, drivers and storemen. Captain SA8 had come into the waste ground with his men in the canvas-covered four-tonners. As he got out of the truck he would say he noticed about four people who had 'obviously been cut off from the main part of "peaceful marchers"', and 'I shepherded [them] to safety from the open ground'. He then moved to the Rossville flats with Major 236, the Company Commander. 'At this time I saw one of our soldiers fire one rubber bullet from an RUC gun into the back of another APC (armoured car) at point-blank range.'

An Englishman called Stewart Clarke, who had moved to Derry, was thrown into the back of the same Pig as Doherty, bleeding from a smashed nose.

Doherty and Clarke were then hauled out and bundled aboard an army lorry for transport to Fort George, the army post in the Strand Road where prisoners were being documented. Two members of a Military Police 'watchdog' team, armed with 9mm Browning pistols, had followed the snatch squads into the waste ground to document prisoners. They took a note of the two men's names but made no mention of the injuries they had suffered.

From a window of his aunt's home in Kells Walk, twenty-five-year-old Tony D (who withheld his full name) watched the Pigs speed across the waste ground and halt virtually in front of him. He saw a youth in a blue denim jacket and jeans standing alone, apparently bewildered by what was going on around him.

A paratrooper close to the flats signalled to another soldier to arrest him. The second paratrooper ran towards the boy, who seemed to be pleading for mercy. Tony saw the paratrooper who had given the signal run back and hit him behind the head with the butt of his rifle. Then the other one grabbed him and marched him off, hitting him all the way with the muzzle of his rifle.

Brian Johnston, who had been on the march from the Bishop's Field and had purposely avoided the rioting, was caught on the waste ground when 'C' Company came through Barrier 14 in William Street. He started running towards the flats but was suddenly confronted by two Paras whacking people as they ran through a gap in a wire fence where Pilot Row used to be. The Paras appeared to have no interest in arresting people and Johnston saw a group ahead of him trying to get through the gap.

When I was six feet from the soldiers, a fellow ahead of me [was] being hit by the soldiers as he passed through the gap. I then saw the soldier on the right raising his rifle butt again. He was looking at me and appeared to be waiting for me. I thought, Jesus, how am I going to get through without them hitting me on the head?

I remember picking up a soft-drinks can from the ground and throwing it at the soldier on the right to distract him so I could get past. I got past safely. I do not remember the soldier doing anything to me as I passed through the gap.

In Chamberlain Street, Otto Schlindwein, who ran a pharmacy in the Creggan, had almost reached the end of the street where it opened into the Rossville flats car park when the first shots rang out. His friend Raymond Cossum shouted at him, 'Jesus, Otto, they're firing live bullets.'

Schlindwein quickened his pace; there were a lot of scared people running down the street. When he got out into the car park he saw Jack Duddy's body lying on the ground, face down and blood pouring out on to his white shirt. He was about to run out across the car park when he was grabbed by Anna Nelis and asked if he could go to the aid of a woman who had been shot in the leg and taken to 33 Chamberlain Street, where the Nelis family lived.

Inside he saw Peggy Deery, whom he knew, lying on the sofa bleeding profusely from the bullet wound in her leg. He bound up the leg with a blanket and told her she needed an ambulance immediately. One came quickly and he helped put Mrs Deery into it. A group of paratroopers had gathered outside the house and one of them told Schlindwein that he was under arrest. The paratroopers then arrested all the other men who came out of Number 33 – about twenty of them.

They were ordered to march in single file, with their hands on their heads, back up Chamberlain Street until they reached William Street and some waste ground. There they were told to kneel down beside each other, still with their hands on their heads. Schlindwein was hit in the side with a rifle butt. One Para seemed surprised to see anyone of Schlindwein's age on the march and asked how old he was. When he said forty-four, the Para laughed. A few minutes later two Pigs arrived to take the group away. They were told to climb into the back and sit on either side; two paratroopers came with them.

In Glenfada Park, Father Denis Bradley was with about twenty-five people huddled against the gable end when the paratroopers arrested them. Everyone was terrified after they had seen Bradley give the last rites to the dying Michael Kelly. Some of them at the gable wall were crying. One youth, Patrick McGinley, recalled a man of his father's age bent down crying like a baby.

The paratroopers suddenly appeared and at the sight of them – faces blackened, rifles raised – everyone threw up their hands. Almost immediately, the troops set about them. Barry Liddy thought they behaved 'like animals that come from the jungle'. He was struck in the chest with a rifle as he tried to protect Father Bradley.

McGinley was going to make a run for the alley when someone put an arm round his neck and pulled him back. He was shouting, 'Let me go you bastard,' because he thought it was a policeman or a soldier. Then he realized it was Barry Liddy, who probably saved his life.

Among those sheltering in Glenfada was Winnie O'Brien, a forty-four-year-old housewife who was a veteran of civil rights marches – 'non-violent that is'. Her father, brothers and husband were all past or present soldiers in the British army. O'Brien had run into Glenfada Park to escape the CS gas and, when shooting broke out nearby, she crouched down behind a flimsy wooden fence. She could hear people shouting that the Paras were coming in and she said a silent prayer.

Suddenly there were shots and O'Brien found herself sprawled on the pavement beneath a heavily built man. At the very moment that Paddy O'Donnell threw himself down to protect her he was shot in the shoulder. He went to put his hankerchief against the wound, but O'Brien had a clean new one in her pocket. She opened O'Donnell's coat and shirt, and pressed it against his shoulder, getting blood on her hands.

Just then they looked up, to see a paratrooper standing over them with a rifle. He ordered them to move, but O'Brien took great exception to the way the wounded O'Donnell was manhandled: 'This Para said "get up against the fucking fence" . . . I said no, I'll never turn my back on a Para or he'll shoot me. He told me "I'll fucking shoot you where you stand" and I said, okay, go ahead. But you'll have to do it from the front.'

Those left at the gable were rounded up, ordered to face the wall and to put their hands on it.

Standing against the wall by Mrs O'Brien was the priest Terence O'Keeffe. He and Father Bradley – who unlike him was wearing a clerical collar – were dragged back by soldiers whenever they attempted to go to the aid of the dead and wounded lying nearby. One Para stuck a gun into Bradley's face as a warning to stay put.

All the prisoners from Glenfada were moved towards William Street, running with hands on their heads while soldiers struck at them with rifles and screamed abuse. Nobody seemed particularly interested in taking Bradley along, but he followed on all the same. He noticed that Paddy O'Donnell looked very dazed and shaky, and tried to draw the paratroopers' attention to his condition. But when O'Donnell turned as if to leave, a Para batoned him, cutting his head open.

Bradley was livid, yanking up O'Donnell's jacket to show his bullet wound.

An officer wearing a red beret gave permission for O'Donnell to leave. Bradley ushered him away to the office of City Radio Cabs, where the owner of a private car agreed to drive him to Altnagelvin. Bradley took the opportunity to head back to Glenfada Park and help with other casualties.

The rest of the prisoners were loaded into a four-ton army truck and driven off towards Fort George. They were forced to kneel facing the front, crushed up against each other, and some were beaten by the soldiers. Father O'Keeffe was appalled by the paratroopers' jubilant mood: they were boasting that they must have killed at least fifty people.

During the journey Winnie O'Brien made her presence felt again. There was blood on the floor of the lorry and a soldier dipped his hand into it, then brought it to her face. O'Brien never flinched: there was blood on her own hands from O'Donnell's wound and she held them up defiantly. She asked the soldier if he thought he was dealing with a bunch of ignorant wogs.

'You lot are worse than fucking wogs,' he replied, threatening her with his baton. 'If you don't shut your fucking mouth, you'll be eating soft food for a month.'

With the arrests in Chamberlain Street and Glenfada Park, plus the handful picked up on the waste ground as they came in, the Paras had scooped up between thirty to forty people, including many older marchers of the type Captain SA8 had earlier 'shepherded away'. In the next group detained, the Paras even picked up some paramedics and charged them with riotous behaviour.

By 4.30 p.m., the Knights of Malta teams were running out of medical supplies and Bernard Feeney was sent to collect fresh kits from an ambulance parked nearby. On the way he fell in with another KoM worker, Charlie McMonagle. As they approached William Street, paratroopers ordered them to stand against a Pig to be frisked.

Their satchels were ransacked and the contents strewn around: when Feeney tried to pick them up he got a boot in the side. The Paras were taunting them about the number of people they had already killed. At that moment an army chaplain appeared and asked why the paramedics were being held.

The Reverend Iain Baillie was attached to the Anglians with the honorary rank of major and was on good terms with the first-aid teams. As the violence in Derry had intensified over the previous months, he was often at the scene of rioting. One day when the CS gas was particularly bad, he invited the KoM commandant, Leo Day, and his two daughters into the back of a troop carrier for a cup of tea.

Baillie gave Feeney and McMonagle permission to move on, but the paratroopers ordered them to stay leaning on the Pig and, called them 'Fenian cunts'. Baillie eventually managed to secure their release and walked away with them, advising the badly shaken pair to try to forget what had happened.

At the top of William Street they found Jim Norris, another KoM worker being threatened by a Para radio operator. A cocked rifle was held to his head after he had called the soldier 'an English bastard'.

Norris had already been through a lot that afternoon. The first casualty he had treated was spitting out broken teeth after being struck full in the face by a CS gas canister, the second was Kevin McElhinney bleeding to death in the entrance to the flats.

Iain Baillie persuaded the paratroopers to release Norris and the KoM workers did not see him again that day. But later in the evening, with darkness falling, Father Bradley was making his way to St Eugene's Cathedral – 'I wanted to be alone for a while' – when he came across Baillie talking to Leo Day. Although Bradley was reluctant to be too hard on a fellow priest, he blurted out that what had taken place was nothing less than an army massacre.

Baillie protested that he had always tried to influence troops to be more sympathetic towards the Catholic community and would not tolerate Derry people being mistreated by anybody, the army included. Before the priests parted, Baillie suggested they said an 'Our Father' together. Bradley agreed willingly: 'I was thankful . . . because it was difficult to pray when people were dying and things were happening so fast.'

The first of the civilians arrested by the Paras, twenty-nine in all, arrived at the Fort George centre around 4.50 p.m. Most of them had been detained in and around Glenfada Park. Exhausted and emotionally drained, some were still feeling the effects of CS gas, others were in shock from injuries. All were understandably apprehensive about what awaited them.

They were met by armed soldiers and a pair of Royal Army Veterinary Corps dog handlers, whose four Alsatians barked furiously and strained at the leash. Inside a compound divided by a barbed-wire fence were a contingent of the Coldstream Guards and a Military Police unit. RUC officers were standing by to handle prisoners once the paratroopers responsible for their arrest provided identification.

Most of the prisoners were bundled unceremoniously off the lorry and forced to run between two lines of paratroopers wielding batons, rubber hoses and rifles. Barry Liddy was reminded of a film where Red Indians made their captives run the gauntlet. Liddy knew Fort George inside out from his work there as a barman in the forces canteen. During the trip there, he was kneeling behind a boy who he reckoned was aged no more than thirteen or fourteen, alone and very nervous. He asked Liddy to look after him and he promised to do so.

As Winnie O'Brien went to clamber down from the lorry, a soldier she thought was a Coldstream Guardsman addressed her as madam, advising her to mind her step. A paratrooper intervened, saying 'fucking chuck her out' and gave her a hefty shove. O'Brien was separated from the rest of the prisoners and searched very politely by a female police officer. Although she was refused permission to use the toilet during the three hours she was held, O'Brien was not mistreated. Released at around 8 p.m., she walked home.

Most of the men were forced to remain spreadeagled in the search position or with hands held behind their heads. Some stayed like that for between two to three hours. It was bitterly cold until a Coldstream Guards officer – 'the only decent human being in uniform' in one prisoner's judgement – told them they could relax. Electric heaters were produced and urns of tea laid on.

The injured William Doherty was now in such a state that Charlie Glenn asked for permission to treat him on the spot. Doherty eventually agreed to let an army doctor put seven stitches into his head wound and thanked him for being gentle. Yet despite being in deep shock and great pain – his arm was black with bruising from the rubber bullet for a month – he was sent back to join other prisoners leaning against a wall. In a moment of compassion, a soldier told him not to bother if it hurt too much.

At around 9 p.m., paratroopers arrived to identify the people they had arrested earlier, as required by law. As prisoners lined up to be photographed alongside them, they were systematically assaulted. A teenage boy was struck in the groin and abdomen so hard that he collapsed and could not get up. O'Keeffe saw him kicked to his feet and placed against the wall to keep him upright.

Two youths were forced to stand for forty-five minutes with their heads strained so far back that their faces were uncomfortably close to electric heaters mounted on tall stands. They were struck every time they tried to shift position, O'Keeffe said. One was told to open his mouth if he wanted a drink: a paratrooper then spat into it.

Charlie Glenn of the KoM, who had been knocked around by the paratroopers when the scoop-up began, was eventually arrested.

After Jackie Duddy died, Glenn had felt that he should make a statement to the police about how Duddy was shot and that he was unarmed. He tried to get through into the centre of town, but all routes were barred. At one barrier he gave his name to an RUC constable who advised Glenn to go to the police headquarters in Victoria Barracks. Then he radioed them:

> There's a Lance Corporal Knights of Malta making his way to Victoria now. Apparently, he said he had witnessed it [Duddy's death] and he's making certain allegations involving the military. Maybe you'd tell all the serials. He's blood all over him, his hands etc and they might think it came from something else.

Glenn did not go to Victoria Barracks. He looked dishevelled and was covered with Duddy's blood. He joined up with another paramedic, and they were stopped by Paras by St Eugene's Cathedral and frogmarched back down William Street, shoved into a taxi and taken with a Para escort on a short drive to a point where military police were herding people into a four-tonner. They were searched and Glenn's first-aid bag and his glasses were confiscated. One of the military policemen said, 'Any money is mine.' Then they were taken by lorry with others to Fort George.

As they got out of the lorry, there were two lines of five or six soldiers forming a corridor between the vehicle and the door to one of the buildings. Glenn recalled, 'We had to run a gauntlet of these soldiers who attacked us with their guns as we ran past. I was hit in the thigh with a muzzle of a gun.

'It was terribly noisy as we entered the building since the Paras were screaming at the tops of their voices and we could hear dogs barking fiercely. It sounded like hell.'

Inside, they were made to stand with their fingertips touching the walls. Glenn could hear thuds and groans from people standing behind him. He never looked back for fear of getting another hiding. Glenn was indignant that none of the other soldiers present nor the police attempted to prevent the Paras assaulting prisoners.

Others found the RUC's conduct more creditable. O'Keeffe singled out one sandy-haired sergeant for his politeness and consideration towards the civilians. The same officer warned a paratrooper aiming kicks at a prisoner that he must not lay a finger on anyone in police custody.

The identification process was a farce, with Paras peering through the barbed wire and picking out people seemingly at random. The soldier who 'claimed' O'Keeffe, a Lance Corporal, was aggrieved to discover that he was a priest. In a pronounced London accent, he asked why he had not been wearing a dog collar. 'I wear my fucking uniform and you should wear yours.'

The paratrooper who identified Charlie Glenn and Sean McDermott could not provide details of the time or place of their arrest, so a Military Police NCO composed his own account for the charge sheet. An RUC officer had to prompt the same soldier when he dithered over describing the offence he saw them committing. He finally decided that they had been among a crowd throwing stones.

Two more groups of prisoners were driven into Fort George during the evening, among them the men arrested at 33 Chamberlain Street. None of them was assaulted while they were there, although Kevin Leonard, a thirty-one-year-old postman, found the army guard dogs so terrifying that he was actually relieved to discover the police were present. When the truck carrying Leonard arrived, one Para told the handlers, 'There's plenty of fresh meat here for you.'

It was near midnight when the last prisoners at Fort George were processed and all of those under arrest were allowed to leave. Charlie Glenn demanded, and received, an RUC escort to walk him out past the Paras.

A Coldstream Guard took him to the gate. 'As we came to the door of the building, the guard turned to me and said, "Don't worry, Coldstreams aren't Paras."'

A small boy who had not been identified by any soldier – probably the lad whom Liddy befriended – asked the army for a lift back to the Creggan as he was scared of being picked up again. A Military Police staff sergeant drove him as far as Craigavon Bridge, where he got out and walked.

Forty-four of the people rounded up by the paratroopers were eventually charged with riotous or disorderly conduct and remanded to appear at the Londonderry Petty Sessions. In normal circumstances, Chief Superintendent Lagan would have decided whether prosecutions should follow. Instead, he forwarded all the arrest files to RUC headquarters for further consideration.

Lagan did not want to bring anyone before the courts. He felt this would only fuel the intense anger among Derry's Catholics. In the public interest, he argued, the events of 30 January should be allowed to recede from the public mind.

The Chief Constable considered that, where sufficient evidence existed, proceedings should go ahead or hooligans would be encouraged to continue rioting 'without retribution'. Among those he wanted to prosecute were William Doherty, Barry Liddy, James McDermott and three juveniles. No action was recommended against George Nelis, Otto Schlindwein, Charlie Glenn or Father O'Keeffe. Winnie O'Brien was never charged with any offence.

It was not until August 1972 that the Director of Public Prosecutions ruled that no evidence would be offered against anyone arrested on 30 January. Summons that had already been issued were withdrawn with permission of the court in Derry. All the arrest files were returned to the Chief Constable's office.

The paratroopers who had remained in 33 Chamberlain Street searched the house from top to bottom, poking around behind an electric fire and rummaging through cupboards and drawers. Nothing was found and the Paras finally withdrew. Anna and Margaret Nelis left their mother in the house and went out, intent on lodging a complaint about the army's conduct and discovering where the men arrested had been taken (they knew nothing yet about the killings so close by).

Walking towards William Street, the sisters encountered a very tall officer (about six foot four, they thought) in a wine-coloured beret and a string cord tied loosely round his neck, whom they took for a senior commander because of his bearing and the deferential entourage around him. Their attempt to talk to him was waved aside. Undeterred, they found another officer in front of Barrier 14, wearing a red beret and camouflage jacket, with longish hair by army standards.

By now very concerned about their brother, they asked him where George and the others could be. He was responsive and suggested they should inquire at the RUC's headquarters on Foyle Road and warned them to take care because there was still shooting in the area. At Victoria Barracks, Anna and Margaret learned that everyone under arrest had been taken to Fort George. It was only while watching a television documentary on the twentieth anniversary of Bloody Sunday that they realized the two officers they had approached were General Ford and Lieutenant Colonel Wilford.

During the short journey to the prisoner processing centre, George Nelis and his brother-in-law George O'Neill were threatened repeatedly by a paratrooper who boasted that he had already killed four men while serving in Belfast. 'I shot the first through the head, the second I shot through the chest, the third I shot in the privates and he died slowly . . . the fourth I just shot in the head.' Nelis was told that he would not live to see another day.

George Nelis would later submit a formal complaint about the soldier's behaviour to RUC headquarters in Derry. He assured the police that he would be able to identify the man in question and an investigation was opened under Chief Superintendent Lagan's supervision. A Private Davidson from 'C' Company was interviewed at the battalion's new base in West Germany.

He denied bragging about killing people in Belfast or threatening Nelis. He insisted that he had never shot anybody, but had himself been wounded in the leg in Northern Ireland. The Para also denied swearing at anyone during the arrest operation.

Like other 'C' Company soldiers, he claimed that the snatch squads had chased rioters into the Nelis house and arrested those whom they recognized. His platoon sergeant acknowledged that some prisoners were brusquely handled. Any swearing was in response to abuse from civilians (and no foul language was used in the presence of women). Lagan ultimately recommended that it would not be in the best public interest to prosecute any of the soldiers involved.

At 5.43 p.m., an entry in the 8 Brigade log read:

SITREP [Situation Report] 1 Para
1. When launched attacked from 3 directions, Little James Street, through barrier 14 and from West.
2. Chased hooligans down as far as low building at Rossville Flats.
3. At this stage came under fire. Fire fight occurred – Para went firm in area. Taken till present to reorg on original line. Full reports of shooting incidents to follow.
4. During fight identified two snipers, shot them and recovered their bodies from outside Rossville Flats.
5. Injuries to 1 Para; 1 man bad back injury having fallen over wall plus two men suffering from acid burns. Acid thrown from Rossville Flats. No of arrests approx 50.

XIV

For God's Sake Hurry Up, I'm Dying

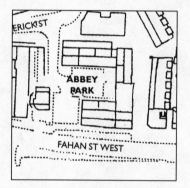

A car has just pulled up to block figure 20. In the car was one dead man and one wounded man.

8 Brigade radio log, 4.30 p.m.

AT 4.30 P.M. a platoon of the Royal Anglians manning a barrier in Barrack Street, to the south of the Rossville flats, saw a group of between thirty and forty people approaching from the direction of the Bogside. Most were smartly dressed women and children; they were on their way to church, they said, and could the barbed wire strung across the road be moved to let them through?

The Anglians were tense, on their guard: shots had recently been fired in the area. The platoon commander at first refused to allow the group to pass, but after some bad-tempered exchanges he relented and instructed his men to clear the way. At that moment two Ford Cortinas, one pale-blue, the other white with a red side flash, swung into Barrack Street and drove briskly up to the barrier.

A third car, an ancient Hillman, then appeared and drew up alongside the Cortinas. The front-seat passenger in the blue Cortina shouted something like, 'Open the fucking barrier, we're late for work.'

When the soldiers motioned him to wait, the passenger called out, 'We've got a dying man in the back here.' The soldiers immediately surrounded the car and ordered the driver to switch off the engine and get out with his passengers. As the Anglians moved to check the two Cortinas, the front-seat passenger in the blue car flung open his door and bolted towards the Bogside.

The soldiers fired a rubber bullet at him and it glanced off his shoulder. The women and children still milling around the barrier began to scream. The Hillman, containing a middle-aged couple, reversed smartly back down Barrack Street and disappeared round the corner. Four men in the Cortinas were hustled up against a wall in the search position, legs apart, hands on the wall, while other soldiers cautiously examined each car.

In the blue one they found Joseph Friel, the Inland Revenue clerk who had been shot in Glenfada Park. He was sprawled across the back seat, his shirt-front drenched with blood, fully conscious but in shock. The second Cortina appeared to have a faulty handbrake and was rolling gently backwards; a soldier grabbed a wing mirror to bring it to a stop. As others came to help, they discovered what appeared to be a dead body on the back seat. It was Gerald Donaghy, the last person shot in Glenfada Park: he was lying motionless, his face ashen, eyes shut.

The car carrying Friel had been borrowed from a neighbour of the Murrays in Lisfannon Road, where Friel was taken after he was shot.

They were going to run him across the border to the hospital in Letterkenny, but he insisted on being taken to Altnagelvin; it was quicker by half an hour and he believed he was dying. James Deehan volunteered to drive him there. Eugene O'Donnell, who worked with Friel at the tax office, and Maddis Morrisson agreed to go along with him. They had set off down St Columb's Wells and then had turned into Barrack Street. Donaghy had arrived at the Barrack Street barrier in the back of Raymond Rogan's car.

It was clear to all who attended Donaghy that he was in a very bad way. Leo Young – brother of John Young who had been shot at the barricade – was the first to reach him. 'His face was pointing upwards and the front of his guts were hanging out, so you could see what he had for dinner,' Young recalled. He opened Donaghy's shirt and saw a wound in his stomach.

Aided by three others, Young carried Donaghy into 10 Abbey Court, Raymond Rogan's home, where he was laid on the carpet in the living room with his feet up on a stool. Rogan had been on the march but peeled off as it reached William Street, fearing there could be serious trouble and worried about his wife and five young children. From his house, he saw people running in panic, then he noticed two bodies near his front door.

Rogan could see that Donaghy was seriously hurt, although there was not a lot of blood. Kevin Swords, a doctor from England who had come to Derry for the march, had helped bring Donaghy in and now examined him carefully, checking eyes and pulse, and feeling beneath his jaw. He and Mrs Rogan searched him for identification, turning out his pockets. All they found was a religious medallion.

Swords thought Donaghy, who let out an occasional groan, might survive if he could be got to Altnagelvin fast. Rogan said he would drive him there in his own car, and Leo Young agreed to go with him. Mrs Rogan said a prayer over Donaghy and placed some rosary beads in his hand. He was laid carefully across the back seat of the car, wrapped in a yellow candlewick bedspread, his head cradled in Young's lap. Rogan was understandably edgy and floored the accelerator along the same route as the car containing Friel.

What happened after the two Cortinas were stopped by the Anglians would be hotly disputed. The soldiers regarded the incident as a routine 'stop and search' that ended with drivers and passengers being arrested and the two men with gunshot wounds driven away in the cars for medical treatment. There was no army brutality, no intimidation, no threats.

But the civilians told a very different story. James Deehan was yanked out of the car so fast that he had no time to put on the handbrake. After his front-seat passenger, Maddis Morrisson, ran away – he was the one hit by a rubber bullet – Deehan was spreadeagled against a wall. A soldier struck him on the head with the butt of his rifle, inflicting a nasty cut. Deehan was extremely frightened by the soldier's behaviour. He recalled him saying, 'I want to shoot you, go on and run, we want to shoot you.' Other soldiers were yelling encouragement, urging him to shoot.

As Leo Young was pulled from his Cortina, where he was sitting beside Donaghy, he asked a soldier, 'What about that dying young fellow?' The soldier replied, 'Let the bastard die.' Young called him an animal and was immediately shoved hard up against some railings. He was warned that if he even blinked, he would get his head blown off.

When Raymond Rogan tried to explain that they were taking Donaghy to hospital, a rifle was raised to his head and a soldier told him, 'One stiff is not enough.' Rogan was used to dealing with the army: as chairman of his local tenants association, he was often called upon to defuse tense situations. He once got a letter of thanks from 8 Brigade headquarters after preventing rioters from dropping a concrete block on the head of an officer knocked down during a confrontation. Now, hands raised as he faced the wall, he had no idea what would happen next.

In the first Cortina Friel was panicking; he was desperate to get to hospital. The Anglians decided to take him to their medical officer on the Craigavon Bridge. When Soldier 104 got into the driving seat, Friel begged, 'For God's sake, hurry up, I'm dying.' They set off for the two-minute drive to the bridge, pausing to collect an RUC escort.

En route, Soldier 104 would claim that Friel had complained about the pain from his wound. 'If you didn't play with guns you wouldn't get hurt,' the soldier claimed to have replied. According to 104, Friel then confessed that he had been carrying a gun when he was hit, but had not fired it and swore that he would never again do such a thing. Friel would later deny vehemently that the alleged conversation ever took place and the RUC officer in the car was never questioned about this.

At the Anglians' first-aid post, an army doctor, a Captain, dressed Friel's wound. Then he was put in a Pig for transfer to Altnagelvin. Another of the wounded, Patrick Campbell, who had been shot in the back making for Joseph Place, had come to the bridge in a private car, which had also been stopped at the Barrack Street barrier. He was put in beside Friel. Campbell was so hot there was steam coming off his coat and Friel thought he must be close to death; the two clasped each other and began to cry.

Gerald Donaghy was also driven to the bridge position where the same army doctor, checked his colour, pupils, breathing and pulse before concluding that he was dead. Then he patched up Friel and Campbell, after which he returned to examine Donaghy more closely. This time he pulled up his shirt and vest, and unzipped the top of the jeans without moving the body from the back seat.

The Captain noticed nothing unusual about the corpse, but five minutes later he heard someone, possibly one of the RUC officers on the spot, saying that a nail bomb had been found on Donaghy. He decided to make no further examination until an army bomb disposal man had seen the body. An Ammunition Technical Officer (ATO), traditionally nicknamed 'Felix', was summoned over the military radio net.

The police also called in their own experts. Shortly after 4.50 p.m., the RUC radio net relayed the following messages:

Delta 7 to November: Send an experienced police officer to the bridge. There is a body there with a nail bomb in his pocket. We want the continuity of the rules of evidence to be maintained.

November to Delta 7: Inspector Bell is on the Bridge, he can deal with that. Suggest you get in touch with him. Over.

The police at the bridge (India 23) then confirmed that 'Felix' had been requested and asked for an RUC photographer to be sent to the scene as quickly as possible.

The police officer who inspected Donaghy's body was a detective sergeant in 'N' Division. He would say that he found a cream-coloured object sticking from the right-hand trouser pocket: observing it more closely, he could see that it looked like a nail bomb enclosed in masking tape. 'Felix' arrived a few minutes later and searched the car for booby traps before turning his attention to Donaghy.

'Felix' claimed later that he had immediately spotted a nail bomb in Donaghy's right-hand trouser pocket and found three more, one in the other pocket of his jeans and one in each of the pockets of his denim jacket. Each bomb contained about a quarter of a pound of high explosive, a two-inch fuse, Number Six detonator and an assortment of nails, all wrapped in sticky tape. While photographers from the army's Special Investigation Branch and the RUC took pictures, 'Felix' removed the explosive components, then handed the bombs over to the detective sergeant.

The journalist from *The Times*, John Chartres, had been invited into the Anglians' post by the unit's press liaison officer and was shown Donaghy's body. Chartres saw one nail bomb – which he could recognize from previous experience – projecting from the jacket pocket of the corpse.

Were the bombs planted on Donaghy's body? None of the civilians who came into contact with him before he was taken to the bridge had seen any sign of a nail bomb. Rogan knew how dangerous such devices were and would never have taken Donaghy into his house if he suspected he was carrying one. Dr Swords had searched him with Mrs Rogan and neither found anything: Swords was certain he would have seen bulky objects in the dying man's close-fitting denim jeans and jacket.

The Anglian soldier who drove Donaghy to the bridge saw nothing in his pockets, even though he leant into the car to feel for a pulse before the medical officer arrived.

The key interval was the five-minute gap between the medical captain's first examination, when he saw nothing unusual about the dead youth, and his return to conduct a second examination.

During this brief period it appears that the body was under the sole control of the RUC.

Only Soldier 104 claimed to have seen a nail bomb on Donaghy before Felix searched him. He said at first that this was immediately after the Cortinas were stopped in Barrack Street, when he noticed it protruding from the front pocket of Donaghy's trousers.

But 104 later changed his story, admitting that he had not looked into the car carrying Donaghy until *after* it arrived at the bridge. It was only then that he saw a bulge in the dead youth's pocket and something protruding slightly. He heard other soldiers talking about nail bombs and realized that this must have been what Donaghy was carrying. He could not explain the discrepancy in his original account.

Especially puzzling is the nail bomb that was said to have been found in the left pocket of Donaghy's denim jacket. The bullet that killed Donaghy went through the lower part of that left pocket. The bomb, made of gelignite wrapped around nails, was four and a half inches long and almost two inches in diameter. If the bomb was deep inside the pocket – as the forensic scientist who examined the jacket in 1972 concluded that it must have been to remain hidden for so long – then the bullet must have hit it.

If that is the case, the bomb would surely have shown marks of having been struck – and it even could have exploded on impact with the bullet. Official photographs of the bombs said to have been found on Donaghy show they were made of a nitroglycerine-based explosive known as Gelamex, which is among the more impact sensitive explosives. The forensic scientists did not describe the condition of the bomb found in the left jacket pocket and a police photo of the four bombs (after they had been defused) appear to show no bullet damage.

Gerald Donaghy's body was finally removed from the Cortina at 6.30 p.m.; two hours after the car had been stopped at the Barrack

Street barrier. 'Felix' blew the lock off the boot to Rogan's car as part of his routine search, but nothing was found. Rogan subsequently received compensation for the damage.

The four men arrested at the Barrack Street barrier – Young, Deehan, Rogan and O'Donnell – were eventually taken to the Anglians' tactical headquarters at the bridge. Their clothes were removed for testing with a hand-held 'gelly sniffer' for contact with explosives. After being photographed and giving a statement, they were transferred to RUC headquarters. All except Young were later released without being charged.

Young spent the night at the Magilligan internment centre, where RUC Special Branch officers questioned him at length before releasing him (he was not charged either). During the interrogation the police had asked how many brothers he had. Young said two, but was told no, only one because 'we got one of them yesterday'. That was how he discovered John had been killed.

The first emergency calls for an ambulance reached the despatchers at Altnagelvin Hospital in the Waterside at 4.15 p.m. The duty crew was directed to Chamberlain Street to pick up a woman (Peggy Deery) with a serious leg injury. Driver William Wilson, and his partner, Norman McElhinney, wove around blocked-off roads until troops at the Castle Gate barrier waved them into Waterloo Street.

The first casualty they found was Jackie Duddy. Father Daly and his helpers had finally escaped from the shooting in the flats' car park and had carried Duddy's body down Chamberlain Street. Round the gable end the little group bumped into John Bierman of BBC TV, with his crew. Daly was never so relieved to see anybody. But soldiers were also there.

Willy Barber, who was helping to carry Duddy, realized he had three rubber bullets in his pocket and he didn't want to be caught with them. He gave them to some girls who were standing in a doorway. 'Keep these for me and I'll collect them tomorrow,' he told them. 'I want them as souvenirs.'

Barber saw a friend and yelled, 'Have you got a car?' And when his friend said 'no' Barber screamed at him irrationally, 'Christ, you never have anything when you're needed.'

It was not until Daly reached the corner of Harvey Street that he felt they were safe. They laid Duddy down on the pavement and Willy Barber took off his jacket and put it under Duddy's head. The others removed their coats and put them round him.

Barber yelled at the soldiers: 'You've killed a fourteen-year-old kid. I hope you're proud of yourselves. I've youngsters growing up. And if this was mine, I'd know how I'd feel. Have you youngsters? How do you feel?'

The soldiers didn't reply.

In nearby Waterloo Street, someone was shouting: 'There's a fourteen-year-old boy shot.' And a voice – it was impossible to tell from where – yelled, 'Keep quiet, or you'll be next.'

Barber yelled at the soldiers again, 'You've killed a fourteen-year-old kid.'

This time one of them replied, 'It wasn't us, it was the Paras.'

Barber could not control himself. He shouted, 'I used to have respect for the British army. I knew quite a few Anglians and they were a decent bunch. But these are murderers.'

A non-commissioned officer tried to pacify Barber.

The Royal Green Jackets manning the barricade and the local 22 LAD commander were still uncertain what had really happened. They were inclined to believe a rumour – from where is not clear – that Duddy had been shot the day before and was a plant.

At 4.35 p.m. 8 Brigade headquarters received the following message from 22 LAD: 'One child's body brought out and dumped on the street. People accused [Barrier] 14 and 15 of shooting child. Not accurate . . . '

The RUC sent the same report: 'We have had a report that a

fourteen-year-old child has been shot dead. He's lying down on the road somewhere . . . by the way it was a pressman who passed that on . . . '

At that moment the officer who had been hit on the chin at the William Street Barrier 14 came up to Barber and said, 'If you need assistance, we'll give it you. If you want an ambulance, we'll get you one.'

Barber did not know that an ambulance was already on its way and was less than a minute away. He screamed at the officer, 'He's dead, he's dead . . . it's no use.'

He paused and then blurted, 'It was a non-violent march.'

'How could non-violent marchers throw stones?' the officer asked. 'How did I get that?' he continued, pointing to the graze on his chin.

'Stones are commonplace in a town like this,' said Barber.

When they laid Duddy's body on the pavement, Father Daly thought he was dead, but he rushed to a house in Harvey Street and asked the owner, Mrs McClusky, to phone for an ambulance.

Then he went back and knelt beside Duddy with the others, and said a prayer for him. There was nothing more they could do. The ambulance came and took Duddy's body away. And a woman asked Father Daly inside her house for a cup of tea.

At 33 Chamberlain Street, the Nelis family's house, a Knights of Malta volunteer, Majella Doherty, was pressing a clean towel to the gaping wound at the back of Mrs Deery's leg, but she was haemorrhaging continuously. Her leg was in such a mess that they could not find an entry wound.

As there was no telephone in the house, Anna Nelis went out to call an ambulance from the home of the Donahue family on the High Street. She found several other people there trying to get help for gunshot casualties. When she got back there was a wounded man lying in the backyard, who she discovered later was Michael Bridge.

Deeply concerned about Mrs Deery, Anna left the house again to see if the ambulance was coming. She found a Pig parked directly outside with two soldiers, whom she later recognized as paratroopers from their winged insignia, standing beside it. Both wore helmets, their faces darkened; one was stocky, hyped up, shouting and swearing loudly.

Asked by Anna to radio for an ambulance immediately, he said, 'Let the whore bleed to death.' He was no more concerned about Bridge. 'Let them all die.'

Afterwards he announced that 'every fucking pig of an Irishman is under arrest'. James McDermott warned him to watch his language. The Para immediately struck him several times with a baton.

Michael Bridge's thigh wound had been dressed by Charles McMonagle, the KoM worker, but he was still in great pain. A Para sergeant booted open the back door to the yard and asked what was going on. Bridge pulled back the blanket covering him to show where the bullet had hit. 'You shot me, that's what,' he replied.

Despite the hostility of some soldiers, an ambulance from Altnagelvin got through to Chamberlain Street and another soon followed. Paras helped to carry out Bridge and Mrs Deery. According to Margaret Nelis, one remarked, 'Are you not dead yet, mate?' as the stretchers passed.

Deery's wound was so severe that surgeons feared the onset of gangrene was inevitable and scheduled the amputation of her leg. In the haste to operate, she was inadvertently given the wrong type of blood. Unconscious and close to death, Deery was rushed to a specialist hospital unit in Belfast, where she spent the next eight weeks.

Her GP, Dr Donal MacDermott, pointed out that if she had received the correct blood, the operation to amputate her leg would probably have gone ahead.

As Michael Bridge was being loaded into the ambulance he saw a woman, whose name he did not know, haranguing the soldiers. Margaret O'Reilly had been standing in Chamberlain Street with her sister and brother-in-law when he was hit in the face by a rubber bullet. He was being treated by a Knights of Malta worker as the Pigs came roaring on to the waste ground. O'Reilly had fled in panic into the nearest house, which was Number 33.

O'Reilly asked one soldier why he smiled when Mrs Deery and Bridge were being carried into the ambulance. 'Because it's a laugh,' he told her. Seeing men arrested in the house being shoved around, O'Reilly lost her temper and shouted at the troops to leave them alone. Bridge eventually persuaded her to leave with him in the ambulance before she got into serious trouble.

Jean Donohue, a qualified nurse, was on her way to help with Mrs Deery but arrived just as the stretchers were brought out. The soldiers were boasting about killing civilians. One told Donahue that it was not nurses who were needed, but blood donors.

The first wounded civilian to turn up for treatment at Altnagelvin was John Johnston, who had been hit with Damien Donaghy by the first Para shots of the afternoon in William Street. Donaghy and Johnston had been bundled into the home of the Shields family in nearby Columbcille Court. There they were attended by Dr Raymond McClean and the Knights of Malta paramedic, Eibhlin Lafferty.

McClean had quickly established that Donaghy's femur was smashed by the bullet that went straight through his thigh. Johnston's wounds were not too serious, he concluded, but his history of a heart condition made it imperative to get him to hospital immediately. Father Joseph Carolan of St Mary's Church in the Creggan, who helped carry Johnston into the house, offered to ferry him to Almagelvin in his own car, a Volkswagen with seats that could be folded flat.

Shortly after they set off, police call sign India 17 asked for a check on 'Volkswagen, red, 7205 HZ'. Moments later, India 7 reported that the car had just crossed Craigavon Bridge, with a priest at the wheel. RUC control advised all units there was no need for further action.

Even so, Carolan had to argue his way through army and police road blocks – at one he began dismantling the barrier by himself – but he eventually delivered Johnston to casualty. As he was leaving, the first ambulances carrying dead and dying civilians began to arrive.

Driving back to collect Damien Donaghy, Carolan was again stopped at checkpoints but refused to submit to being searched. After dropping off Donaghy at casualty, he remained at the hospital for a while to offer spiritual help.

Carolan would recall later that the day before the march he confided to the renowned Irish tenor Josef Locke in Dublin his fear that it could turn into a bloodbath. He had been worried about wholesale tear gassings, showers of rubber bullets and mass baton charges. 'But it turned out to be a bloodbath with the real stuff.'

When Dr McClean had sent Johnston and Donaghy off to hospital, a man came into the Shields' house saying that someone had been shot dead right outside, in Glenfada Park. McClean followed him out of the house to where Gerry McKinney was lying on the ground in Abbey Park. He had lost a lot of blood, but two paramedics were trying to resuscitate him. McClean checked him over and found that he was dead, but told the paramedics to keep trying to bring him round. McClean thought it was better to keep them occupied; he did not want to create any more panic than there already was.

Then he went to 8 Abbey Park – the Carrs' house – where Michael Kelly, already dead, was on the living-room floor and lying next to him was Jim Wray. He was also dead. Again, he told the paramedics to keep up their efforts at resuscitation.

Then he went next door where he found William McKinney lying on the floor. He was quite conscious, pale and shocked but calm. 'I'm going to die, doctor, am I?'

McClean lied a bit and said, 'You have been hit badly, but if we can get an ambulance and get you to hospital quickly, I hope you will be all right.'

McClean saw Father Mulvey in the hall and asked him to be with McKinney. McClean also stayed until he lost consciousness and died.

Father Mulvey had been at the Rossville Street barricade when paratroopers in a Pig drove through it, then reversed to where the bodies of John Young, Willie Nash and Michael McDaid were lying. They had picked them up by the hair of the head and their feet and tossed them into the back of the Pig. Mulvey had tried to stop them, but was ignored and now he was extremely angry.

It was almost forty minutes since the paratroopers had started shooting and Altnageluin's despatchers were struggling to handle the 999 calls. Shortly after 4.50 p.m. the RUC radio net instructed all units not to interfere with ambulances ferrying casualties to hospital. Moments later, this message was relayed to police control: 'There's ambulances running in and out of here wholesale, there's one after coming out with a man injured and two bodies, do you want us to check them? Over.'

The curt response was: 'I thought I had made it very clear to everyone. Do not bother checking any more ambulances coming from that area. Out.'

With emergency calls pouring in, ambulance crews were coming under severe pressure. John Rutherford and Ronald Moore started their shift at 1 p.m. and around 4.30 p.m. they were directed to Rossville Street, following a circuitous route to avoid the barriers. The first person they picked up had suffered a heart attack but was stable. A Knights of Malta team borrowed one of their two stretchers and returned with a dead man.

The crew were asked if they could take another casualty. Rutherford agreed to fit one more on the floor and the KoM workers brought out a corpse, which he wrapped in blankets. Back at the hospital, he and Moore had to hose blood out of the interior of the ambulance and get a change of blankets. Five minutes later, at around 5.15 p.m., they were instructed to collect more shooting victims from the Rossville Street area.

Dr McClean met them there and explained he had a badly shocked woman nearby but she would not need hospitalization. An onlooker informed the crew there was an injured man in Lone Moor Gardens, so they picked him up. It was Danny McGowan, who had been shot in the leg in Joseph Place; he told them he was hurt playing football – in case he was stopped by the police.

Two more ambulance men, John Rafferty and Samuel Hughes, arrived at the main entrance to block 1 of the Rossville flats to find a body lying under a blanket drenched with blood. Bystanders told them it was Barney McGuigan. They were waiting for Alana Burke, the girl hit by a Saracen, to be brought down from the flats when six men carried over another body with a chest wound.

At that moment there was a rattle of gunfire and people dived to the ground. A twenty-five year-old student from Magee University, Colm O'Dohmnaill, had been standing over Barney McGuigan's corpse, feeling utterly helpless. A teenage boy asked to see the dead man's face in case it was his uncle and O'Dohmnaill pulled back the coat laid over McGuigan's shattered head, then replaced it (it was not the boy's relative).

O'Dohmnaill thought the shooting came from the direction of a Pig on the waste ground and was shocked that the army would open fire at an ambulance. He saw Father Mulvey standing bolt upright, shouting at the soldiers at the top of his voice, 'Stop firing, you stupid bastards.' The shooting ended abruptly and the stretcher was loaded into the ambulance. As far as O'Dohmnaill could see, nobody was hit.

With a few students, he made his way into William Street, heading towards St Eugene's Cathedral. They passed a group of

Paras and one of the girls with O'Dohmnaill asked if they were feeling bad after shooting down civilians. A soldier replied, 'It'll be double figures tonight.' As they drove off, the Paras yelled, 'Fuck off, cunts.'

Eibhlin Lafferty was beside the ambulance when the firing began. Someone pushed her down and held her medical bag over her for flimsy protection. When she got up again she saw that one of her brothers had McGuigan's shoes in his hands. Thinking the troops might mistake them for a weapon or bomb, she grabbed the shoes and carried them to the ambulance herself, holding them out at arm's length.

With Altnagelvin's crews working flat out, Vinny Coyle, who owned one of the few private telephones in the Brandywell, was pleading for an ambulance to be sent in from Letterkenny hospital. He was told that the army would never let it pass over Craigavon Bridge. In frustration, Coyle called St Eugene's Cathedral and startled the priest who answered by shouting at him, 'For fuck's sake get down here, people are being killed.' The priest did not respond immediately, so Coyle told him, 'Get the fucking bishop.'

James Chapman, a former regular in the British army who lived in Glenfada Park, was watching as the Para's Pig drew up a few feet from the barricade. He saw them jump out, lift the bodies by the hair and legs, and throw them into the back of the vehicle. From the window of his mother's flat, directly overlooking the barricade, William B (who requested anonymity) saw the three corpses tossed into the back 'like coal into a bunker'.

Father Irwin had been attending to casualties in the area and was approached by a woman in great distress on the first floor of the Rossville flats. She told him she had seen three men, either dead or badly injured, being dumped into the back of a Pig. Accompanied by Bernard Feeney of the KoM, Irwin ran down-stairs and asked a Para NCO if this was correct.

The NCO told him there were no dead soldiers there. Irwin explained that he was not looking for army casualties and the NCO repeated that there were no dead or injured. The priest went back upstairs, where the same woman pointed out the vehicle containing the bodies. Irwin and Feeney hurried down again, to find Father Tony Mulvey on the scene.

With the permission of a Para officer they approached the Pig. When the rear door was pulled open they saw three men sprawled on top of each other. McDaid was on top of the pile. Father Irwin annointed him and Young, then moved their corpses so Mulvey could do the same for Nash who was at the bottom.

As Irwin remonstrated with the Paras, Leo Day of the KoM arrived with his colleague Alice Long. She was complaining that soldiers would not let ambulances through to collect casualties around the flats. Day persuaded an officer to allow this, then a woman bystander told him there were bodies in the back of a Pig 'and one of them may still be alive'.

The officer allowed Day to check: he found a tangle of bodies with blood running across the floor. When he tried to get inside, the Para stopped him. At that moment Alice Long heard a moaning sound from inside the vehicle. She reached forward and grabbed at the rear door, only for a soldier with a blackened face to kick it shut.

It would be twenty-seven years before Alice Long could bring herself to describe what she saw next. She pulled the door open again and the foot of one of the shot men gave a slight but discernible twitch. Day noticed the movement too and they realized that at least one person in the Pig was still alive. A paratrooper kicked the door shut again and ordered the KoM pair not to look inside. According to Long, he then raised his rifle so that it was pointing downwards, poked it through an open vision flap and fired three rapid shots.

Long claimed that the soldier, who seemed very pleased with himself, said something like, 'They'll not make any more noise now.' Day told her there was no point in remaining any longer, but as they went to move on, she noticed two discarded bullet cases on the ground. When she picked them up, Long saw that the front of each casing had peeled back in four sections, splitting open like a flower.

The soldier who fired into the vehicle immediately cocked his rifle and ordered Long to give him the cases. He warned her she would be the next casualty if she did not comply and Day told her to hand them over. As they left, the soldier shouted some sort of threat.

The Pig was driven back to 'C' Company's forward location where a Royal Army Medical Corps private attached to the Paras examined them. He would say they were placed side by side on the floor in a position which would have allowed them to breath freely were they still alive. At approximately 6.15 p.m. the bodies were delivered to the morgue on the ground floor at Altnagelvin. There was no evidence of more than one gunshot injury to each of them.

Jim McLaughlin was helping with identification of other bodies when the Pig arrived. He said the dead men were 'piled in like lumps of meat', but that the soldiers were more respectful unloading them in front of civilian witnesses. Father Irwin was already in the morgue. He found that McDaid's body was still warm.

At least two people were wounded by gunshot and never went to hospital. Dr Donal McDermott was in the Bogside in his car late in the afternoon when someone, whose name he cannot recall, asked him to come to the aid of a wounded youth.

In a house between Westland Street and the Old Bog Road, Dr McDermott treated a young man for a gunshot wound in his leg. The bullet had gone straight through the flesh, leaving the bone untouched. The entry wound was on the inside of the top of his thigh and the exit wound at the back – much like Mrs Deery's wound only nowhere near as messy. Dr McDermott cleaned it, sprinkled it with antiseptic powder and applied a dressing. Then, he recalled, the young man 'got up and ran out of the door like a hare'.

The other injured man was a member of the Provisional IRA who received flesh wounds during the firefight with Anglians around Barrack Street.

XV

Going Home

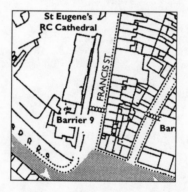

That was the first time I'd ever sworn in front of
my father

Mrs Deery's niece Rita after police
joked about the killings

THE BOGSIDE WAS eerily quiet as people made their way home. Families gathered to swap stories of the day, coal fires were lit and chimney smoke drifted up the hill to the Creggan.

By 7.30 p.m., the level of dread among those with relatives not yet back from the march was almost tangible.

A stream of people called Father Daly at the parochial house to ask what he knew about the shootings, if he had seen a son or a husband or could put any names to the dead. Exhausted and grieving, his hands and clothes still splashed with blood, Daly was desperate to talk to somebody about what he had been through.

On impulse he telephoned Peter McCullagh, an RUC Superintendent who had been at school with him. To his astonishment, McCullagh appeared to believe that the march had passed off without serious trouble and only a handful of minor injuries. Daly told him that he had personally anointed six people and knew of many others who were badly injured. 'I said I saw those bodies myself, with my own eyes.'

Still unconvinced, McCullagh rang Altnagelvin; ten minutes later he called to tell Daly that the hospital had eleven bodies in the morgue. Daly was furious that the names of those under arrest were still being withheld by the army. Without this list, it was impossible to eliminate them from the list of dead and wounded, ensuring that some families would only discover their loss in the most harrowing circumstances.

When Paddy Doherty's wife, Eileen, heard rumours that live

271

bullets had been fired at civilians, she rushed home to make sure that her family was safe. On the way a relative told her that Paddy had been shot.

Eileen got a lift to Altnagelvin, where she found Father Tom O'Gara. The priest told her that he thought Paddy fitted the description of a wounded man, but it turned out to be someone else. When O'Gara went to the morgue, Paddy was the second corpse he saw. Eileen went home to tell the children their father was dead.

Her son Tony, then nine years old, learned of his father's death before his mother arrived home. He and another small boy were playing marbles in the street when his friend told him that his father had been killed. The 'snapshot' memory of that moment would be with him for ever. Uncertain whether to believe his friend, Tony felt he should not pass on the news to the rest of his family. 'So I was stuck with that knowledge for two or three hours, until people came back from the hospital.'

Gerry McKinney's wife, Ita, was alarmed by reports of the killings on the 6 p.m. radio news. Her husband always telephoned if he was going to be late back from work, but she had heard nothing from him. Then a man she did not know called at her house to say he believed that Gerry was taken to Altnagelvin after suffering a heart attack.

At that moment Ita realized that her husband had probably been killed, because he had never had heart trouble before. She could not bear to go to the hospital, so friends went on her behalf. At around 8 p.m. they returned to the house. 'I didn't need to ask, their faces were sad enough to tell me that Gerry was dead.' Two days later police ticketed an old car that McKinney had parked outside his home.

News of the shooting of John Johnston reached his brother-in-law, John Duddy, as he was walking away from Barrier 14, soaked with purple dye from the water cannon. Duddy went home for a change of clothing, then set out to drive to Altnagelvin with his sons. Not far from St Eugene's Catholic Cathedral paratroopers stopped the car, pulled them out and asked what they were up to.

Very angry, Duddy replied that he was going to the hospital, 'to see my brother-in-law, who you bastards shot'.

A soldier said, 'That bastard stands for four hours' and Duddy was spreadeagled and searched. Nearby, a priest named Father Byrne was railing at the Paras, accusing them of murder.

The paratroopers pulled out five to ten minutes later and Duddy drove on to Altnagelvin. He found Johnston being treated for wounds to the leg and arm, shocked and very subdued. Duddy was terribly shaken to discover later that his former workmate Barney McGuigan, to whom he had chatted earlier in the afternoon, was now lying in the hospital morgue.

McGuigan's son, Charlie, then sixteen, was walking home when he noticed that he was receiving some uncomfortable looks from people he knew. When he reached St Mary's Church in the Creggan a friend, Neil McLaughlin, told him to get home quickly because his father had been wounded.

A group of people outside the McGuigan house told Charlie, 'Don't be worried, he has only been shot in the leg.' But Charlie now feared the worst. When he went into the house he found his mother distraught; she had no information about Barney, only rumours that he had been shot. Three of his uncles, Hugh, Liam and Paddy, then arrived and took his mother to the hospital where Paddy identified Barney's body in the morgue.

Later, back at home, Charlie's mother cleared a space in the kitchen and made him kneel under the Sacred Heart picture and swear to her that he would never do anything about his father's death that would bring shame on the name of the family. She asked Charlie to think of his three sisters, aged fourteen, ten and nine, and of his two brothers, aged twelve and six. Having lost her husband, his mother was determined that she would not lose any other member of the family as a result of what had happened.

At the home of the Nash family an aunt of Willie's became hysterical when she learned he had been killed and his father wounded in the space of a few minutes. Two KoM workers, John O'Kane and Angela Coyle, went to look after her. She was the last person they treated that day. Then they dragged themselves home, bone weary and sick at heart.

Relatives of the missing were also phoning John Hume, who had spent the march at his Westland Park home in the Bogside. Some also came calling personally at his front door. Ivan Cooper turned up with a story of six people being shot dead, but they could not find out anything from the hospital on the phone, so they borrowed a car from a neighbour and drove over there. They had had trouble getting through the army roadblock on the Craigavon Bridge.

The police log recorded their journey with a warning message from headquarters to the duty officer at Altnagelvin: 'November to India 38: Messrs Hume and Cooper are on their way to the hospital . . . just to warn you to be on your guard for them . . . make contact with local inspector and provide whatever duty he requires there.'

At the hospital, Hume and Cooper found soldiers swarming around the premises. The first person Hume met was Mrs McGuigan, which was doubly shocking for him since they had grown up in adjacent streets in the Bogside and she was now in a terrible state.

Hume's first priority was to compile a reliable list of the dead and wounded, and inform their relatives. He found out that McGuigan, Doherty, Gilmore and McKinney were already in the morgue. With heavy heart, Cooper informed their anxious families. McGuigan's wife was so overcome with grief that she flew at a soldier standing nearby.

The dead were laid out on the floor of the morgue covered with a white sheet. Hugh Gilmore's brother and sisters went to identify him. Each time the sheet was lifted and they saw it was not Hugh their hopes were raised that he was still alive. But as they approached the last body, which was separate from the rest, they saw a hand sticking out from under the cover and it was engrained with black marks. They knew it was Hugh; he worked at the tyre factory on William Street and always had black rubber marks on his hands.

Charlie Nash identified his brother, Willie, who was fifth in the line of corpses. He could see he had been shot and he looked up at a policeman who had accompanied them into the morgue and said, 'That's my brother.' The policeman had a smirk on his face and Charlie lunged at him; there was a fracas, right there in the morgue.

Jim Wray's brother, Liam, had rushed to Altnagelvin with Rosemary Doyle of the KoM. She had gone there with Wray's body in an ambulance after examining him in the house where he lay dying alongside Michael Kelly. A priest gave her a lift back to the Bogside and she went to tell his family of his death.

At the morgue, hospital officials and police asked Doyle if she recognized any of the five other bodies there. She identified four of them, but although she knew John Young, his face was so ·disfigured that she could not be sure it was him. Later that night, she treated five members of Wray's family for shock.

As eleven-year-old Owen Deery, one of Peggy Deery's fourteen children, was going home after the march, his friends kept coming up to him saying something had happened to his mother, but they did not know whether she was missing or dead. When he got home, the family had decided to go to the morgue, after a television newsflash provided an emergency telephone number for inquiries about casualties. Peggy's niece Rita and Rita's father went to the hospital to look for her. A doctor confirmed that Peggy had been wounded but could provide no further details. While they waited for information, Rita went downstairs to get cigarettes from a vending machine.

The ground floor was deserted. A man dressed in a white coat, white cap on his head, appeared and Rita saw he was wearing a clerical collar. Father Tom O'Gara had just come from the morgue where he counted thirteen bodies. He asked Rita if she would try to identify them, but she couldn't bear it. When she and her father left the hospital later, they came across RUC officers singing 'It's a beautiful day'. Rita could not contain her fury. 'That was the first time I'd ever cursed in front of my father,' she would admit.

The ordeal of Michael McDaid's family was the cruellest of all. Shortly after 7 p.m., when the family realized he was missing, his brothers John and Danny drove to Altnagelvin. By then the hospital was under heavy guard by police and paratroopers. A local GP, Dr Thomas McCabe, counted a dozen RUC officers in flak jackets when he examined the body of his former patient John Young (he discovered two souvenir rubber bullets stuffed inside Young's jerkin).

Although McDaid was already in the morgue, his brothers were assured by hospital staff that he was not among the dead. They returned home and told their mother that 'Mickey' was alive. But still anxious, the family joined the crowd that gathered at Hume's house when he and Cooper returned from the hospital at around 8 p.m.

By then, the MPs had established that at least twelve people had been killed. McDaid was not on their list, although Hume had learned about a thirteenth dead male who was still unidentified. Badly rattled himself, Hume read out the names of all the known dead from a handwritten sheet of paper. 'There is one more,' he said, turning to the McDaids to add, 'It won't be yours, it's very unlikely.'

Both Cooper and Hume attempted to reassure the family that Michael was probably under arrest somewhere. One of his sisters was convinced that she had seen him alive on television, being bundled into a Pig. Shortly before 10 p.m., with no further information coming through from the hospital, the McDaids put on their coats and went home.

Five minutes later, the hospital rang Hume's house to say that Michael was the thirteenth victim. He had apparently been confused with Danny Gillespie, who was lightly wounded but did not go directly to hospital for treatment. It fell to Hume to break the crushing news to the family (three months later, he found his list crumpled in the pocket of the suit he had been wearing).

Father Daly was devastated to hear of Michael's death. Earlier in the evening, he had personally assured Mrs McDaid that her son was not on any of the casualty lists. After identification was confirmed, Daly could not face her again and asked another priest to go to the family home in his place.

McDaid's brothers returned to the morgue, pushing their way in past the guards. John lifted a white sheet to see Michael's face. There was a triangular mark on his cheek and the back of his head was thickly matted with blood.

As bodies began arriving at Altnagelvin, two detectives and a scene-of-crime specialist from the RUC station in the Waterside were despatched to handle the casework. They obtained official certification of each death from the duty casualty officer, Dr Ian Gordon, then set about securing formal identification of the victims. All thirteen corpses were locked up in the mortuary overnight to await post-mortems.

Next morning Dr Vincent Cavanagh was among local physicians who attended as three state pathologists set to work in the overcrowded morgue. He was given complete freedom to examine his former patient, Gerry McKinney. Cavanagh saw that McKinney had been shot in the back at around the level of the tenth rib, with the bullet ploughing on through the gut to exit on the other side of his body.

Before the autopsies took place, Cavanagh saw RUC officers carrying out swab tests on the victims' hands and pinning swatches of their clothing to sheets of paper. Each stage in the process of building up a dossier on the thirteen corpses was meticulously recorded in the dispassionate prose of men familiar with violent death.

Patrick Doherty's file opened with a precise description of the damage done by the bullet that killed him: 'Entry wound on the right buttock circular and 7cm in diameter centred 13cm from mid-line of back, exit wound 5cm x 3cm on left side, 10cm below nipple and 5cm behind it.' A track through the body connected the wounds 'passing from right to left at an angle of 45° to the horizontal'.

Police notes recorded that Doherty was dead on arrival at Altnagelvin, where 'life was pronounced extinct by Dr Gordon'. He was identified by James Gallagher in the presence of a Detective Constable. The post-mortem was carried out by Dr Carson, Northern Ireland's deputy state pathologist. Two RUC photographers, responsible for compiling a detailed album on all the dead, were present throughout.

When the pathologist had finished with Doherty, a scene-of-crime officer, took charge of a blood sample and eight swabs previously taken from his hands, together with his clothes. Two days later this evidence was delivered to the Department of Industrial & Forensic Science in Belfast.

It was already cutting things close for the Department's experts to uncover any compromising evidence. Experience showed that the first forty-eight hours were vital for detecting traces of explosives on clothing, especially when bombs were wrapped in sticky tape. In the event, nothing was discovered to link Doherty with firing a gun or handling a bomb.

Since none of the wounded treated at Altnagelvin was accused of having committed any offence that day – and none featured in the files of the Special Branch – the RUC had no power to order swab tests. To the chagrin of the police, sympathetic hospital staff allowed journalists to interview most of the wounded as soon as they were well enough. All denied vehemently that they had been carrying weapons or explosives and insisted that nobody else on the march had done so.

Each of the wounded was subsequently interviewed by police, usually in the presence of a chosen clergyman or solicitor. Michael

Bridge was livid when a Detective Sergeant and a colleague arrived at his bedside to take a statement. 'Get the fuck out of here, you bastards,' he told them. 'I'll fucking talk to you nothing.' He changed his mind later and gave a statement in the presence of Father Tony Mulvey.

But Bridge remained fiercely hostile to the police. When officers arrived to interview Alex Nash in an adjacent bed without anyone there to advise the old man, he got so worked up that he burst into tears. Initially, Nash was just as prickly, telling one policeman: 'The IRA are too generous with you fuckers.' Next day he relented and spoke to a Detective Sergeant with Father Mulvey present.

All those who were treated for wounds also received a police questionnaire prepared under Chief Superintendent Lagan's guidance. It asked, 'Were you injured on Sunday January 30 by gunshot; where were you when this occurred; how did you receive your injuries; what were you doing in the area at the time; who was with you at the time?' There was no obligation to complete it, but most did.

Hours after the last troops pulled out of the Bogside, people were still struggling to come to terms with what had happened. In community centres, in the parlours of terraced houses, on street corners, they gathered for comfort, some stunned by grief, others raging and vowing vengeance. A small group formed at the bottom of Westland Street and Brigadier MacLellan radioed his units to see if trouble was brewing again from the young Derry hooligans. The message came back: the crowd was made up of men, not yobbos.

To the schoolboy Don Mullan it seemed as if the entire Catholic section of Derry was deeply traumatized. He would never forget the silence that descended on his home town. It struck him that the aftermath of an earthquake must be a bit like this.

Delayed shock was setting in now, affecting people in ways they would least have expected. Big Paddy Walsh – the quiet, shy family man – was dismayed to find himself raving and swearing in front of his wife and children. Walsh did not get back from the march until around 10 p.m. and his wife, frantic with worry, was waiting to give him a piece of her mind.

But then she saw his face – 'sad and mad at the same time' – and understood that he must have been through something terrible. After Walsh calmed down he told her about the killings he had witnessed, never mentioning how he risked his own life to go to the aid of Paddy Doherty and others. Mrs Walsh only found out about that a week later, when the *Sunday Times* published photographs showing Walsh beside the dying Doherty.

It took Walsh days to recover something of his old cheerful self. His black mood was not helped by overhearing Protestant workmates gloat about the killings ('thirteen is not enough', one observed). At night, Walsh would jerk and shudder, muttering in his sleep.

Leo Day always expected his Knight of Malta paramedics to provide detailed reports of their activities at public events and no exception was made for Bloody Sunday. Some volunteers found that writing things down helped them to cope with their searing experiences. Teenage girls like Alice Long and Antoinette Coyle, more accustomed to treating cuts and bruises after routine bouts of rioting, drafted moving accounts of their efforts to save men with devastating gunshot wounds.

In a careful hand, Coyle described how she carried on administering first aid and comforting distraught people as the bullets flew. She kept calm enough to diagnose a possible spine fracture when Alana Burke (struck by a Pig) complained she had no feeling in her legs. Coyle instructed others present to make sure that she was not moved.

After Coyle had helped open up an army barrier to allow an ambulance through, paratroopers shoved her up against a wall to be searched. She protested vehemently and was told that her white uniform made a perfect target. When the last of the dead and dying had been removed, Coyle returned with a stretcher to pick up

Burke. There was one last case of shock waiting for treatment and Coyle applied the KoM remedy of placing a spoon wrapped in clean cloth in the patient's mouth while the legs were raised.

It was only when Long, who had joined the KoM at the age of ten and was now a superintendent, finally got home that she began to realize just how bad the day had been.

At the Shields' flat in Columbcille Court, Long had seen the bath in which Damien Donaghy was laid until a tourniquet could be applied to his leg wound. It was still full of blood.

By the Rossville flats telephone box, Long came across the body of Barney McGuigan. The blanket covering him was already soaked through with blood and Long placed another brought out by a woman from the flats over his terrible head wounds. She could not bring herself to look too closely at McGuigan.

Later, thirteen-year-old Michael Rooney and John Duffy, aged fourteen, found part of an eyelid sticking to the concrete wall of block 2 of the flats by the phone box where McGuigan was killed. It was about five feet up on the wall. They put it into a Bo-Peep matchbox and reverently laid it to rest on the bloodstained Civil Rights flag now covering the spot where McGuigan had fallen.

Less haunting images lingered on for others caught up in the tumult of the afternoon. Vinny Coyle remembered how his first sight of the paratroopers in battle order had reminded him irresistibly of his acting days, 'blacking up' for a musical about Al Jolson in Blackpool. 'I thought, what nice new red berets and aren't they going to get dirty because all of them have blacked-up faces.'

A local art teacher recalled that while he was watching bodies being loaded into the ambulances, a fellow with a terrible stutter had begun ranting against Faulkner, Paisley and Protestants in general. It was too much for him. 'What with the stutter and the deaths, I got quite angry [and] told him, for God's sake, shut your mouth.'

Brian McColl's abiding memory was of the girl who became

hysterical as Hugh Gilmore died in front of her. 'She just screamed and roared, and the more she roared, the more the army fired.' On impulse, McColl slapped her face. Instantly, she fell limp and silent across his knee.

And after it was all over, sixteen-year-old Malachy Coyle, who had seen Jim Wray shot dead, was running home, still frightened, when he encountered three men with dogs near St Eugene's Cathedral. They were Protestants. 'The soldiers are shooting everyone in sight,' blurted Coyle. The men had heard about the killings and were also shocked. One of them said he would never again support the Prime Minister, Brian Faulkner. They let Coyle walk with them so that he wasn't stopped at the army checkpoint. Coyle thanked them and ran home.

Later that night, several young Derry Provos were driving through the Bogside when they came across a group of men and women boarding the bingo bus to Buncrana. They told them they should be ashamed of themselves, going to bingo after thirteen people had been shot dead and they walked off the bus and went home.

Dr Donal MacDermott arrived home at his house in Clarence Avenue to find paratroopers in the armoured cars playing loud jazzy music on their radios. Unionist neighbours came out and gave them tea and buns.

At one point, a paratrooper knocked on MacDermott's door and told him to put out all the lights in his house and draw the curtains. He assumed the Paras were concerned about IRA snipers. He refused, and instead turned on all the lights he could find. It created quite a beam, since his house had thirty-three windows.

As the army units pulled down the barriers and the Paras were preparing to return the three miles to their original location at Drumahoe, Brigadier MacLellan was trying urgently to get through to Wilford: 'Hello 65 this is Zero, go ahead and telephone me on the civil line when you are finished with it over. Roger, out.'

MacLellan called again: 'Hello 65, this is Zero, reference my last message it is a matter of priority that you contact Seagull [Brigade HQ] as soon as possible, over.'

'65 roger, will try to ring you but the number is engaged at the moment, will keep trying.'

Seconds later the Paras got through, apparently, because they then sent a follow-up message over the open line: 'Hello Zero, this is 65, reference our last message to Seagull on other means confirmed over 200, over.'

MacLellan: 'Zero, roger.'

Dropping their guard on the secure means now the action was over, the army revealed that a land line telephone had been one of the so-called secure links. But what did the Paras mean by 'confirmed over 200'? Two hundred what? It was not arrests – there were only forty-three. It was not shots fired against them, since there were probably fewer than twenty. Could it have been bullets fired by the Paras? But they would say they only fired 108 live rounds and sixty-four rubber bullets.

Shortly afterwards the Paras were ordered to leave for Drumahoe. Their departing message was about the secure link land line: 'Hello Zero, this is 65, I take it we take our secure means back with us now, over.'

'Zero, wait out, Zero, yes.'

As the Paras arrived back at Drumahoe, all units who had been on active duty in Derry that day were warned by the army's public relations office that they would be expected to 'select suitable soldiers who could present an intelligent battle picture as they saw it, soonest'. The guidelines were as follows:

1. Good 1st hand evidence ref on this afternoon's activities. Members of 1 Para and other regiments are required – soldiers may have to speak on television.
2 Details of dead which may link with the ungodly [IRA] and their activities.

3 Full report on all other shooting incidents.

The Paras did not respond. At 11.43 p.m., they requested radio silence for the night, but left a telephone number, just in case. Telephone link only: Derry 61838. They were still 8 Brigade's first reserve force and on thirty minutes' notice.

The last army radio message, at ten minutes to midnight, recorded that the men who had gathered at the Bogside Inn had also gone home.

Epilogue

At around 7 p.m. on Sunday evening, while the hospital secretary at Aitnagelvin was still trying to convince incredulous journalists that thirteen people were dead, an urgent confidential signal for Edward Heath came chattering over the teleprinter at Chequers, the Prime Minister's country residence. Despatched from 10 Downing Street by Lord Bridges, his private secretary, it informed him that the Ministry of Defence was reporting at least five civilian fatalities during rioting in Londonderry. Bridges said there was no confirmation of media claims of significantly higher casualties but promised to keep Heath posted.

The next message followed almost immediately. The MoD could now confirm that at least twelve civilians had been killed and another fourteen wounded. The army was insisting that the Paras had come under indiscriminate sniper fire after intervening to arrest hooligans. Bridges told Heath that one of the dead had already been identified as 'a wanted man' and that another was carrying four nail bombs.

By then, prominent Catholics had begun coming forward to denounce the conduct of the army on television and radio. The Bishop of Derry, Neil Farren, had telegraphed Downing Street demanding an immediate public inquiry: the Primate of All Ireland, Cardinal Conway, did the same. And late that night Heath's Irish counterpart, Jack Lynch, telephoned from Dublin to warn that there would be a furious public reaction in the Republic. A fractious conversation ended abruptly when Heath blamed the bloodshed in Derry on the IRA.

285

At army headquarters in Lisburn, meanwhile, the MoD's feeble response to the growing barrage of allegations against the Paras was dismaying senior officers. Uncomfortably aware that the military's side of the story was not being put across effectively, they decided to draft in Colonel Maurice Tugwell, General Ford's special adviser on information policy. Around midnight on Sunday he recorded an interview with BBC radio intended to put a more positive 'spin' on events in Derry ahead of Monday morning's newspapers.

Tugwell began his damage limitation exercise by dismissing out of hand eyewitness reports of the Paras shooting indiscriminately at civilians. He was adamant that shots had been aimed only at identifiable gunmen and bombers: all of those killed were males 'of arms-carrying age', one of whom had nail bombs in his pockets. Tugwell also claimed that four of the dead had been on the army's wanted list, although he did not provide any names.

Next morning Heath presided over a meeting in Downing Street to discuss how his government should handle the increasingly damaging fallout from Operation Forecast. The Republican publicity machine was already gearing up, spreading damning accounts of Bloody Sunday around the world. The feeling was that only a full-scale Tribunal of Inquiry would suffice, but Heath was concerned about the publicity that the allegations against the Paras had already received. In the circumstances, he suggested, 'selected defence correspondents' could be given the army's account of what happened.

The MoD had already received a confidential report on the Derry killings prepared by Ford's staff in Lisburn and agreed to provide a briefing for media defence specialists in London. The officer chosen to present it was Colonel Harry Dalzell-Payne of MO4, the department most directly concerned with military operations in Northern Ireland. In a chillingly lucid analysis written a few days before the NICRA march, he had predicted that troops might have to open fire because all other existing methods of crowd control had already failed.

Following Tugwell's lead, Dalzell-Payne took the offensive, announcing that a preliminary investigation had already established that all shooting by the army conformed entirely to the requirements of the Yellow Card. He insisted that the Paras did not shoot 'until lead bullets were fired at them' and ruled out any possibility that they fired recklessly, 'because they have bloody good NCOs and men who know the form'. And he repeated Tugwell's claim that four of the dead civilians were being sought by the security forces at the time they were shot.

In fact, none of the victims had ever been on any wanted list. Four were known to the security authorities simply because they had previously been arrested for riotous conduct (only one, Gerald Donaghy, was eventually convicted). That did not prevent the same damaging allegation from being recycled by the British Information Services offices in New York on 1 February. Heath was worried about reactions among the large Irish-American community, although he thought his good relations with President Nixon would count in Britain's favour. The BIS statement faithfully relayed the military line; it would be weeks before the MoD acknowledged its mistake and offered a muted apology.

Unsurprisingly, many Catholics were inclined to suspect an orchestrated campaign to discredit the Paras' victims by leaking stories favourable to the military to friendly journalists. Their misgivings would have grown had they known that General Sir Michael Carver, the Chief of Staff, appeared to take seriously reports that one of the dead in Derry might actually have been killed some time before the NICRA march took place.

At a meeting of the MoD's Northern Ireland Policy Group on 31 January, Carver noted that army witnesses were claiming that the body of a youth of about fifteen had been shoved out of a doorway into the street during the confrontation with the Paras. It was possible, he said, that this person had actually died in a shooting incident the previous day; an autopsy should be able to establish the approximate time of death. Carver also mentioned the possibility that other casualties – including IRA gunmen, by some media accounts – had been evacuated to Letterkenny hospital. But although background notes prepared for Dalzell-Payne's briefing also referred to 'a fifteen-year-old boy shot on the Saturday and locals brought the body from the Bogside', not a shred of evidence was ever produced to back up this macabre theory. The only victim who bore any resemblance to the description provided by the army was young Jack Duddy. Yet numerous eyewitnesses had seen him dying from a gunshot wound to the chest shortly after the Paras had launched the arrest operation.

The importance that Heath attached to winning the public relations battle over Bloody Sunday was underlined after the Lord Chief Justice, Lord Widgery, agreed to conduct the inquiry into the killings. On the evening of 31 January he was invited round to Downing Street to discuss what it should cover and how it should proceed. It had been a trying day for the Prime Minister: a mob of angry protesters had earlier burned the British embassy in Dublin to the ground while the Irish police stood by.

The confidential minute of the meeting was taken by Heath's Principal Private Secretary, Robert Armstrong. In the presence of the Lord Chancellor, Lord Hailsham, the Prime Minister raised a number of issues that he thought Widgery (a former army brigadier) might take into account. He wanted the Tribunal to get under way without delay, while events were still fresh in the minds of people involved, and to deliver its findings speedily. He also believed that the need for public hearings generally outweighed any potential risk to security force witnesses.

Widgery apparently saw nothing irregular about being lobbied by the head of the government that had just appointed him to carry out an independent public inquiry. In fact, he suggested to Heath that it would be helpful if his investigation were restricted to what actually happened during the brief period when the Paras were shooting. 'This would enable the Tribunal to confine evidence to eyewitnesses,' he pointed out. Left unsaid was the fact that such an approach would rule out any searching examination of the political and military planning behind the decision to endanger the lives of civilians.

In his memoirs, Heath would insist that 'there was no attempt to interfere in Lord Widgery's deliberations'. But the official minute records that he had one last piece of advice for the Lord Chief Justice. Heath urged him to bear in mind that in Northern Ireland, Britain was 'fighting not only a military war but a propaganda war'.

The government's concern that public opinion could swing against continued military involvement in the province surfaced again at a Cabinet meeting on 3 February, when ministers expressed alarm about the lack of progress towards a political solution. Next day Brian Faulkner attended another crisis gathering in Downing Street. Heath told him that there would be immense political pressure for 'a change of course' if, as army intelligence was predicting, further serious trouble erupted at a NICRA anti-internment rally scheduled for Newry the following Sunday, 6 February.

Faulkner responded sharply that if this was allowed to go ahead it would be virtually impossible to stop the Orange Order from staging its own illegal processions. Carver involved himself directly in the planning of a massive security operation in Newry, flying over the proposed route of the march by helicopter. He and Tuzo ensured that the RUC would be in the front line this time: troops were ordered to adhere rigidly to the Yellow Card rules on opening fire, even if army barriers were in danger of being overrun. In the event, the march passed off peacefully.

Under Britain's stringent contempt of court rules, Widgery's appointment effectively prevented the mainstream media from publishing anything further about what had happened in Derry. But journalists in the Irish Republic were able to comment and some newspapers there – most also on sale in Britain – were openly accusing the army of pre-meditated murder. For policy reasons, Ford and Wilford were refused permission by the MoD to sue after one Irish newspaper alleged libellously that they had conspired to shoot all men of military age in the Bogside.

Behind the scenes there was growing official unease about the interviews that army personnel had given before the reporting ban had taken effect. Complaints about biased coverage of the march by BBC TV on Bloody Sunday were aired when the Northern Ireland Policy Group discussed its public relations strategy. One assessment noted worriedly that Ford had been pressured into providing an off-the-cuff account of the situation after being 'cornered' by journalists at the William Street barrier around 5.15 p.m.

Ford had just met up with Colonel Wilford, the Paras' commander, who told him that his men had been shot at before returning fire and that at least two people were dead. The *Sun* newspaper's correspondent, Harry Arnold, heard Ford tell the BBC that he understood the army had fired three shots and hit two men. Another journalist said that he had already seen three bodies himself. 'We shall have to find out who shot them,' Ford replied.

Wilford was subsequently interviewed on ITN's *News at Ten* programme. By his own account the Paras' commander was now feeling on top of the world, the undisputed military master of the Bogside. He was asked first if he felt that his men had inflicted an unacceptably large number of casualties during the arrest operation.

Wilford: Well, I suppose five is quite large in these circumstances, it's unfortunate but after we got up there ... towards Rossville flats, we came under fire. We came under fire from the flats, we were also petrol-bombed from the flats and some acid in fact was poured on us from the top of the flats.

ITN: Local people are saying that you used excessive force when you went in there [to the flats].

Wilford: Well, what is force? If you're being fired at you return the fire and they know that perfectly well.

ITN: How many gunmen do you feel you have hit in the Bogside?

Wilford: Well, I'm told from my quick ... you must understand that it's a very quick sitrep, that three gunmen were hit. We have not yet got the weapons, but this is the usual thing, we saw people come forward. I'm not going to say that I saw weapons being taken because I haven't yet spoken to the men on the ground.

ITN: You have no worries about this action?

Wilford: None at all.

Harry Arnold also spoke to Wilford, who confided that he had originally hoped to arrest about 300 people but that a 'tactical delay' had made the Paras seventeen minutes late going into action. Wilford thought they had ultimately detained about sixty civilians (the true figure was closer to forty). Arnold found it difficult to understand how anyone could have removed weapons from bodies lying in full view of the paratroopers at the foot of the Rossville flats.

On BBC radio later that night, Wilford claimed that a man armed with an M1 carbine (a weapon favoured by the IRA) had been seen on a balcony in the Rossville flats. He suggested that some of the civilian casualties might have been caused by indiscriminate firing by the IRA. But as the Paras' commander later explained, he had not personally seen any gunmen; his subsequent explanation of the M1 'sighting' sounded singularly lame: 'I did not say this was true, I said it was possibly true.'

During another television interview, Lieutenant N – who had been in charge of the mortar platoon – volunteered that he had spotted a man with a rifle firing from a position beside the Rossville flats:

Interviewer: So you saw him?

Lt N: He'd just been engaged, yeah.

Interviewer: And you saw him firing?

Lt N: Yeah, absolutely.

But Lieutenant N's account was actually based on what one of his men had told him he had seen. During the same interview, another Para was asked if he was sure all of the thirteen dead were gunmen. 'Personally, maybe not,' he replied. As for talk of civilians being shot in the back – 'well, we don't deny this, but who is to say that it was not a ricochet?' If people got hit by a bullet aimed at a gunman, he maintained, there was nothing the army could do about it.

Within days of Bloody Sunday, Chief Superintendent Frank Lagan became the target of a vicious whispering campaign against him in military and police circles in Belfast. He was accused of causing 'particular problems' over the gathering of evidence from Altnagelvin hospital and letting reporters interview the wounded before the police had a chance to take statements or swabs. It was also claimed that he had turned away extra police help sent from Belfast, 'distorted the truth' over his exchanges with MacLellan at the time the order was given to send in the Paras and been impossible to contact for the twenty-four hours after Bloody Sunday. Finally, there were insinuations that his sympathies lay too closely with his fellow Catholics and that he had lost the confidence of most of his men. An aggrieved Lagan stood up to the blasts and survived, eventually being promoted to Assistant Chief Constable. He retired from the force at age 60, and still lives in Derry.

The Para commander, Lieutenant Colonel Wilford, was decorated six months after Bloody Sunday, receiving the Queen's award of the Order of the British Empire. Inevitably that strengthened the conviction of Catholics in Derry that the British establishment had endorsed the killings. Yet despite being exonerated by Widgery, Wilford's fast-track career was effectively over; he was never promoted again and following a frustrating decade on the sidelines, he tossed his OBE into a cardboard box and quit the army after more than thirty years' service.

As a civilian, Wilford would turn to painting, grow his hair in a pony tail and embrace a mildly bohemian life-style. He blamed the pressures of being forever associated with that afternoon in Derry for the break-up of his twenty-two-year marriage and estrangement from his son, an officer in the Parachute Regiment. After the Saville Inquiry was announced, Wilford broke his long silence, accusing the army of making him the scapegoat, but he would never falter in defence of his men.

Brigadier Pat MacLellan relinquished command of 8 Brigade within a year of the killings, was promoted to Major General and was also decorated, becoming a Commander of the British Empire (CBE, one up from OBE). He was subsequently promoted to Major General and for the next five years he gloried in the title of Resident Governor and Keeper of the Jewel House at the Tower of London. His superior in Northern Ireland, Lieutenant General Robert Ford, would remain in the province long enough to command the massive invasion of the Bogside and the Creggan in August 1972. Ford was subsequently given a knighthood.

General Sir Michael Carver retired as Chief of the Defence Staff in 1973, when he was given the rank of Field Marshal; four years later he was made a life peer.

Life for the citizens of the Bogside became more hectic and more dangerous. Youngsters who had watched their friends die that day flocked to join the IRA – despite their parents' urgings not to seek revenge and disgrace the family name. Some of them died. In 1987, Peggy Deery's son, Paddy, was killed when a bomb being carried in a car he was driving blew up. Peggy, who had never fully recovered the use of her wounded leg, died three months later.

Sean Keenan's son Colm, an IRA volunteer, was shot dead by

British soldiers in June 1972. A few weeks later Sean was released from internment. He died in 1993.

On 30 December 1972, Martin McGuinness, then twenty-two years old, was arrested with his deputy, Joe McCallion, in County Donegal; they were charged with possession of 250 pounds of gelignite and 4757 rounds of .303 ammunition found in an abandoned car. McGuinness and McCallion were imprisoned for six months. McGuinness told the court,

> For over two years, I was an officer in the Derry Brigade of the IRA. We have fought against the killing of our people. Many of my comrades have been arrested and tortured and some were shot unarmed by British troops . . . I am a member of Oglaigh na Eireann (IRA) and very, very proud of it . . . We firmly believe we were doing our duty as Irishmen.

McGuinness was arrested again as an IRA member in Donegal in February 1974, and served nine months of a twelve-month sentence. At the end of 1999, he became Education Minister in the Northern Ireland power-sharing executive.

Dr McClean was mayor of Derry in 1973–74, the first Catholic mayor since the gerrymandering. He still practises medicine there.

Father Edward Daly became Bishop of Derry and has since retired. Father Mulvey died, so did Father O'Gara.

Of the other wounded, Mr Johnston died later that year, not from his wounds, but people say the wounds contributed to his death and count him among the dead that day. Alex Nash could not hear a British army helicopter overhead without becoming agitated and some of the time he would imagine all soldiers were Paras, or undercover agents out to get him. He died last year.

John Hume shared the 1998 Nobel prize for Peace for his part in nurturing the 'peace process'.

Although the families of those killed on Bloody Sunday lodged legal claims for compensation from the British government soon after the Widgery Tribunal's report appeared, it would take almost two years before a settlement was hammered out. Despite advice from the Attorney General that most claims would succeed, the Ministry of Defence fought a long rearguard action to contest all the cases. Its lawyers argued that it could not be held liable for any deaths 'where it can be shown that the person concerned recklessly and negligently exposed himself to danger'. This hard line dismayed the Northern Ireland Office: one of Whitelaw's advisers noted sharply that some observers might consider that the army was 'lucky not to have fared worse' at Widgery's hands.

On 14 December 1974 the terms of the settlement were finally agreed. While any legal liability on the part of the MoD and the army was still firmly denied, Her Majesty's Government formally acknowledged that all those killed were innocent and 'withdrew unequivocally any allegation to the contrary' it had made previously. It also apologized to the next of kin of the deceased and publicly expressed sympathy with them for their loss.

The following ex gratia payments were made to the relatives of the dead 'in a spirit of goodwill and conciliation':

Patrick Joseph Doherty	£16,575.35p
Gerald Vincent Donaghy	£850
John Francis Duddy	£2,422
Hugh Pius Gilmore	£250
Michael Gerald Kelly	£250
Michael Martin McDaid	£250
Kevin Gerard McElhinney	£250
Bernard McGuigan	£3,750
James Gerard McKinney	£13,770
William Anthony McKinney	£1,350
William Noel Nash	£250
James Patrick Wray	£1,500
John Pius Young	£250

Acknowledgements

This book could not have been written without the cooperation of the people of the Bogside and the Creggan. When we first invaded their homes, twenty-eight years ago, many were grieving the loss of relatives and neighbours on Bloody Sunday; others were angry and sought revenge. All were stunned by what had happened on that day. For weeks, they lived in disbelief that the British paratroopers had used live rounds and killed unarmed citizens.

In their shock and confusion, they let us into their homes, calmly told us their stories and frequently extended warm hospitality. We admired them, then, for their extraordinary fortitude, and when we returned in 1988 we found that same strength undiminished by almost three decades of the Troubles.

In 1972, Bridget Bond, the indomitable leader of the Derry Civil Rights Association was our central source of information about the march. She made time for us even when her front room was already packed with eyewitnesses giving statements; in 1999 we were sad to find out she had died. Dr Raymond McClean and his wife Sheila welcomed us back in 1999 as though we had never gone away. Roisin Keenan, Sean's daughter, and her son Colm Barton were invaluable guides back into history. Bishop Daly – he was Father Daly in 1972 – recalled the terrifying moments when he and four others carried the body of young Jackie Duddy out of the firing line; his insightful recollections of the tragedy helped us to reconstruct the day. Charlie McGuigan, Barney's son, who was sixteen in 1972, described the pain families have been through to find justice for their loved ones.

In many of our interviews at the time, and still today, we pledged not to reveal the names of those who gave us information. They know who they are, and we thank them.

This time, we owe a debt of gratitude to a new group of people in Northern Ireland – among them Patricia Coyle, Des Doherty, Noirin Doherty, Patrick L. Doherty (Paddy Bogside) and Peter Madden. A special thanks to Don Mullan, who is the foremost expert of Bloody Sunday. We were delighted to find a new colleague, Paul Greengrass.

The *Derry Journal* kindly helped us find material published between 1969–72 and the British Library's Newspaper Library assisted us in finding relevant articles.

Thanks to Jean and Hugo Hegarty for their warm hospitality and support, and to Elaine Smith for looking after us at our favourite hostelry in Derry.

In London, Lena Ferguson, whose diligent research for Channel Four produced two ground-breaking reports on Bloody Sunday, was very helpful. The Press Office of the Public Record Office guided us through the maze of the Widgery Tribunal Report.

Several army and police officers spoke of their experiences in Northern Ireland on the understanding that they would not be identified. Regimental associations of the Royal Green Jackets, the Royal Anglians and the Glosters helped us trace former soldiers.

We thank Field Marshal Lord Carver and General Sir Frank Kitson for the letters.

Special thanks to our old friend, Gilles Peress, for allowing us to use his stunning photograph of Barrier 14 and the sequence of the death of Paddy Doherty. Thanks to Trisha Ziff for helping us track down other photographers who kindly let us reproduce their pictures – Fulvio Grimaldi, Robert White and the Bloody Sunday Trust, and Jeff Morris.

Our former colleagues at the *Sunday Times* who were involved, directly or otherwise, in the original Bloody Sunday investigation encouraged us to complete this work. We are particularly grateful to Harry Evans, who took the decision to keep us in Derry to carry out a two-month investigation, and to John Barry, then editor of Insight, and our peerless researcher Parin Janmohamed. Thanks, also, to John Butterworth, John Fielding, Ron Hall, Phillip Knightley, Bruce Page, Magnus Linklater, Cal McCrystal, Brian Moynihan, Mark Ottaway, and Tony Geraghty.

Clive Priddle, our editor at Fourth Estate, masterminded the structure of the book and gave up weekends to keep us on schedule. We are full of admiration for his expert editing, and for the support of the unflappable Catherine Blyth.

In the final stages, as in our other collaborations, we imposed on our families a regime of permanent uncertainty and general chaos for which we apologize; we will try to do better next time.

Selected Bibliography

Bardon, Jonathan, *A History of Ulster*, Blackstaff, Belfast, 1992

Bew, Paul, Gibbon, Peter and Patterson, Henry, *Northern Ireland, 1921–1994: Political Forces and Social Classes*, Serif, London, 1995

Carver, Michael: *Out of Step*, Hutchinson, London, 1989

Curran, Frank, *Derry, Countdown to Disaster*, Gill and Macmillan, Dublin, 1986

Dash, Samuel, *Justice Denied, A Challenge to Lord Widgery's Report on 'Bloody Sunday'*, International League for Human Rights, New York, 1998

Devlin, Bernadette, *The Price of My Soul*, Pan, London, 1969

Evelegh, Robin, *Peace-keeping in a Democratic Society, The Lessons of Northern Ireland*, C.Hurst & Co, London, 1978

Geraghty, Tony, *The Irish War, the Military History of a Domestic Conflict*, HarperCollins, Guildhall Press, Londonderry, 1998

Hamill, Desmond, *Pig in the Middle, the Army in Northern Ireland 1969–85*, Methuen, London, 1986

Hastings, Max, *Ulster 1969, The Fight for Civil Rights in Northern Ireland*, Victor Gollancz, London 1990

Irish Government, *Bloody Sunday and the Report of the Widgery Tribunal, The Irish Government's Assessment of the New Material*, presented to the British government in June 1997

Kitson, Frank, *Low Intensity Operations*, Faber & Faber, London, 1971

Lacey, Brian, *Siege City: The Story of Derry and Londonderry*, Blackstaff, Belfast, 1991

Lindsay, John (ed.), *Brits Speak Out, British Soldiers' Impressions of the Northern Ireland Conflict*, Guildhall Press, Londonderry, 1998

McCafferty, Nell, *Peggy Deery, An Irish Family At War*, Attic Press, Dublin, 1988

McCann, Eamonn, *War and an Irish Town*, Penguin, London, 1974

McCann, Harrigan, Bridie and Shiels, Maureen, *Bloody Sunday in Derry: What Really Happened*, Brandon, Kerry, 1992

McClean, Raymond, *The Road to Bloody Sunday*, Ward River Press, Dublin, 1983, 1997; revised edition, Guildhall, Londonderry, 1997

McKittrick *et al*, *Lost Lives*, Edinburgh, London, 1999

McMahon, Bryan, 'The Impaired Asset: A Legal Commentary on the Report of the Widgery Tribunal', *Le Domain Humain*, V1,3, Autumn, 1974

McMonagle, Barney, *No Go, A Photographic Record of Free Derry*, Guildhall, Londonderry, 1997

Mullan, Paul, with John Scally, preface by Jane Winter, *Eye-witness Bloody Sunday*, Wolfhound Press, Dublin, 1998

O'Brien, Conor Cruise, *States of Ireland*, Hutchinson, London 1972

O'Dochartaigh, Niall, *From Civil Rights to Armalites, Derry and the Birth of the Irish Troubles*, Cork University Press, 1997

Purdie, Bob, *Politics in the Streets. The Origins of the civil rights Movement in Northern Ireland*, Blackstaff, Belfast, 1990

Sunday Times Insight Team, *Ulster*, Penguin, London, 1972

Taylor, Peter, *Provos, the IRA and Sinn Fein*, Bloomsbury, London 1997

Toolis, Kevin, *Rebel Hearts: Journeys Within the IRA's Soul*, Picador, London, 1995

Walsh, Dermot, The Bloody Sunday tribunal of Inquiry, a Resounding Defeat for Truth Justice and the Rule of Law, paper for the Law department, University of Limerick, January 1997.

Winchester, Simon, *In Holy Terror: Reporting on the Ulster Troubles*, Faber, London 1974

Ziff, Trisha (ed.), *Hidden Truths, Bloody Sunday 1972*, Smart Art Press, Santa Monica, California, 1999

Note on Sources

We began the research on this book in 1998 shortly after learning that the Saville Inquiry had obtained from the *Sunday Times* our notebooks, witness statements, memos and files from 1972. The Saville Inquiry (Saville) asked us to prepare to be interviewed and sent us a single CD-ROM (No. 5) containing our material. Subsequently, we obtained another nine Saville CDs. These contained documents from the Cabinet Office, the Treasury Solicitor, the Ministry of Defence (MoD), The Northern Ireland Office (NIO), and the Royal Ulster Constabulary (RUC). This extraordinary archive includes interviews with approximately five hundred civilian eyewitnesses and several hundred army personnel, RUC and government officials, in Derry, London and Belfast, who participated in Bloody Sunday, plus more than one thousand photographs, maps and diagrams.

The archive is repetitive – the same statements from civilian eyewitnesses, soldiers and policemen often appearing more than once on the same CD – and then again on the other nine. The new interviews are of mixed value.

Our original material is 'primary source' – we conducted interviews within a few days, or weeks, of the event, as journalists, not as officials of a government-sponsored inquiry. We were free to ask whatever questions we thought needed answering to put together the first independent account of what happened on that day. Our report was published in the *Sunday Times* (ST) on 23 April 1972 – five days after the publication of the report of the British government's official inquiry by the Lord Chief Justice, Lord Widgery (Widgery).

Twenty-seven years later, Saville investigators went back to the original interviewees' interviews and then added new ones – including soldiers who were part of the military force surrounding the Bogside, but who did not fire and had not been called to give evidence at the time. The additional testimony widens the investigation of the killing ground, bringing in more background and detail, and confirms what the first inquiry concluded: that the thirteen who were shot dead were unarmed. So were the fourteen who were wounded.

Newly declassified documents fill important gaps in the military preparation for the march, the execution of the scoop-up, and the immediate aftermath.

In some respects the new testimony confuses rather than clarifies. For example, instead of one dead body allegedly with nail bombs, the soldiers now speak of three. Although these could all be one and the same incident, it is not clear and will take time for the new inquiry to unravel. In another incident, a witness in a second statement sees a soldier fire into a Pig containing three dead bodies, an event that was not mentioned in the first statement.

During the relatively short life of the Saville Inquiry, several key official documents (MoD, Cabinet Office, NIO) have been declassified, adding significantly to an understanding of the military strategy behind the use of paratroopers in Derry and the part played by the British and Stormont governments.

We have combined original archive material with new military, government and Saville material. We have included material from interviews taken from IRA members. Following the ruling on anonymity for the soldiers we have excluded their names although many are now known (we have named those senior officers already named), and we have also excluded the names of IRA members who told us in 1972 what the IRA did on that day.

In each chapter we have identified the key contested issues which the Saville Inquiry will face. As our book went to press, Saville had not released its statements from the soldiers who fired on that day, nor those from the key government officials and military officers. We requested interviews with the following: Sir Edward Heath, Lord Hailsham, Field Marshal Lord Carver, General Sir Robert Ford, Major General Pat MacLellan, General Sir Frank Kitson and Chief Superintendent Frank Lagan. All declined to speak to us in advance of giving testimony to Saville.

PROLOGUE
We have repeatedly asked Saville for the correspondence between the Inquiry and the *Sunday Times* that led to the handing over of our notebooks, memos, etc. At the time of going to press these requests had been denied.

I THE ALARM
Eileen Doherty graciously gave us an interview in 1972 and she also talked to Joanne O'Brien in *Hidden Truths, Bloody Sunday*, 1999. The background to Peggy Deery is based on Nell McCafferty's *Peggy Deery, An Irish Family At War*, Attic Press, Dublin, 1989, plus our interviews at the time. Charlie McGuigan, Barney McGuigan's son, spoke with us and gave a statement to the Saville Inquiry. The beginning of the march is reconstructed from civilian eyewitnesses (1972 and Saville), an updated interview with Bishop Daly, plus the army radio log of 8 Brigade.

II CITY UNDER SIEGE
Background to the civil rights struggle in Derry is drawn from several histories – *Ulster by Insight*, Penguin, London, 1972; Eamon McCann, *War and an Irish Town*, Penguin, London, 1974; Bob Purdie, *Politics in the Streets, The origins of the civil rights movement in Northern Ireland*, Blackstaff Press, 1990; From Civil Rights to Armalites, Niall O'Dochartaigh, Cork University Press, 1997;

Devlin, Bernadette, *The Price of My Soul*, Pan, London, 1969; Hume, John, *A Memoir*; Brian Lacey, *Siege City, The Story of Derry and Londonderry*, Blackstaff, Belfast, 1999, plus Insight interviews with NICRA leaders, and updated interviews with Dr Raymond McClean, Paddy 'Bogside' Doherty and Bishop Daly.

III Operation Forecast

Accounts of the army's deepening involvement in Derry come principally from statements and evidence given to Widgery by Ford and MacLellan. Key documents include Ford's December 1971 analysis of military options, *Future Military Policy for Londonderry, An Appreciation of the Situation by CLF*, and his memorandum on *The Situation in Londonderry as at January 7,1972*. The army's plans for the NICRA were set out in 8 Brigade Operational Order 2/72, 27 January 1972. Lord Carver's anecdote regarding Lord Hailsham about the shoot-to-kill policy was provided in a letter to the authors. Chief Superintendent Frank Lagan provided a more comprehensive statement to the Saville Inquiry. Lieutenant Colonel Wilford has robustly defended his Paras in media interviews (especially *Guardian*, 7 July 1999).

IV The Decision to Put Civilians At Risk

Discussions between MacLellan and Lagan on how to handle the NICRA march were set out in their conflicting evidence to Widgery. Lagan's most recent statement to Saville deepens the division. MacLellan's dealings with Ford and his description of events at Ebrington barracks on Bloody Sunday are also from original evidence to Widgery, as is Ford's account of his movements in Derry that day. Wilford's preparations and briefings to 1 Para are from evidence to Widgery; other officers from the battalion, including Major 236, also testified. The debate within the British government over the march is described in Cabinet minutes (especially 11 January and 27 January 1972) and also features in the memoirs of Sir Edward Heath and Lord Carver.

The controversy over I Para's methods in Belfast was first reported in the *Guardian* 25 January 1972. Supporting material is from the *Sunday Times* archive and Saville statements from soldiers not previously interviewed.

V Barrier 14

The sketch of Dr McLean and his battle over CS gas comes from interviews with him in Derry in 1999 and from his book, *The Road to Bloody Sunday*, Guildhall Press, Dublin 1983, revised 1997. The first transcription of the Porter tapes was made by the authors in 1972. Porter also gave a long interview to the Saville inquiry. Statements by Major General Robert Ford were made to the Widgery Inquiry, to reporters at Barrier 14 and to Observer A, also in Widgery. Also, Insight interviews with Magee students and Willy Barber 1972. The evidence of 'customizing' or 'doctoring' rubber bullets comes from Saville interviews with esp. INQ1282 and INQ954, Riflemen from 2nd Royal Green Jackets.

VI How Could Anyone Pick on Me as a Gunman?

The question of who fired first that afternoon will be a contentious issue in the Saville Inquiry. The army's brigade log records a shot at 3.55 p.m. from 'the direction of the Rossville flats' which hit a drainpipe on the Presbyterian church. Before or after this shot, paratroopers of the machine-gun platoon of Support Company shot and wounded Damien Donaghy and John Johnston. These shots – five in all, according to the soldiers – are not recorded in any of the logs submitted to Widgery or Saville, as far as we know. Civilian eyewitnesses (supported by our IRA interviews) say a freelance Official IRA gunman fired a single shot at the paratroopers in the area of the Presbyterian church – but *after* the shots that wounded Donaghy and Johnston. Key evidence, as yet not fully analysed, is also provided by David Capper's BBC tape recording of the shots.

VII Move! Move! Move!

One of the most hotly debated issues to be addressed by Saville will be whether the order to send in the Paras was given solely by Brigadier MacClellan, why it was sent; how it was sent (secure radio, land line telephone, or some other means?) to Lieutenant Colonel Wilford and whether he exceeded the order. Essential to demonstrating that there is a mystery are the following documents: 8 Brigade radio log, 1 Para battalion log and HQ Northern Ireland log. Saville will be examining original statements by MacLellan, the Brigade Major, Lieutenant Colonels Steele and Wilford. Steele said that the log keeper wrote down the order accurately and it was limited to one company through Barrier 14.

A related issue is whether the secure link was working or, as Porter theorized later, was stuck on send. Several soldier statements elaborate on the various radio links in operation – Company, Battalion or Regiment and Brigade, but none of them addresses the problem, which there clearly was, of a breakdown in secure link communications.

VIII Shoot Me! Shoot Me!

Several reporters, photographers and television crews – including the BBC and ITN , Harry Arnold of the *Sun*, Jeff Morris of the *Daily Mail* and Colman Doyle of the *Irish Press* – were at Barrier 14 and gave statements to Widgery or to Insight. Gilles Peress gave his own interview to Widgery. The Paras, Lieutenant N and Major 236's statements to Widgery are important. Of the civilians who were wounded there are Insight statements and/or interviews from 1972 with Peggy Deery, Michael Bridge, Michael Bradley and Patrick McDaid.

Father Daly described seeing the pistol man at the end of Chamberlain Street. But the key issue here for Saville is whether the paratroopers came under fire immediately they jumped out of the Pigs. There appears to be a key inconsistency between the testimony of soldiers taken immediately after Bloody Sunday, and those taken later – i.e. by Saville. Several of the soldiers who had not given statements before say there was no automatic fire, such as from a Thompson sub-machine gun. The majority of the eyewitness accounts still say there was no automatic fire directed at the troops.

IX THE RUBBLE BARRICADE

A key issue here is whether three of those shot at the rubble barricade could have been shot by soldiers on the city walls. The autopsies suggest that they could have been shot from the walls because of the 45 degree downward track of the bullets through the body. If they were shot from the walls, they must have been standing up. It seems to us, taking into account eyewitness testimony and soldier evidence, that they were shot by the paratroopers at Kells Walk, and they were crouching behind the barricade at the time they were shot.

Peter Taylor's unedited interview for BBCl with Support Company's CSM raises the question of whether the Paras who fired first and were wearing gas masks were able to see their targets properly. The CSM said, 'You can't see a bloody thing . . . [and wearing the masks] . . . added a hundred per cent to the confusion.' Another unresolved issue is whether Hugh Gilmore was shot by one bullet, or two.

Father O'Gara saw the gunman on the Glenfada Park side of the barricade.

X DON'T MOVE, PRETEND YOU'RE DEAD

New evidence from Saville – the testimony of Danny Craig – raises the issue of whether there were nail bombs in the hands of civilians in Glenfada Park.

As we wrote in our original Insight article, there is a good selection of photographs in the Insight archive, plus eyewitness testimony, that permits the placing with some confidence of the bodies of Willie McKinney and Jim Wray. Malachy Coyle's statement to the Saville Inquiry is additional testimony to Wray's last moments.

The issue of Private H's 19 bullets through a bathroom window is still open.

XI CAN'T STAND THIS ANY LONGER

The key issue here is where Paddy Doherty was shot. Gilles Peress's pictures, which were sold to the *Sunday Times*, were interpreted by the Magnum agency in Paris and by the *Sunday Times* as showing that Doherty had been shot on the car park side of the flats, as he was crawling through the alley between blocks 2 and 3. But this ignored the civilian eyewitnesses who say they saw him shot in the forecourt of the flats, in front of the shops. We favour this explanation. The reason is that Peress could not say for sure that Doherty had been shot on the car park side, he only took this view because Doherty looked as though he might have been shot in Peress's second frame. Also, the soldiers firing from Glenfada Park could have had a direct line of sight to Doherty as he was crawling across the flats' forecourt. It is more difficult to see how he was shot from the Paras in the car park.

XII A TOKEN RETALIATION

This incident is reconstructed primarily from interviews the authors conducted at the time with commanders of the Official and Provisional IRA in Derry, plus the handful of civilian eyewitnesses who saw the IRA arrive in the Bogside after the Paras had started shooting. The IRA commanders gave their interviews in confidence. The civilian eyewitnesses have been named.

XIII I'LL NEVER TURN MY BACK ON A PARA

Accounts of being arrested by the Paras and held at Fort George are from statements given to NICRA following Bloody Sunday. Some have now been updated under Saville. Knights of Malta paramedics on duty in the Bogside and other eyewitnesses, such as Father Bradley, provided additional material. The key question here is whether the Paras were excessively brutal in making arrests. The decision not to prosecute anyone arrested was set out in official correspondence, as was the complaint submitted to the RUC by George Nelis. The army's version of events was contained principally in statements from soldiers of 1 Para and other regiments submitted to Widgery. These are basically confirmed by the soldiers' statements to Saville we have seen.

XIV For God's Sake Hurry Up I'm Dying

Events at the Barrack Street barrier were described in statements from soldiers and civilian eyewitnesses. The key question here is whether nail bombs were actually found on Gerald Donaghy's body, as is alleged, or whether the bombs were planted. As mentioned above, new testimony from soldiers who have not previously given statements is confusing. The Donaghy dossier was re-examined for Saville by forensic expert J.B.F. Lloyd.

A new question is posed by Alice Long's account of the Para shooting into the Pig containing the bodies of Young, Nash and McDaid. This comes from her statement to Saville. In previous accounts Long did not mention any such incident, nor did other civilians present. Long told Saville that Leo Day, her KoM commandant who is now dead, had urged her not to report this shooting in order to spare the families further anguish.

XV Going Home

Father Daly provided the story of his conversation with McCullagh. The account of John Hume and Ivan Cooper comes from interviews with Insight. Descriptions of how families learned about the deaths are from NICRA and other interviews. Tony Doherty's story is from *Hidden Truths, Bloody Sunday*. Rita Nicols' story is from Nell McCafferty's biography of Peggy Deery. Material from individual post mortems on victims is from RUC dossiers and statements by doctors. The description of Provisionals stopping the bingo bus comes from *Rebel Hearts* by Kevin Toolis.

EPILOGUE: THE LAST CASUALTY

The minute of Prime Minister Heath' s talks with Lord Widgery on 31 January 1972 was discovered in the Public Records Office by Dessie Baker and Jane Winter (British–Irish Human Rights Watch). The briefing for defence correspondents is from the Saville documents. Correspondence on the compensation issue is also from Saville documents.